THE ADVANCED WORKBOOK

FOR SPIRITUAL & PSYCHIC DEVELOPMENT

A COURSE COMPANION

HELEN LEATHERS & DIANE CAMPKIN

PUBLISHED BY SPREADING THE MAGIC

Copyright Helen Leathers & Diane Campkin 2011
Helen Leathers & Diane Campkin assert the moral right to be identified
as the authors of this work.

ISBN 978-0-9930513-1-9

First Published in 2011 by Spreading The Magic
www.spreadingthemagic.com

Cover Design by Titanium Design Ltd.
www.titaniumdesign.co.uk

All rights reserved. No part of this publication may be reproduced, stored in a retrieval system,
or transmitted, in any form or by any means, electronic, mechanical,
photocopying, recording or otherwise, without the prior
permission of the publishers.

Please note that while we are happy for handouts to be copied for use in your circle,
group or workshop, the copyright remains ours and full credits must remain on each copy.
Copies of these can be downloaded from the 'Readers' Resources' section
on www.thepsychicworkbook.com

There is always more to learn,
There are always unexplored avenues,
Keep an open mind and an open heart,
Venture outwards, look inwards,
Find your own truth.
We trust that this book will assist on your path to discovery.

Also by Helen and Diane

Help! I Think I Might Be Psychic
101 Frequently Asked Questions About Spiritual, Psychic & Spooky Stuff
(paperback & ebook)

The Spiritual & Psychic Development Workbook
A Beginners Guide

The Spiritual & Psychic Development Workbook
A Course Companion

The Advanced Spiritual & Psychic Development Workbook

The Spiritual & Psychic Development Meditation Collection
The Advanced Spiritual & Psychic Development Audio Collection
(CD & MP3)

Also by Helen Leathers

Bright Blessings

The Power In Your Hands
The Power In Your Hands Audio Collection
(CD & MP3)

See the back of this book for more details and how to order these products
or go to www.stmpublishing.co.uk

CONTENTS

INTRODUCTION 7
BEFORE YOU START: A REMINDER 9
FOR DISCUSSION: KEY CONCEPTS OF SPIRITUAL & PSYCHIC DEVELOPMENT 15

LESSONS

LESSON 1:	DEEPER MEDITATION	19
LESSON 2:	ENERGY WORK	29
LESSON 3:	INCREASING YOUR SENSITIVITY	39
LESSON 4:	'3RD EYE' CHAKRA DEVELOPMENT	51
LESSON 5:	ANGELIC ENERGY	63
LESSON 6:	PSYCHOKINESIS	75
LESSON 7:	AUTOMATIC WRITING	87
LESSON 8:	PSYCHIC ART	99
LESSON 9:	MANIFESTATION	109
LESSON 10:	PAST LIVES	119
LESSON 11:	TRANCE MEDIUMSHIP	131
LESSON 12:	OUT OF BODY EXPERIENCES	141

WHERE NEXT? 155

APPENDICES

HANDOUT 1:	INTRODUCTION	157
HANDOUT 2:	BODY/CHAKRAS OUTLINE	159
HANDOUT 3:	SENSING PROMPT	161
HANDOUT 4:	ANGEL CARDS	163
HANDOUT 5:	DOWSING CHARTS FOR PAST LIFE RESEARCH	169
HANDOUT 6:	FACE OUTLINE	179
HANDOUT 7:	BASIC COLOUR INFORMATION	181
HANDOUT 8:	PAST LIFE INTERVIEW SCRIPTS	183
HANDOUT 9:	TRANCE MEDIUMSHIP SCRIPTS	185

CONTENTS

ABOUT THE AUTHORS 186
RESOURCES 188
ACKOWLEDGEMENTS 189
ABOUT 'SPREADING THE MAGIC' 190
OTHER PRODUCTS FROM HELEN & DIANE 191

INTRODUCTION

INTRODUCTION

Spiritual and psychic development is a huge subject. Our 'Beginner's Guide' covered basic elements essential to form the foundations of good practice, but the variety of subjects and skills that can be discussed is vast, so we always knew that a follow-up, advanced workbook would be on the cards - so to speak.

In the 'Beginner's Guide' we started you off with the key skills that you would need to get going, along with a variety of core subjects to spark your interest and help you find out where your natural abilities lie and what kind of work you enjoy most. It's always good to develop the things you enjoy and are good at first. This will give you confidence and experience that you can then take with you as you try new things. This 'Advanced Workbook' helps you to continue your journey of discovery, much like a map to help you work out which road to take next. We'll build on the basics, and we'll look at more advanced subjects and exercises that will challenge your abilities and also, we hope, help you continue to develop your own personal spiritual philosophy about life, the universe, etc.

ABOUT THIS BOOK

This is a step-by-step workbook with lessons that you can literally follow through to the letter. We know from experience that there are many people who wish to develop their psychic abilities but don't have ready access to courses, workshops, development circles or personal teachers. Our aim in writing this is to provide everything that you need to continue your spiritual and psychic development journey with more advanced subjects. We have essentially created it as a tool to be used in a group setting or development circle.

Based on the ideal of working once a week, this workbook gives you a three month course to follow. In each lesson you will work through the detailed format. Everything is included for you, so you don't have to do too much preparation or rely on someone coming up with fresh ideas each week. We know how challenging and time consuming that can be. It's been designed so that each subject helps you to progress to the next one. Some subjects follow on naturally from those we've already covered in the 'Beginner's Guide' and therefore take less explanation. Others are quite different so we go into more theoretical detail. You will also notice that some of the exercises from the first book are repeated in this one; this is deliberate. Each time you revisit subjects and exercises you'll not only improve your skills, taking them to a higher level, but you'll also recognise just how far you've come on your journey. This should give you a feeling of both accomplishment and confidence in yourself.

For each subject we'll give you theories along with some practical exercises. 'Other things to try' is a new section that we've added since the first workbook. It's up to you what to do with it. You can use it to build on the practical work, create extra exercises and experiment further within the lesson. Alternatively, save it for another time (and make the book last longer!). Some suggestions in this section, depending on the subject, may be more appropriate as homework for further research and devlopment in combination with the section 'And another thing...'.

As new skills and concepts are introduced they are added, where appropriate, to the lesson structure to assist your development further. We've also added a 'For discussion' section at the end of each lesson with suggested points to focus on.

Many of the visualisation exercises and meditations are available as MP3 downloads or on CD as part of the 'Advanced Audio Collection'. Full details about this audio collection will be published on the website www.stmpublishing.co.uk. So you can either read out the exercises or simply hit play on your CD or MP3 player. (Please note that, where indicated, some of the exercises require that at least one group member acts as a facilitator and does not 'go off' with the rest of the group. Please don't overlook this just because you're using the audio products and don't have to do the reading.)

PSYCHIC VS. SPIRITUAL DEVELOPMENT

It's important to understand that psychic and spiritual development are different concepts. Being psychic basically means that you can 'read' a person through their energy field. In our case, working on a spiritual basis, or mediumistically, means that you connect with Spirit, such as a Guide or loved one who has passed over, who helps to pass on messages or do work on this plane of existence. Spiritual development also involves developing your own thoughts on the different levels of existence and all aspects of life and physical death, our reason for being and our interactions with others.

It's possible for a person to be 'psychic' but not to develop spiritually and sometimes this can lead to their work being ego-centred. However, when you develop spiritually you connect with people on a deeper level, in a more empathic way. Your work is heart-centred. You will also find that you naturally develop psychically at the same time.

We believe that the best way to approach this type of work is from a spiritual direction whilst actively seeking to develop psychically at the same time. By doing this we bring harmony and balance into our lives as we integrate all aspects of our being and become whole again. As this happens we see the world, other people and our relationships on every level in a different light, it opens our eyes and our souls. It causes us to remember who we really are and why we are here. All in all, we believe that it makes the world a nicer place to be.

OUR ETHOS

To re-iterate what we said in our 'Beginner's Guide' by writing this book we do not wish to portray ourselves as the definitive experts. We are the first to admit that we still learn something new every day. Nor are we saying that our beliefs or opinions are the right and only way. They are simply ours and they may change in time, after all, who says you have to hold the same ideas forever? As with all books of this nature, some parts of it will resonate with you more strongly than others. However, even the parts that don't resonate so strongly will provide a base of knowledge that will help you to develop your own belief system further.

Sometimes we need time to discuss and formulate our beliefs (one of the reasons we have added a discussion section to the lessons). So as well as the twelve lessons we have written a short 'For discussion' essay about, what we consider are key elements for spiritual and psychic development. We'd suggest that you take a look at this with your group and spend a session discussing it before you progress to the lessons.

HOW THIS BOOK COULD CHANGE YOUR LIFE

Having both grown up with psychic and spiritual experiences punctuating our childhood and teenage years, we have actively sought to develop our skills and work in the areas of psychic readings, mediumship, healing, and 'rescue' work. We believe that any degree of personal, spiritual and psychic development can help a person to change their life for the better. You can understand yourself and those around you on new levels, develop your intuition, help yourself and others through difficult times, learn to engage with the energy of living and, with experience, help to bring things about that will improve the world around you, as an individual, for your family and for the larger community.

If you've been working on your spiritual and psychic side for a while already you will probably have realised that this type of work changes you, your outlook on life, and occasionally the way that others are with you. You become more sensitive, see the world differently, and are more touched by and connected with many elements of the universe, people, places and events. You may also have noticed that you can begin to see the bigger picture, step outside of the chaos of living and see things in a little more of a detached, philosophical way. As you progress further you will begin to see how we all play our part. Keep an open mind and an open heart and accept all that the universe sends you.

In love and light always,
Helen & Diane

BEFORE YOU START - A REMINDER

Let's review the rules we work by and have a reminder of the basics before we get going.

RULES

There are three rules that we insist on when working spiritually and psychically:

1) Do not mix your spirits!

In other words, no alcohol, or other mind-altering substances for that matter! Being under the influence whilst working in circle affects your ability and judgement. It also lowers your energy vibration and your defences (in much the same way as it lowers inhibitions). This can leave you and the rest of the group open to less positive energies or influences. This rule is non-negotiable.

2) Confidentiality.

Anything of a personal nature must not be spoken of outside of the group. This will allow everyone to work with trust and develop a safe and supportive environment. This does not mean that spirit are going to divulge your innermost secrets to everyone, they don't work like that, but discussions can arise which can bring up sensitive issues and everyone needs to know that they can be open and honest with each other.

3) Stay Positive!

This is extremely important. Positive energy is essential when working. Although working with spirit must be taken seriously, it can also be fun and indeed laughter can help to raise the energy vibrations and facilitate your work. If you feel negative, depressed or simply under the weather, take a break and do something else instead. We will describe how to bring yourself out of a meditation should you feel the need, and if you ever feel worried or uncomfortable during any work with spirit, stop, ground yourself, ask spirit for extra protection to be placed around you and if necessary take a break. If you feel uncomfortable while working in a group and others appear to be fine, you must still mention it. It may be wise, as a group, to change the subject for a few minutes or to lighten the mood a little before proceeding. If necessary, close down, ground and finish the session. You can always repeat the exercise another time. Put some music on, have a laugh, make some tea and eat chocolate biscuits. No one should ever feel negative or uncomfortable while working with spirit and you should always feel confident enough within the group to voice your concerns and have them accepted by all. It's important as a group that you always adhere to this rule.

WORKING WITH OTHERS

You may already be working with a group (which is great) so you may know some of this already, but it's worth reminding yourselves before we go on.

While you can have a go at some of the exercises on your own, you will need to work with at least one other person for some of the work. However, working with others is not only rewarding, but when a group of people work together with the same intentions, they develop faster than if they worked on their own. A group of people working together for psychic development is referred to as a development circle.

In a development circle, all are equal, every person brings their own unique qualities, energy and experiences to the group and they all learn from each other. They all contribute to the energy of the group and the higher the level of energy, the higher the spiritual connection and the better and faster the development becomes. It could be likened to connecting to the Internet via broadband rather than 'dial-up'. The group becomes a supportive family-like environment that is eventually much more than it starts out to be.

If you wish to form a development circle, you should aim to have between 3 and 12 members, meeting weekly or fortnightly on the same day and time, and if possible, at the same venue. It's best to keep to the same people while you're becoming established and only introduce those who you all feel comfortable

with and whose energies gel with the group. In our experience you shouldn't overly worry about this as those whose energies or intentions are not in harmony with the group don't usually stay long!
Please remember the following points when working with others:
- It's vital that you develop the harmony of the group. This takes time but meeting regularly and feeling that it's a safe and confidential environment are essential. This allows open and honest discussion and builds trust and support.
- Everyone must feel comfortable with every activity that you undertake. No one must ever feel pressurised into taking part in an activity with the group. We would suggest that when you are starting out, if one person doesn't want to do a particular exercise, they don't do it, no questions asked. If they feel uncomfortable with a whole subject, they can simply choose not to take part in that session.
- Everyone should feel that they have a voice, and any problems or concerns should be discussed openly and confidentially with all group members.
- If you're in an established group, have a quick chat about the subjects covered in this workbook to ensure everyone is happy with participating in all of the lessons.
- This is our advanced workbook so if this is the first you have seen and are just forming a group please read the next section - 'HOW TO USE THIS BOOK'. You may want to take a look at our beginners workbook: 'The Spiritual & Psychic Development Workbook - A Course Companion'. More information can be found on page 192.

HOW TO USE THIS BOOK

Once you have a number of like-minded people who wish to work together to develop their psychic abilities and have arranged a convenient time and place to meet, you're ready to begin your course of study.
- Ensure that you have read the 'Introduction' and 'Before You Start' sections of this workbook.
- Photocopy the 'Introduction' (Handout 1) on page 157 and give a copy to each person in the group.
- Arrange and hold a pre-start meeting to discuss any issues that may have come up.
- Ensure that everyone has scheduled the regular meetings into their diaries to encourage commitment.
- Gather the basic tools together and you're ready to begin.
- A few days before each lesson, read through the Preparation Guide and ensure that you have all of the required tools. Remind any other members of the group who agreed to provide certain things at the end of the previous lesson. You will also need to photocopy the required number of handouts listed in the Preparation Guide.
- On the day of the meeting ensure that the room is prepared, there are enough seats for everyone and you have enough room for the work you're about to undertake. Open the windows, bring in some flowers or burn some incense to freshen the air. Gather together the tools that you require for the lesson you're working on and set out some water and glasses. It's important to keep hydrated when working.
- At each meeting simply work through the appropriate lesson as detailed in the next section of the book. All the words and meditations are written for you. The exercises are detailed for you and further study ideas are suggested. At the end of each lesson there's information about the next one so that everyone knows what's coming up and whether there's anything that they need to bring to the meeting. As each lesson covers a different subject there will be a varying amount of theory, practical and discussion each time. So, although the opening and closing sections will remain the same each time, there will always be something new to learn about, experience and do.
- It's inevitable that discussions will start during the lessons, and should be encouraged. They're important for your own understanding of the subject, your personal growth and for the bonding of the group. However, it's also important to keep on track and these discussions can always be continued afterwards over a cup of tea. We know how easy it is to carry on way in to the night.
- Please note that while we are happy for handouts to be copied for use in your circle, group or workshop, the copyright remains ours and full credits must remain on each copy. The worksheets/handouts in the back of this book can also be downloaded for free from our website www.thepsychicworkbook.com,

simply click on 'Readers' Resources'. No other part of this publication may be reproduced, stored in a retrieval system, or transmitted, in any form or by any means, electronic, mechanical, photocopying, recording or otherwise, without the prior permission of the publishers.

OUR SUGGESTIONS
- Food - it's not advisable to eat a large meal just before doing work of this nature, equally a rumbling tummy during a meditation can be off-putting! A small meal one or two hours beforehand is best.
- Health - if you're unwell it isn't advisable to do any of the work in this book as your energy levels will be low. If you are suffering from depression, anxiety or similar mental health issues or are on medication for any of these conditions, we would strongly suggest that you avoid working with spirit. You're more vulnerable and may end up having a negative experience. You should concentrate on getting well before developing in this way.
- Sharing - please do! If you're doing an exercise with someone don't be worried about saying something silly. It may well be relevant to the person you're working with even though you might think it's not. Give what you get, even if it sounds silly.
- Comparing - please don't! Everyone develops at different rates and finds certain things easier than others. Don't feel that you have to be the same as someone else or that you're not good enough. You will find that each person excels at or is drawn to different types of work. Learn from and encourage others who are on a similar journey.

SEEKING SUPPORT
It's a good idea to know how and where to find support and advice from like-minded people. Your local spiritualist church is often a good point of contact with some very experienced members. You may want to go along to some evenings of clairvoyance for some inspiration - you could even get a message of guidance for your endeavours. They may run courses and workshops and can prove to be very beneficial in pursuing your spiritual path and psychic abilities. But they're not for everyone. They're generally Christian based, so be aware of this if it's an issue for you.

It's also useful to have contacts should you have any questions or problems. If you come across anyone who you suspect may have a spiritual problem such as a haunting, point them in the direction of the spiritualist church. They 'get' the whole spirit communication thing and will, hopefully, be understanding and sympathetic to their needs or problems. They usually run or know of a local rescue circle that can provide healing and advice or can put you in touch with an appropriate medium who is experienced in, and can help with more serious concerns. When you first start out it can be exciting and tempting to try and help them yourselves, but it isn't something you should attempt without a lot of experience.

AN IMPORTANT POINT
During the course of this workbook we do talk about communication with spirit, however, we appreciate that this may be a cause of concern for some people. Our golden rule is always to work with positive and highest intentions. Spirit should never hurt you or encourage you to do anything harmful to yourself or others or to act inappropriately. If at any time you're at all concerned by your experiences you should seek help from an experienced and reputable medium, healer, or if necessary a medical practitioner.

BARE ESSENTIALS
Protection of your energy field before and during your work, and closing and grounding at the end of it, are absolutely essential. **NEVER FORGET TO DO THESE TWO THINGS.** These were covered in detail in our 'Beginner's Guide' and are built into each lesson for you but but here's a quick reminder.

Protection
Imagine some form of protective shield around you and your aura. This could be a force field of bright

white light, a bubble, an egg, mirrors reflecting away from you or you could see yourself inside a hollow crystal filled with light. Know that you're safe, completely sealed in and protected from outside influences. Helen always visualises a circle of light blue flames, like a gas burner on a hob, around herself, or the group she's working with. They're safe for us but keep out any negative energy. We find that it's good practice to use a visualisation followed by a protection request, which can be said mentally to yourself, or out loud if you are working with others.

Protection Visualisation:
- Visualise your aura around you as though it is a giant egg shape and you are inside it.
- See it as being filled with pure white light.
- Now imagine that the outside edge hardens like a shell around your egg, and turns to metallic silver reflecting any negative intentions or energy that comes your way.
- Know that nothing can get in or out.

As you practise and become adept at visualisation you may be able to give yourself a trigger word that will allow this state of protection to be created instantaneously. It may be 'protect', 'shields up' or something similar. Don't use this every day as it's a powerful visualisation; only use it when you need it. In general daily activities knowing that your loved ones, spirit guides and angels are around you and can offer protection, should be more than sufficient.

Protection Request:
- Take a moment to close your eyes and calm your mind.
- Concentrate on your breathing, allowing the breath to become deeper and slower.
- Mentally ask your spirit guides and angels to draw close and offer their assistance using the following script:

"I call upon my spirit guides, angels and loved ones in spirit to draw close to me and to create a circle of protection around me ensuring that I am safe and protected at all times and on all levels, while I work and afterwards. I ask for your protection, guidance and wisdom. I am happy to work with guidance from the spirit world and to communicate with them, but I do so only in love and light and with the highest intentions. I ask that anyone from the spirit world who wishes to assist or communicate does so with the same intentions, and that my guides and angels enforce this on my behalf."

Closing and grounding visualisation:
For use after specific work or meditations when you have consciously 'opened' your energy field.
- Sit in a comfortable position and close your eyes.
- Bring your attention to your breathing and focus on this for a few breaths.
- Take your awareness to the invisible energy field surrounding your physical body. If you can't sense it, simply imagine it as a bubble a few inches around you.
- Visualise it drawing in and closing around your physical body like plastic shrink-wrap.
- Take your awareness to the area just above your crown and see a sphere of light sitting here.
- Imagine that sphere of light shrinking in size until it's tiny and then sinking down through the crown of your head.
- See it slowly descending down past the brow into the throat.
- Then following the line of the spine, down, through your body, towards your heart area.
- Down to your solar plexus, through the abdominal area, to the base of your spine.
- Now visualise the sphere of energy either leaving through the base of your spine, or dividing in two and sinking down through your legs and leaving through the soles of your feet.
- Feel this energy leaving you and connecting with the earth.
- Have a sense of downward movement, deep into the earth.

- Become more aware of your feet and your physical body.
- Take a moment to thank your spirit guides, angels and loved ones in spirit for their presence, protection and wisdom whilst you've been working, knowing that they will always be on hand should you need to call on them.
- Now bring your awareness back to your physical body, the chair you are sitting on, your contact with the floor.
- Begin to bring some movement back into your fingers and toes.
- In your own time, open your eyes, fully awake and aware and in the physical world.

SOMETHING NEW - CLEANSING YOUR WORK AREA

As you begin to work with more advanced subjects it can be beneficial and sometimes necessary to know how to cleanse an area either before or after you work.

Cleansing before you work is a good idea as you may not be aware or in control of what has gone on in the room before. It could be that there's been an argument there that day which can leave a negative residual energy behind and isn't really conducive to our type of work. You may wish to cleanse the room afterwards so that anyone using the area subsequently doesn't feel uneasy or uncomfortable if they pick up on the work you have been doing, Not that the work will leave anything negative behind but if people sense an energy that they're not used to and cannot explain, often the not-knowing can make them feel uneasy rather than the energy itself.

How to cleanse an area:
- Firstly, physically clear the area so that it isn't cluttered, open windows and doors and freshen it up. Light a candle and put on some incense if you like.
- Then use one of the following tools, hold the intention of cleansing in your mind and ask your guides or angels for their assistance. (Don't forget to thank them afterwards.)
- Move around the room ensuring that you pause at each corner, either:
- Clap your hands (a clear bright clapping sound indicates that the energy is clear; you will hear the sound change as it clears).
- Ring a small hand bell (again the clarity of sound will indicate how 'clean' the area is).
- Sprinkle a little salt or salt water (you can vacuum it up afterwards!).
- Smudge the area. Smudge is a native American bundle of herbs. You can buy these in new age shops and online. Simply light the end of the herb bundle and then blow on it gently until it is smouldering and smoking. Hold the bundle in one hand and waft the smoke around the room or area with your other hand or a feather (which is the traditional way).

If you're a reiki practitioner, remember you can use reiki symbols to cleanse the area.

FOR DISCUSSION

KEY CONEPTS OF SPIRITUAL & PSYCHIC DEVELOPMENT

In our 'Beginners Guide' we looked at practical, physical and energetic basics that you need to understand in order to successfully develop your intuitive, spiritual and psychic skills. However, as you progress, there are other elements that are also important to understand. These concepts not only assist in developing your skills but in becoming more calm, reacting more positively to situations that occur in life and living with a more spiritual outlook. We have both discovered that this journey causes your life to become more fulfilling and less stressful, and this in turn allows life to flow better and it appears to become easier and more successful. So they are concepts that are certainly worth spending time on. It's up to you how you approach this but we felt that they would make a good topic for discussion during a group meeting. So before progressing to our advanced lesson subjects have a session based on the following.

STEP 1 - read out
STEP 2 - discuss
STEP 3 - plan for progress

STEP 1 - read out the following to the group
In our 'Beginners Guide' we looked at practical, physical and energetic basics that you need to understand in order to successfully develop your intuitive, spiritual and psychic skills. However, as you progress, there are other elements that are also important to understand. These concepts not only assist in developing your skills but in becoming more calm, reacting more positively to situations that occur in life and living with a more spiritual outlook. We have both discovered that this journey causes your life to become more fulfilling and less stressful, and this in turn allows life to flow better and it appears to become easier and more successful. So what are these concepts? We believe that your development and spiritual evolvement depends on these three things:

Have Patience – Have Acceptance – Have Faith

All three are needed, but are not total. By this we mean that you can have varying degrees of each, you don't need to be fully accomplished in one before you can move on to the other (thankfully), and it's okay to slip up occasionally too! They're also all linked, so each helps to enhance your grasp of the others.

Patience is essential as it takes time, practice and commitment to be good at the techniques that we show you in both of our development workbooks. We still practise all of them and don't pretend that they're all easy to learn, or that we're the best in the world at them. We're confident in our abilities but know that we need to continue to practise and develop.

Next you need to accept that all is as it should be and that you learn at the pace that's right for you. Events and lessons along the way help you to develop your understanding of how things work, how everything falls into place exactly as it should. Although in the early days of your journey you can't always see this. (Check back with yourself later though, hindsight is a wonderful thing.) In time, you come to know this more readily and be accepting of all that happens, as it happens.

When you start developing the first two of these three key elements - patience and acceptance - you can connect at a much higher level and start to understand the bigger picture of how things are. Even if you cannot verbalise that understanding, you can feel it, you can resonate with it, you can understand it in your heart and feel comfortable with it. You can then work in alignment with it and this allows you to develop at a faster rate. This is when you start to have faith. We aren't referring to a religious faith, but a deep understanding or inner knowing. An interesting point of note is that if you foster a sense of faith, however small and perhaps undefined, right from the outset, the whole process to develop true faith happens much quicker and more simply. This is because you're emitting the essence of faith to the universe and you must therefore attract it right back to you. You must have faith in yourself, in your place in creation and in your universal awareness, It allows you to listen for guidance and answers and to recognise when you hear them, to make the best choices and take responsibility for your actions.

Having a more philosophical view of how everything works together is powerful. It doesn't mean, however, that you should allow yourself to be a martyr or a victim, believing that it's part of the bigger picture. As soon as you recognise that this is what you're becoming or have become, we believe that it's up to you to acknowledge what you've learnt from the situation and get the hell out of there! Learn your lessons as quickly as possible and move on. This will help to avoid falling into similar negative cycles of behaviour and will ensure not only your happiness but that you're setting a good example to others who may be in a similar situation. Every single person can inspire others by their actions. Use your wisdom, your acceptance and your faith to be the best you can be, this will inspire others to positive change. You will illuminate the way for them through your own inner light.

STEP 2 - discuss
Make your own personal notes as you discuss each of the concepts in turn. Consider the following points:
- How do you feel about this essay in the whole, and about each of the concepts?
- What does this concept mean to you and where are you now with it?
- How might this concept help you in your life, in daily life and in more spiritual pursuits?
- Share any poignant thoughts or stories that come to mind regarding these concepts.
- How has you spiritual journey so far affected you in relation to these concepts?
- How might you go about improving this concept within your life and your relationahip with it?

STEP 3 - plan for progress
Read out the following:
There are a number of ways that you can develop these key concepts. Here are our tips:
- Practically you can increase your level of patience by setting yourself little tasks, such as watching a timer for a full minute. Helen found that she always used to take food out of the oven or microwave before the set amount of time had fully elapsed. 'Five seconds left on the microwave timer? That's nothing, just open the door!' So she set herself the task of waiting until it was fully finished every time. Then wait for it to reach zero, and count to five, slowly, before taking the food out. Just these simple exercises really helped. She noticed that she grew less impatient generally, and at the same time, more accepting that everything was just as it should be. Yoga, tai chi, relaxation and breathing exercises will all help to increase your patience.
- To help with your acceptance think about a situation in the past that hasn't gone to plan initially. Write about it in your journal if you're using one to track your development. What had you wanted to happen and why? What went wrong or didn't happen? Now think carefully about the outcome, what did you learn as a result? Was there a different or more beneficial outcome? Once you've looked at one experience, take another, and another. Do this exercise as many times as you can until you start to really believe that everything has happened just as it should. This will help you to accept that when things don't go quite to your plan in daily life, there's always a good reason for it. You may never know what that reason is, but trust that it's for the best. And use your notes or memories of past experiences as backup to help. After all, if it worked out for the best in the past, why wouldn't it in the future? You will eventually stop becoming quite so frustrated at being held up at red lights, or strangely losing your keys as you're about to leave home, and accept that you were meant to be delayed for some reason. (But please don't use this as an excuse for laziness, or being consistently late; respect for others is also important.)
- Spending time with yourself, both out in nature and in meditation helps too. Being out in nature takes away the noise and stuff of everyday life and helps you to connect with the universe. Medita-

tion helps you to still the body and still the mind. In stillness you go beyond your physical self, beyond your own thoughts and desires. You can connect deeply and profoundly with yourself and with the universe.

- Start a gratitude book, or get into the habit of regularly, perhaps daily, writing in your journal what you're grateful for in your life. Start by listing five things each day that you're grateful for. They may be simple, or very general at first. (If you're stuck with this, what about, 'I can breathe'.) Eventually you will start to appreciate lots of wonderful things that happen to you every day and can add these to your book. (For example; I spent time with wonderful friends today, I found some money in an old coat, I received a compliment, a stranger smiled at me on the bus etc.) If you haven't read or listened to 'The Secret' or 'The Power' by Rhonda Byrne we think that this would be worth doing to help you along your journey.

Come up with some actions points and ideas to assist in your development relating to these key concepts. You may want to share and swap your ideas. If you're keeping a journal these notes should be added to it so that you can track your journey.

LESSON ONE
DEEPER MEDITATION

PREPARATION
Well in advance of your meeting ensure that you have all of the tools that you require for this lesson. If not, find out if another group member has access to what you need.

Regular tools:
- Healing book
- Pens and pencils
- Paper
- Candles & matches if desired
- Box of tissues

Tools for this lesson:
- At least one candle in a sturdy holder (or more depending on the layout and size of the room) and some matches.

Extra tools if you want to do 'other things to try':
- Collection of crystals such as blue apatite, fire agate, gold or yellow calcite, opal aura quartz and sodalite.
- A recording / CD of a single drum beat, or a heartbeat.
- One or more small drums that you can play with your hands.

On the day of the meeting ensure that the room is prepared:
Are there enough seats for everyone and enough room for the work you are about to undertake?
Open the windows or burn some incense to freshen the air.
Cleanse the area.
Gather the required tools together. Call and remind anyone who has promised to bring something.
Set out some water and glasses.
Prepare some relaxing background music.
Ensure that the room isn't too cold or too warm.
Ensure that you're not going to be interrupted. Unplugging the phone and turning off mobiles are good ideas.

At the beginning of the meeting:
As people arrive ask them to add the names of anyone they know who needs some healing to the Healing Book. Remember that you don't need to put their full names and private information, first names, initials or nicknames will suffice. Whoever you intend to send the healing to, it will reach.

Once everyone has arrived and is comfortable then you can start.
Work your way through the script and exercises for this lesson as detailed on the following pages.

Read the following script out loud to the group. It's a time of meditation so keep your voice calm and relaxed, reading in a fairly slow and controlled manner. Instructions are in brackets and italics.

OPENING & PROTECTION

- Let us take a moment to close our eyes and calm our minds.
- Concentrate on your breathing, allowing the breath to become deeper and slower. *(Pause to allow everyone to take a couple of breaths in and out)*
- Let us all mentally ask our Spirit Guides and Angels to draw close and create a circle around our own.
- We let it be known that we are happy to work with Spirit and that we only work in love and light. We ask that anyone from the spirit world who wishes to contact us only does so in love and light and with the highest intentions.
- We ask for your protection, guidance and wisdom as we blend our world with yours. *(Pause)*
- Let us blend and harmonise our energies as we sit together in circle.
- Let us send out a note of harmony to the person on our left. Visualise this as a pale pink mist coming from your heart area and moving towards the heart of the person sitting on your left. *(Pause)*
- As you continue to do this, become aware of receiving the same loving energy from the right.
- As we send and receive this energy, be aware of any changes in the atmosphere within the circle. *(Pause)*
- Have a sense of oneness with the group. *(Pause)*
- Now bring your attention back to yourself and the centre of your being, the lower abdominal area.
- Focus on your breathing; become aware of the rise and fall of your abdomen. As you inhale it will gently rise and as you exhale it will fall. *(Pause to allow everyone to take a few breaths in and out)*
- Have a sense of warmth here and in your mind's eye allow a symbol or shape to form. Imagine that this symbol or shape is sitting at and represents your centre. It may be a simple glow of light, a flame or a flower.
- With each in-breath visualise your symbol becoming larger, stronger or more open whichever is appropriate.
- With each out-breath, imagine that you are exhaling any negativity left from your day, or worries that you may have. *(Pause to allow everyone to take a few breaths in and out)*
- Now take your awareness to the soles of your feet, feeling their contact with the floor. Visualise lines of energy extending out from your feet and down into the ground. In your mind's eye, see these lines of energy as roots extending deep into the earth.
- Earth energy also travels back up through these roots revitalising and nourishing you.
- See this energy entering through the soles of your feet and travelling up through your legs to the base of your spine.
- At the base of the spine imagine that the energy becomes a sphere of deep red mist or light, as you visualise it, it becomes more vibrant in colour. *(Pause)*
- From this point a beam of energy leaves the red sphere and travels up towards the sacral area, just below the belly button. Here it forms a sphere of vibrant orange mist or light. As you focus on it, it becomes stronger in colour. *(Pause)*
- Gradually a beam of energy leaves the orange sphere and travels up towards the solar plexus, where it forms a sphere of clear yellow. With each breath, this yellow becomes stronger and brighter. *(Pause)*
- Once more a beam of energy leaves this sphere and continues its journey up to the heart area. Here a sphere of mist or light begins to form, which you may see as either green or pink. Focus on this area for a few breaths allowing the energy to grow stronger and clearer and to expand. *(Pause)*
- Gradually a beam of energy leaves the heart area and moves upwards to the throat. Here it forms a sphere of clear blue. Once more, as you focus on this area, allow the colour to expand and increase in strength. *(Pause)*
- Now, visualise a strand of energy leaving the throat area and linking with the third eye area, just between and slightly above the eyes. Here energy will begin to form as before. You may see this

energy as either a rich indigo or violet, whichever you prefer. Concentrate on this energy and visualise it increasing in strength. *(Pause)*
- Again, a beam of light extends upwards from this area moving to the crown. As it does so, become aware of another beam of energy coming down from above to meet the first. As they meet at the crown a sphere of pure energy begins to form. You may see this energy as either violet or pure white light. This connects you with the higher realms of Spirit.
- As you hold this vision for a few breaths the light grows and strengthens. And as it does so, the beautiful pure light begins to overflow down and around you, surrounding you in its wonderful energy. It fills your aura, cleansing, balancing and strengthening it. You feel safe and comfortable. You feel relaxed and light. *(Longer pause before moving on to the Healing script below.)*

HEALING
- Slowly open your eyes and join hands with those sitting to either side of you. This increases the flow of healing energy.
- We know that our Guides, Angels and loved ones in Spirit have come forward and that they surround us with their healing energies. We ask them to help us as we send out our healing today. *(Pause)*
- Visualise a pool of brilliant white light forming and growing in the middle of our circle. *(Pause)*
- This is a pool of healing energy from which we can all draw when we need to. Know that this universal healing energy will find its way to all of those for whom we request healing.
- We ask for healing for each of us here, for our minds, bodies and spirit.
- *(If there are absent members: We ask for healing for the members of our group who cannot be with us today.)*
- We ask for healing for all of those on our Absent Healing List. Take a moment to visualise them standing in the healing pool.
- I would also like to ask for special healing for _____
- *(Mention anyone else that you feel healing is really important for today. Gently squeeze the hand of the person to your left to indicate that it's their turn. Let everyone have a turn at saying this part before continuing with the script.)*
- We send our healing thoughts to Mother Earth and to the plant and animal kingdom.
- Thank you.
- Release your hands and slowly open your eyes.

THEORY: DEEPER MEDITATION
The following 'theory' section should be read aloud to the group. You may want to get others to join in and take it in turns to read.

Meditation is a very powerful tool for spiritual and psychic development. In fact, if you do nothing else, learn to meditate; it's the one thing that will improve your development above all else. The benefits of meditation are wide-ranging and work on many levels, they include:
- physical, mental and emotional relaxation,
- helping to put things into perspective,
- allowing you to connect with and develop your intuitive side,
- helping you to be more at peace with and understand yourself,
- improving your focus and concentration,
- relieving physical tension,
- lowering blood pressure and heart rate,
- increasing serotonin levels,
- controlling your thoughts,
- learning forgiveness,
- increasing productivity and creativity,

- having a more positive attitude,
- increasing your empathy and listening skills,
- reducing your tendency to worry,
- increasing your patience and tolerance,
- assisting you to enter into a state where spirit communication can occur if you wish.

In a meditative state you can also re-program your brain to get rid of negative thinking and self-talk, or beliefs that have been drummed into you over the years that don't serve you or hold you back in some way. Deep meditation is used for affirmations, recalling memories, venturing into past lives, deep inner healing, deeper personal understanding and moving into trance mediumship which is covered in lesson 11.

The deeper the meditation, the greater the ability to develop your psychic and intuitive abilities and the more it heightens your spiritual awareness. The different levels of meditation can be measured by the frequency of the brainwave rhythms:
- Beta waves - normal waking state, conscious, working & alert state of mind.
- Alpha waves - slower brainwave, physically and mentally relaxed with awareness, obtained in light meditation, a reflective state of mind.
- Theta waves - often mixes with alpha but is a deeper meditation, reduced consciousness, a free flowing, creative state of mind.
- Delta waves - sleep state, higher delta brainwaves occur when dreaming (during REM) and the lower delta brainwaves occur during the dreamless state.

In lighter meditation you will experience relaxation, drowsiness, a relaxed mind, your arms and legs may feel heavy, you may find yourself staring blankly, you probably won't want to move. It's the starting point for spiritual development as it helps keep a perspective on things, you can develop your visualisation skills, and it generally helps you to become more open-minded, especially to connection with spirit.

In a deep meditation there's an enhanced sense of oneness with others and with the world. You may also discover that there's an altered sense of time and space. Time spent in deep meditation will greatly enhance your psychic and intuitive powers and also allow a sense of detachment that can help you work out solutions to problems in your life and see the bigger picture. You may lose track of time, and awareness of your own body and the people and things around you while in this state. You will probably be very reluctant to move or speak. You may also experience involuntary twitching and a sense of heaviness in your physical body.

A meditation is a great way to start a development session whether you're working on your own or in a group. It switches you away from everyday stuff and demonstrates your intention to work on the more spiritual level.

Discuss any personal experiences or thoughts on the subject (but keep any eye on the time).

PRACTICAL WORK
Read out each exercise, one at a time to the group so that you're all clear as to what you're doing, then allocate a time to complete the exercise.

Stage 1 - Simple Physical Relaxation
Before you begin, find a position that you feel comfortable in and can maintain for the duration of the meditation. You can lie down if you wish, but if you're tired this can encourage sleep. It's best to be upright in a chair or cross-legged on the floor, perhaps supported by a cushion if required.
- Ensure that you're physically relaxed before you begin meditating. This can be done very simply by taking your attention to each area of your body in turn, starting with your feet and working upwards, including your face and head. Slowly and systematically focus your attention on each muscle group

tensing and holding it for a few seconds and then consciously releasing it. Take your time and don't rush through, you may want to repeat this exercise a second time. Read out the following:
- Ensure you're sitting or lying comfortably.
- Take your awareness to your hands, make a tight fist, hold for a count of 3, 2, 1, and release.
- Tense your lower arms, hold for 3, 2, 1, and release.
- Tense your upper arms, hold for 3, 2, 1, and release.
- Tense your shoulders, lifting them up towards your ears, hold for 3, 2, 1, and release.
- Take your awareness to your neck: pull your chin toward chest but keep it from touching chest, hold for 3, 2, 1, and then relax.
- Take your awareness to your lower face and jaw, bite hard and pull back the corners of your mouth hold for 3, 2, 1, and then relax.
- Screw your eyes up and wrinkle your nose, hold for 3, 2, 1, and then relax.
- Move your awareness to your forehead, lift your eyebrows as high as possible, hold for 3, 2, 1, and then relax.
- Take your awareness to your upper torso, pull your shoulder blades together hold for 3, 2, 1, and then release.
- Tense your stomach muscles, pulling your bellybutton towards your spine, hold for 3, 2, 1, and then release.
- Take your awareness to your legs tense your thigh muscles, hold for 3, 2, 1, and then release.
- Pull your toes towards your head tensing your calf muscles, hold for 3, 2, 1, and then release.
- Taking your awareness to your feet, point and curl your toes downwards, hold for 3, 2, 1, and then release.
- Tense your whole body at once, hands, arms, face, neck, chest, stomach, thighs, calves and feet, screw your eyes up, hold for 3, 2, 1, and completely release.
- *(Move straight on to the next stage.)*

Stage 2 - The Breath
- Take your awareness to your breathing, preferably through your nose as this is more relaxing.
- Ensure that you're breathing slowly and deeply.
- As you inhale, your abdomen will gently rise. And as you exhale it will fall.
- If your mind drifts or you lose track during this exercise bring your attention back to refocus on your breathing.
- Take a long, slow, deep inhalation for a count of 1 - 2 - 3 - 4, hold for 1- 2 and exhale for 1 - 2 - 3 - 4.
- In 2 3 4, Hold (pause), Out 2 3 4
- In 2 3 4, Hold (pause), Out 2 3 4
- In 2 3 4, Hold (pause), Out 2 3 4
- In 2 3 4, Hold (pause), Out 2 3 4
- In 2 3 4, Hold (pause), Out 2 3 4
- Continue breathing slowly and deeply until you're ready to move on to the next stage. It's not a race or a competition, just a way of relaxing and focusing your mind on the moment.
- *(You can start to lengthen the breath once you're used to this exercise, increasing the inhalation and exhalation to 5 or 6 counts. Take your time though.)*

Stage 3
Exercise 1 - Candle Gazing
Start by doing this exercise for just couple of minutes and then gradually increasing as you wish for up to 15 minutes.
- Place a candle in a stable holder on a flat surface so that each person can sit about two to three feet away from it. It should be just at or below eye level when you're seated. You may use one candle in the middle of a circle. Or, depending on how much room you have, more candles in different places with fewer people focussing on each one.
- Light the candle(s) and ensure that you're sitting comfortably and with good posture. Your back

should be straight and your hands resting gently, palms up, on your knees. Read out the following:
- Close your eyes and take a few deep inhalations and exhalations allowing your body to relax.
- Slowly open your eyes and with a soft gaze look at the flame of the candle in front of you.
- Let any thoughts that you may have drift from your mind as though they were a wisp of cloud floating in a clear blue sky.
- Don't try to analyse these thoughts, but take your focus back to the candle's flame.
- Keep your eyes relaxed. You may blink if needed.
- Close your eyes for a moment or two and see if you can visualise the candle's flame in your mind's eye. *(Pause for a moment.)*
- Open your eyes again and continue to gaze at the flame itself.
- Enjoy the stillness and the peace. *(Pause for a moment)*
- Close your eyes.
- Place your hands together and rub your palms to warm them.
- Place them over your eyes gently allowing them to warm the muscles around your eyes.
- Slowly remove your hands and in your own time, open your eyes.
- *(Briefly discuss your experiences.)*

Exercise 2 - Guided visualisation for deeper meditation
- Ensure that you're sitting comfortably with your hands on your knees, palms facing upwards.
- Close your eyes. Take a deep inhalation, and breathe out slowly. Continue to breathe slowly and deeply.
- During this meditation you will always be safe and protected, you will feel relaxed and comfortable. If, however, there is anything that does make you feel uneasy, or you wish to come back out of the meditation, you can do so at any time by counting backwards from 3 to 1 and taking a deep breath in and out. You can then bring your awareness back to your physical body, particularly your feet and open your eyes.
- For now though, continue to breathe slowly and deeply, your body feels relaxed and your mind is clear.
- As you breathe, images may begin to form in your mind's eye. Don't try to manipulate or analyse them, simply observe them. If you don't automatically see these images, simply imagine or sense them.
- Ahead of you lies a staircase or series of ten steps. Move towards them. At the bottom you can see a doorway. We're going to slowly go down these steps towards the door feeling safe and confident at all times. So moving down the steps on my count,
- 10, 9, 8, with each step feeling lighter and lighter.
- 7, 6, 5, feeling calm and peaceful,
- 4, 3, relaxed and light
- 2 and 1, you find yourself standing in front of the door. Reaching out you open the door and as you do so, a wonderful, warm light shines through from the other side, bathing your whole being in its rays.
- As you stand in this light for a few moments, your physical body is warmed through and your energy body is nourished and energised. This gives you a sense of comfort and completeness and offers further protection on your journey. *(Pause for a short while.)*
- Today's journey is to help you to experience a deeper state of meditation. To encourage deep calm and oneness with yourself and the universe.
- The rays of light subside and you can now see through the doorway to the other side.
- As your eyes adjust to the change in light, colours begin to form shapes. You can see your sanctuary on the other side of the doorway.
- You step through, closing the door behind you and make your way through your sanctuary to the exit that leads to your outside space, or your sanctuary may be an outside space itself.
- Venturing into your outside space you will see a pathway leading away from your sanctuary. It may have a light glow about it.
- This pathway will lead you to a place that you associate with a sense of deep serenity and reverence.

LESSON ONE – DEEPER MEDITATION

- It may be a sacred spot or a place of worship, a building or an outside place.
- Follow the path enjoying the scenery as you go. The path slopes slightly downhill. The further you travel down this path the more relaxed and content you feel.
- After a short while you come to your sacred spot.
- Take a moment to observe it and feel its energy. *(Pause for 30 seconds.)*
- As you enter the area or building you can see candles placed randomly around it. Each candle is lit and gives off a gentle glow.
- Sit somewhere comfortable, take in your surroundings and enjoy the peace and tranquillity. *(Pause for 30 seconds.)*
- This place and the candle light are soothing and as its energy envelops you, you have a sense of comfort and wellbeing. You lie down.
- Your eyes become heavy, allow them to close as you lie here, safe and content.
- Your body feels as though it is floating. Within this meditation you drift off into a deep sleep.
- Deeper and deeper.
- You dream of lying on a soft white cloud, floating downwards, you feel lighter and lighter. It feels natural to let go and enjoy this sensation.
- Deeper and deeper.
- The deeper you go, the better you feel.
- *(Pause for a couple of minutes)*
- The floating sensation lessens and you gently open your eyes to find yourself lying in your sacred place once more. You feel refreshed and calm.
- As you lie here, you can see a beautiful crystal lying just in front of you. Reach out and hold the crystal. It has been placed here for you as a gift from this special place.
- This crystal is a magical object to help transport you in to a deeper state of meditation whenever you visualise that you're holding it.
- Hold your crystal against your lower abdominal area, the centre of your being.
- Close your eyes once more and take yourself back to your sanctuary, visualise lying in a comfortable and safe space in your sanctuary. You will be instantly transported to it.
- Thank your guides and loved ones in spirit for your magical crystal then place it in a special place in your sanctuary where you will be able to return to it whenever you like. You are able to bring the essence of this gift with you as you return to the physical world. You may also wish to find a similar stone in the physical world to help in your meditations.
- Now make your way to the doorway leading to your stairwell.
- Open the door. Step through closing the door behind you.
- Know that your sanctuary is your own space that you can return to at any time for relaxation, guidance and healing.
- And keeping your sense of calm and wellbeing, it is time to head back up the stairs. So moving back up the stairs on my count,
- 1, 2, 3, breathing slowly and deeply,
- 4, 5, 6, your body is starting to feel heavier,
- 7, 8, bringing your awareness back to your physical body,
- 9 and 10, on that top step now and when you're ready, step off the top step.
- **Bringing your awareness completely back to your physical body and this room, your contact with the chair, your feet with the floor. Slowly begin to move your fingers and toes, and in your own time, opening your eyes, fully awake and aware and in the physical world.**

(If you are reading this aloud for someone else, watch for them starting to wriggle fingers and toes. If they appear not want to come back to the room simply repeat the last paragraph, in bold, but raising your voice so that it's said slightly louder and firmer. Repeat a third time if necessary moving over to the person and at the end just saying their name and asking that they come back now into the room, placing your hand gently on their shoulder.)

- Spend a few minutes sharing experiences of the meditation or making notes about it if you're keeping a personal journal. Don't forget to date the entry.

CLOSING & GROUNDING
Once you have completed the exercises everyone should sit comfortably and complete the following meditation to close and ground their energy. Read out the following:
- Sit in a comfortable position and close your eyes.
- Bring your attention to your breathing and focus on this for a few breaths. *(Pause)*
- Take your awareness to the invisible energy field surrounding you and visualise it drawing in close around your physical body. *(Pause)*
- Take your awareness to the area just above your crown and see a sphere of light sitting here.
- Imagine that sphere of light shrinking in size until it's tiny, then sinking down through the crown of your head.
- See it slowly descending down past the brow. *(Pause)*
- Into the throat. *(Pause)*
- Then following the line of the spine, down, through your body, towards your heart area. *(Pause)*
- Down to your solar plexus. *(Pause)*
- Through the abdominal area. *(Pause)*
- To the base of your spine. *(Pause)*
- Now visualise the sphere of energy either leaving through the base of your spine, or dividing in two and sinking down through your legs and leaving through the soles of your feet.
- Feel this energy leaving you and connecting with the earth.
- Have a sense of downward movement, deep in to the earth. *(Pause)*
- Become more aware of your feet and your physical body.
- Let us take a moment to thank our Spirit Guides, Angels and loved ones in Spirit for their presence, protection and wisdom whilst we've been working. Knowing that they will always be on hand should we need to call on them. *(Pause)*
- **Now bring your awareness back to your physical body, the chair you are sitting on and your contact with the floor.**
- **Begin to bring some movement back in to your fingers and toes.**
- **In your own time opening your eyes, fully awake and aware and in the physical world.**

(Watch for them starting to wriggle fingers and toes and keep an eye on anyone who doesn't do this. If a member of the group appears not to want to come back to the room simply repeat the last three points, in bold, but raising your voice so that it said slightly louder and firmer. Repeat a third time if necessary moving over to the person and at the end just saying their name and asking that they come back into the room now, placing a hand gently on their shoulder.)

Check to ensure that everyone feels grounded before you finish the session. If not, get them to walk around for a little while. Stamping your feet or jumping up and down helps to bring you back to the physical world. If these don't do the trick, you can ground your energy very readily by eating a small amount of food such as a biscuit.

OTHER THINGS TO TRY:
- Using crystals: Simply hold them in your hand or place them in your lap while meditating in whichever way you prefer. Crystals that will encourage a deeper meditation are blue apatite, fire agate, gold or yellow calcite, opal aura quartz and sodalite.
- Using healing energy: Receive healing energy from an individual or group while meditating to encourage a deeper meditative state.
- Black Out: Try meditating in complete darkness.
- In a beat: Meditate to a recording of a simple drum beat or heartbeat. Have it playing while you

work through a physical relaxation and breathing exercise then simply focus your attention on the beat for as long as you wish.
- Bang it out: Try drumming out a simple rhythm on a small drum over and over again with your hands - if you have enough drums for each person in the group to do this it's very powerful. Go past the boredom point and just keep going. Allow your consious mind to be taken out of the equation. You will go in to a state of deep meditation.

AND ANOTHER THING...
- Meditate in complete silence.
- Meditate with white noise. White noise is designed to cut out background and external noises and interruptions. You can get CDs and downloadable MP3s of white noise tracks and also white noise machines. Take a look at the website www.whitenoisemachine.co.uk.
- Try a binaural beat recording designed for inducing a deep meditation. There are many types available online including ranges from 'Hemisync', 'Holo sync' and 'Life flow'. There are also single MP3 tracks that you can download from some websites.
- Methods of sensory deprivation, such as using a flotation tank can also encourage a deeper meditative state.

FOR DISCUSSION
- What have we got from this lesson? Best bits? Tricky bits?
- Key Concepts - how are we getting on with patience, acceptance, faith?
- Healing - feedback from those in the healing book? Success stories?

Next Time...
The next lesson will be covering ENERGY WORK.
You will need to arrange for the following tools to be brought along:
- An item of jewellery or something similar if you're planning on doing some psychometry after the exercises for building up the energy.

Extra tools if you want to do 'other things to try'
- Collection of crystals such as clear quartz, rose quartz, sodalite, amethyst, black tourmaline, black obsidian and haematite.

LESSON TWO
ENERGY WORK

PREPARATION
Well in advance of your meeting ensure that you have all of the tools that you require for this lesson. If not, find out if another group member has access to what you need.

Regular tools:
- Healing book
- Pens and pencils
- Paper
- Candles & matches if desired
- Box of tissues

Tools for this lesson:
- An item of jewellery or something similar if you are planning on doing some psychometry after exercises for building up the energy.

Extra tools if you want to do 'other things to try':
- Collection of crystals such as clear quartz, rose quartz, sodalite, amethyst, black tourmaline, black obsidian and haematite.

On the day of the meeting ensure that the room is prepared:
Are there enough seats for everyone and enough room for the work you are about to undertake?
Open the windows or burn some incense to freshen the air.
Cleanse the area.
Gather the required tools together. Call and remind anyone who has promised to bring something.
Set out some water and glasses.
Prepare some relaxing background music.
Ensure that the room isn't too cold or too warm.
Ensure that you're not going to be interrupted. Unplugging the phone and turning off mobiles are good ideas.

At the beginning of the meeting:
As people arrive ask them to add the names of anyone they know who needs some healing to the Healing Book. Remember that you don't need to put their full names and private information, first names, initials or nicknames will suffice. Whoever you intend to send the healing to, it will reach.

Once everyone has arrived and is comfortable then you can start.
Work your way through the script and exercises for this lesson as detailed on the following pages.

Read the following scripts out loud to the group. It's a time of meditation so keep your voice calm and relaxed, reading in a fairly slow and controlled manner. Instructions are in brackets and italics.

RELAXATION
- Ensure you're sitting or lying comfortably.
- Take your awareness to your hands, make a tight fist, hold for a count of 3, 2, 1, and release.
- Tense your lower arms, hold for 3, 2, 1, and release.
- Tense your upper arms, hold for 3, 2, 1, and release.
- Tense your shoulders, lifting them up towards your ears, hold for 3, 2, 1, and release.
- Take your awareness to your neck: pull your chin toward chest but keep it from touching chest, hold for 3, 2, 1, and then relax.
- Take your awareness to your lower face and jaw, bite hard and pull back the corners of your mouth, hold for 3, 2, 1, and then relax.
- Screw your eyes up and wrinkle your nose, hold for 3, 2, 1, and then relax.
- Move your awareness to your forehead, lift your eyebrows as high as possible, hold for 3, 2, 1, and then relax.
- Take your awareness to your upper torso, pull your shoulder blades together hold for 3, 2, 1, and then release.
- Tense your stomach muscles, pulling your bellybutton towards your spine, hold for 3, 2, 1, and then release.
- Taking your awareness to your legs tense your thigh muscles, hold for 3, 2, 1, and then release.
- Pull your toes towards your head tensing your calf muscles, hold for 3, 2, 1, and then release.
- Take your awareness to your feet, point and curl your toes downwards, hold for 3, 2, 1, and then release.
- Tense your whole body at once, hands, arms, face, neck, chest, stomach, thighs, calves and feet, screw your eyes up, hold for 3, 2, 1, and completely release.
- Now take your awareness to your breathing, preferably through your nose as this is more relaxing.
- Ensure that you're breathing slowly and deeply.
- As you inhale, your abdomen will gently rise. And as you exhale it will fall.
- If your mind drifts or you lose track during this exercise bring your attention back to refocus on your breathing.
- Take a long, slow, deep inhalation for a count of 1 - 2 - 3 - 4, hold for 1- 2 and exhale for 1 - 2 - 3 - 4.
- In 2 3 4, Hold (pause), Out 2 3 4
- In 2 3 4, Hold (pause), Out 2 3 4
- In 2 3 4, Hold (pause), Out 2 3 4
- In 2 3 4, Hold (pause), Out 2 3 4
- In 2 3 4, Hold (pause), Out 2 3 4
- Continue breathing slowly and deeply.
- *(Move on to the script below.)*

OPENING & PROTECTION
- Let us take a moment to close our eyes and calm our minds.
- Concentrate on your breathing, allowing the breath to become deeper and slower. *(Pause to allow everyone to take a couple of breaths in and out)*
- Let us all mentally ask our Spirit Guides and Angels to draw close and create a circle around our own.
- We let it be known that we are happy to work with Spirit and that we only work in love and light. We ask that anyone from the spirit world who wishes to contact us only does so in love and light and with the highest intentions.
- We ask for your protection, guidance and wisdom as we blend our world with yours. *(Pause)*
- Let us blend and harmonise our energies as we sit together in circle.
- Let us send out a note of harmony to the person on our left. Visualise this as a pale pink mist coming from your heart area and moving towards the heart of the person sitting on your left. *(Pause)*

LESSON TWO - ENERGY WORK

- As you continue to do this, become aware of receiving the same loving energy from the right.
- As we send and receive this energy, be aware of any changes in the atmosphere within the circle. *(Pause)*
- Have a sense of oneness with the group. *(Pause)*
- Now bring your attention back to yourself and the centre of your being, the lower abdominal area.
- Focus on your breathing; become aware of the rise and fall of your abdomen. As you inhale it will gently rise and as you exhale it will fall. *(Pause to allow everyone to take a few breaths in and out)*
- Have a sense of warmth here and in your mind's eye allow a symbol or shape to form. Imagine that this symbol or shape is sitting at and represents your centre. It may be a simple glow of light, a flame or a flower.
- With each in-breath visualise your symbol becoming larger, stronger or more open whichever is appropriate.
- With each out-breath, imagine that you are exhaling any negativity left from your day, or worries that you may have. *(Pause to allow everyone to take a few breaths in and out)*
- Now take your awareness to the soles of your feet, feeling their contact with the floor. Visualise lines of energy extending out from your feet and down into the ground. In your mind's eye, see these lines of energy as roots extending deep into the earth.
- Earth energy also travels back up through these roots revitalising and nourishing you.
- See this energy entering through the soles of your feet and travelling up through your legs to the base of your spine.
- At the base of the spine imagine that the energy becomes a sphere of deep red mist or light, as you visualise it, it becomes more vibrant in colour. *(Pause)*
- From this point a beam of energy leaves the red sphere and travels up towards the sacral area, just below the belly button. Here it forms a sphere of vibrant orange mist or light. As you focus on it, it becomes stronger in colour. *(Pause)*
- Gradually a beam of energy leaves the orange sphere and travels up towards the solar plexus, where it forms a sphere of clear yellow. With each breath, this yellow becomes stronger and brighter. *(Pause)*
- Once more a beam of energy leaves this sphere and continues its journey up to the heart area. Here a sphere of mist or light begins to form, which you may see as either green or pink. Focus on this area for a few breaths allowing the energy to grow stronger and clearer and to expand. *(Pause)*
- Gradually a beam of energy leaves the heart area and moves upwards to the throat. Here it forms a sphere of clear blue. Once more, as you focus on this area, allow the colour to expand and increase in strength. *(Pause)*
- Now, visualise a strand of energy leaving the throat area and linking with the third eye area, just between and slightly above the eyes. Here energy will begin to form as before. You may see this energy as either a rich indigo or violet, whichever you prefer. Concentrate on this energy and visualise it increasing in strength. *(Pause)*
- Again, a beam of light extends upwards from this area moving to the crown. As it does so, become aware of another beam of energy coming down from above to meet the first. As they meet at the crown a sphere of pure energy begins to form. You may see this energy as either violet or pure white light. This connects you with the higher realms of Spirit.
- As you hold this vision for a few breaths the light grows and strengthens. And as it does so, the beautiful pure light begins to overflow down and around you, surrounding you in its wonderful energy. It fills your aura, cleansing, balancing and strengthening it. You feel safe and comfortable. You feel relaxed and light. *(Longer pause before moving on to the Healing script below.)*

HEALING
- Slowly open your eyes and join hands with those sitting to either side of you. This increases the flow of healing energy.
- We know that our Guides, Angels and loved ones in Spirit have come forward and that they surround us with their healing energies. We ask them to help us as we send out our healing today. *(Pause)*
- Visualise a pool of brilliant white light forming and growing in the middle of our circle. *(Pause)*
- This is a pool of healing energy from which we can all draw when we need to. Know that this universal healing energy will find its way to all of those for whom we request healing.
- We ask for healing for each of us here, for our minds, bodies and spirit.

(If there are absent members: We ask for healing for the members of our group who cannot be with us today.)
- We ask for healing for all of those on our Absent Healing List. Take a moment to visualise them standing in the healing pool.
- I would also like to ask for special healing for _____

(Mention anyone else that you feel healing is really important for today. Gently squeeze the hand of the person to your left to indicate that it's their turn. Let everyone have a turn at saying this part before continuing with the script.)
- We send our healing thoughts to Mother Earth and to the plant and animal kingdom. Thank you.
- Release your hands but keep your eyes closed so that you remain relaxed and peaceful as we go in to our meditation. *(Brief pause before moving on to the script below.)*

MEDITATION
- Ensure that you're sitting comfortably with your hands on your knees, palms facing upwards.
- Close your eyes.
- Take a deep inhalation, and breathe out slowly. Continue to breathe slowly and deeply.
- During this meditation you will always be safe and protected, you will feel relaxed and comfortable. If, however, there is anything that does make you feel uneasy, or you wish to come back out of the meditation, you can do so at any time by counting backwards from 3 to 1 and taking a deep breath in and out. You can then bring your awareness back to your physical body, particularly your feet and open your eyes.
- For now though, continue to breathe slowly and deeply, your body feels relaxed and your mind is clear.
- As you breathe images may begin to form in your mind's eye. Don't try to manipulate or analyse them, simply observe them. If you do not automatically see these images, simply imagine or sense them.
- Ahead of you lies a staircase or series of ten steps. Move towards them. At the bottom you can see a doorway. We're going to slowly go down these steps towards the door feeling safe and confident at all times. So moving down the steps on my count:
- 10, 9, 8, with each step feeling lighter and lighter.
- 7, 6, 5, feeling calm and peaceful,
- 4, 3, relaxed and light
- 2 and 1, you find yourself standing in front of the door. Reaching out you open the door and as you do so, a wonderful, warm light shines through from the other side, bathing your whole being in its rays.
- As you stand in this light for a few moments, your physical body is warmed through and your energy body is nourished and energised. This gives you a sense of comfort and completeness and offers further protection on your journey. *(Pause for a short while)*
- Today's meditation is to help you feel your connection with the universe and your own inner light.
- The rays of light subside and you can now see through the doorway to the other side.
- As your eyes adjust to the change in light, colours begin to form shapes. You can see your sanctuary on the other side of the doorway.
- You step through, closing the door behind you

- Move through your sanctuary to a place that you would like to sit or lie to enjoy your time here. You will be safe and comfortable, warm and relaxed.
- Ask your spirit guides and angels to draw close and to help you to understand the essence of universal energy.
- As you sit or lie in your sanctuary you become deeply relaxed and at peace.
- Place your hands gently on your abdomen. You may become aware of a sense of warmth here.
- In your mind's eye you start to see, or sense, a pure bright light within you, it can take any form you wish, a flame, an orb, whatever comes to mind or makes sense to you.
- This is your own inner light.
- As you focus your thoughts on it it becomes larger and more intense. It's brilliance causes your whole body to glow with the same energy and light.
- You know in your soul that every living thing has this light, this essence within them. Some nurture it, others are unaware of it's existence. This light is a small part of the universal energy, it is a part of the whole. It is what draws us back together again.
- Our light energises and inspires us, it illuminates the dark corners within and without.
- The more you acknowledge this part of you, the brighter it becomes. The light seeps through into your auras and extends far beyond your physical body.
- You are a being of light, an integral part of the universe.
- You contain a spark of the universal light. And the universal light contains you.
- Enjoy this moment. *(Pause for 1 - 2 minutes)*
- Your connection with the universe is undoubted.
- We're all a part of it.
- It's only our level of awareness of this connection that differentiates one being from another.
- Bring your awareness back to your own being, to the light within you.
- You will bring this feeling, this knowing and understanding back with you and incorporate in to your feeling for and understanding of others and the world around you.
- Thank your guides and angels for helping you with your comprehension of this energy connection.
- It's now time to return.
- Get up and move through your sanctuary to the doorway that leads to your stairwell.
- Open the door. Step through closing the door behind you.
- Know that your sanctuary is your own space that you can return to at any time for relaxation, guidance and healing.
- And keeping your sense of calm and wellbeing, it is time to head back up the stairs. So moving back up the stairs on my count,
- 1, 2, 3, breathing slowly and deeply,
- 4, 5, 6, your body is starting to feel heavier
- 7, 8, bringing your awareness back to your physical body,
- 9 and 10, on that top step now and when you're ready, step off the top step.
- **Bringing your awareness completely back to your physical body and this room, your contact with the chair, your feet with the floor. Slowly begin to move your fingers and toes, and in your own time, opening your eyes, fully awake and aware and in the physical world.**

(Watch for them starting to wriggle fingers and toes and keep an eye on anyone who doesn't do this. If a member of the group appears not to want to come back to the room simply repeat the last paragraph, in bold, but raising your voice so that it said slightly louder and firmer. Repeat a third time if necessary moving over to the person and at the end just saying their name and asking that they come back now in to the room, placing your hand gently on their shoulder.)

Spend a few minutes sharing experiences of the meditation. Remember that it's okay if someone fell asleep, could see nothing or did their own thing. If you're keeping a personal journal, you may wish to take some time to record you experience. Don't forget to date the entry.

THEORY: ENERGY WORK

The following 'theory' section should be read aloud to the group. You may want to get others to join in and take it in turns to read.

Understanding and working with 'energy' is one of the most fundamental parts of spiritual and psychic development. It helps you maintain your own energy levels, and understand how you can be affected by and have an effect on others. You use it to help connect with other people, spirit and your surroundings. You can also learn to create and sustain high levels of energy for advanced subjects and group work.

In the past, and possibly still today, when potential mediums joined a development circle there would be only one potential medium. The rest of the group were already established and were there purely to provide energy for the novice's development. Most of what you do in this type of work involves tapping into universal energy to either gain information and guidance from the collective conscious or creating energy that can be used for the work you do. For example if you choose to work with spirit, you effectively allow them to feed off the energy the group has created to let them make their presence known. You also use this energy for healing, automatic writing and manifestation projects. As you progress through these advanced subjects, being able to create and sustain high levels of energy becomes essential. It's also something that's required if you want to begin looking at 'rescue work'. Rescue work is helping spirit to move over into the light if they're stuck here on the earth plane. When we do this type of work, we work with our spirit guides and create high levels of energy so that we can re-create the portal or 'light' that's required for them to move on to the next plane of existence.

Creating and maintaining a conscious connection to universal energy is one of the most powerful skills you can master. It's just like putting a battery into an item to complete a circuit and create power. When you first start to work on your own development it's sufficient to connect to the higher realms through the crown chakra and then at the end of your work, to ground through the feet, But as you progress you tend to find that you need more energy to do the work that you want to do. This could manifest by feeling really tired during or after practising, or not being as successful at the exercises as you would like, or perhaps feeling as though you've more potential than you're seeing in your results. A conscious connection at both the feet and crown throughout your work will mean that you can create a greater more controlled and focussed energy flow. If during your work you start to lose focus, become tired, feel less energy flowing or need an extra boost, then re-establishing your conscious connection will remedy this. It's a very simple exercise but don't underestimate the difference it will make to your work and abilities.

This chapter is building on the work you did on auras and chakras in our 'Beginner's Guide'. You can practise these exercises on your own but it's infinitely better, and you'll develop faster, if you work in a group. In a group energetic harmony is vital so we will look at how to develop this as well.

Discuss any personal experiences or thoughts on the subject (but keep any eye on the time).

PRACTICAL WORK

Read out each exercise, one at a time to the group so that you are all clear as to what you are doing, then allocate a time to complete the exercise.

This gives an excellent three-step process to go through at the beginning of every session from now on. But be aware that it may take some time to sense the energy fully and to understand the impact that it has on your psychic and spiritual development. It's a good idea to appoint someone to lead these exercises from one to another and then on to other work so that everyone isn't sitting wondering what's going on next.

Step 1 - Conscious Connection Visualisation

You can sit comfortably either cross-legged on the floor or upright in a chair or you can stand. Try connecting using this exercise and then simply sit or stand allowing the energy to flow, observing any sensations.

- Sit in a circle so that you're ready to move on to step 2 and 3 without moving around too much. Read out the following:
- Take your awareness to the soles of your feet, feeling their contact with the floor. Visualise lines of energy extending out from your feet and down into the ground.
- In your mind's eye, see these lines of energy as roots extending deep into the earth. Maintain this feeling of energy at the feet and be aware of earth energy moving up through these roots entering your energy system, revitalising and nourishing you. It may help to see them beginning to glow with light as the energy travels up from the earth and enters your energy system.
- Now take your awareness to the crown of your head.
- Imagine that you're being suspended by a piece of string from this point. The piece of string hangs from a point far above you, so far above you that you're unable to see its origin.
- You should have a sense of being lifted upwards.
- In your mind's eye, the string is a brilliant white light, a magical connection with higher realms. Its brilliance and its power connects with and enters into your energy system.
- You can sense this energy entering your energy system through your crown chakra. It feels amazingly empowering.
- *Briefly discuss your experiences.*

Step 2 - Harmonising exercise

This exercise helps you to connect and harmonise as a group and is done at the start of each session of working in the 'Opening & Protection' section. This harmonisation process can also be done on its own and will help with generating higher levels of energy for your work.

- Sit comfortably in a circle, either in a chair or cross-legged on the floor.
- One person in the group should say the following:
- "Let us blend and harmonise our energies as we sit together in circle. Let us send out a note of harmony to the person on our left by visualising a pale pink mist or light coming from our heart area and moving towards the heart of the person sitting on our left. As we continue to do this, become aware of receiving the same loving energy from the right. As we send and receive this, an energy circle is formed that encompasses all of us. Be aware of any changes in the atmosphere within the circle. Have a sense of oneness with the group."
- *(Pause for a minute or so to experience the sensation then read the following)*
- Now slowly open your eyes bringing your awareness back to the room.
- *Briefly discuss your experiences.*

Step 3 - Creating an energy source as a group

This exercise is a good one to do prior to any form of mediumship but particularly if you're asking for sound or movement to occur to confirm connection with your guides or a particular spirit.

- Ensuring that you're sitting comfortably, join hands in order to focus and build up the energy.
- Read out the following:
- Close your eyes and take your awareness to either your feet (if seated) or the base of your spine (if sitting on the floor). Imagine roots extending out through this point and down deep into the earth.
- See these roots glowing with a bright white light. This is the powerful earth energy that nourishes all living things. The roots glow so bright and carry this energy all the way up to you and your contact with the ground. This wonderful energy enters your energetic system at this point. It moves up through your body and along the line of your spine to the centre of your being, just below the belly button. *(Pause)*
- Once you feel the energy here take your awareness to a point just above the crown. Visualise a beam

or funnel of pure white light coming down from the heavens. This is heavenly energy from the spirit realms. It enters your energetic body through the crown chakra and streams down through your head and neck towards your centre.
- As these two streams meet and become one at your centre, feel the energy building up, a powerful warmth may be felt. *(Pause)*
- Become aware of the palms of your hands and the connection you have with the group. You should feel warmth or tingling as your focus encourages the energy to be pulled from your centre to your hands.
- Maintain your contact and simply let the energy flow around the circle passing from hand to hand. You may get a sense of it moving round in a particular direction. You may also experience different sensations such as your arms wanting to 'float' or move, or 'power surges' where your body, arms or hands shudder slightly. This is quite normal, just let the energy flow.
- You can continue to create this battery effect for as long as you wish, or as long as you feel comfortable.
- *Either briefly discuss your experiences or move straight on to Step 4.*

Step 4 - Things to do with all that energy
Go on to use this energy for mediumship (see the example below), healing or psychometry within the group. Pay special attention to any different sensations that you may experience. Does your connection to spirit feel stronger or different in any way?

Using the energy to assist your mediumship
Follow step 3 again but this time request that the energy draw your spirit guides and loved ones in spirit closer and that they pass on any messages or visions that they wish to. During this time, you may get a sense of a spirit presence, hear sounds, see things in your mind's eye, smell fragrances, or have things simply pop into your head. It's fine to discuss what you feel and see while maintaining the flow of energy. Although this might feel a bit awkward at first you will get used to it. Once established, you won't affect the energy connection or flow by talking calmly to each other. If anyone feels uncomfortable at any point they should stop working and close and ground their energies. Make notes during or after this exercise so you can review the information you've received at a later date.

Step 5 - To finish
When you're finished visualise a small door sliding across the crown, closing your connection with the heavens (although it will never truly close this helps you to state your intention that you're finishing your work). Also visualise the bright white roots turning to dark brown. Close and ground your energies.

CLOSING & GROUNDING
Once you have completed the exercises everyone should sit comfortably and complete the following meditation to close and ground their energy. Read out the following:
- Sit in a comfortable position and close your eyes.
- Bring your attention to your breathing and focus on this for a few breaths. *(Pause)*
- Take your awareness to the invisible energy field surrounding you and visualise it drawing in close around your physical body. *(Pause)*
- Take your awareness to the area just above your crown and see a sphere of light sitting here.
- Imagine that sphere of light shrinking in size until it's tiny, then sinking down through the crown of your head.
- See it slowly descending down past the brow. *(Pause)*
- Into the throat. *(Pause)*
- Then following the line of the spine, down, through your body, towards your heart area. *(Pause)*
- Down to your solar plexus. *(Pause)*
- Through the abdominal area. *(Pause)*

- ○ To the base of your spine. *(Pause)*
- ○ Now visualise the sphere of energy either leaving through the base of your spine, or dividing in two and sinking down through your legs and leaving through the soles of your feet.
- ○ Feel this energy leaving you and connecting with the earth.
- ○ Have a sense of downward movement, deep in to the earth. *(Pause)*
- ○ Become more aware of your feet and your physical body.
- ○ Let us take a moment to thank our Spirit Guides, Angels and loved ones in Spirit for their presence, protection and wisdom whilst we've been working. Knowing that they will always be on hand should we need to call on them. *(Pause)*
- ○ **Now bring your awareness back to your physical body, the chair you are sitting on and your contact with the floor.**
- ○ **Begin to bring some movement back in to your fingers and toes.**
- ○ **In your own time opening your eyes, fully awake and aware and in the physical world.**

(Watch for them starting to wriggle fingers and toes and keep an eye on anyone who doesn't do this. If a member of the group appears not to want to come back to the room simply repeat the last three points, in bold, but raising your voice so that it said slightly louder and firmer. Repeat a third time if necessary moving over to the person and at the end just saying their name and asking that they come back into the room now, placing a hand gently on their shoulder.)

Check to ensure that everyone feels grounded before you finish the session. If not, get them to walk around for a little while. Stamping your feet or jumping up and down helps to bring you back to the physical world. If these don't do the trick, you can ground your energy very readily by eating a small amount of food such as a biscuit.

OTHER THINGS TO TRY:
- Using crystals to help - Clear quartz is perfect for helping you to connect with, harmonise and channel energy. Rose quartz and sodalite in a group environment will assist in harmonising the group's energies and bring about mutual respect, love and trust. Both clear quartz and amethyst can help to activate the crown chakra and connect with spiritual energy. If you have trouble grounding at the end of all this, hold a piece of either black tourmaline, black obsidian or haematite.
- Why not spend some time experimenting with these different crystals to see how they make you feel and what affect they have on your energy?

AND ANOTHER THING...
- Practise the conscious connection if you're feeling a bit spaced out or are lacking in confidence at any point. It helps to re-align your energies and makes you feel more in control.
- Channelling energy around your own body (as in step 3b) can really help to warm you up if you get cold. Try it next time its chilly out, you don't even have to remove your gloves.
- Take a look at Helen's book 'The Power In Your Hands' and the associated audio products and video micro-workshops available from www.thepowerinyourhands.co.uk or www.stmpublishing.co.uk. (More information can be found on page 193.)

FOR DISCUSSION
- What have we got from this lesson? Best bits? Tricky bits?
- Key Concepts - how are we getting on with patience, acceptance, faith?
- Healing - feedback from those in the healing book? Success stories?

Next Time...

The next lesson will be covering INCREASING YOUR SENSITIVITY.
You will need to arrange for the following tools to be brought along:

- Large sheets of white paper – a cheap flipchart pad is perfect
- Drawing pins or 'Blu Tac'
- Sheets of paper
- Crayons or colouring pencils
- An item of jewellery or something similar if you are planning on doing some psychometry.

Extra tools if you want to do 'other things to try'
- A couple of different plants.
- A book or two on the metaphysical properties of crystals.
- Collection of crystals such as clear quartz, petalite and moonstone to enhance your sensitivity. Plus others in your collections to have a play with.

LESSON THREE
INCREASING YOUR SENSITIVITY

PREPARATION
Well in advance of your meeting ensure that you have all of the tools that you require for this lesson. If not, find out if another group member has access to what you need.

Regular tools:
- Healing book
- Pens and pencils
- Paper
- Candles & matches if desired
- Box of tissues

Tools for this lesson:
- Large sheets of white paper – a cheap flipchart pad is perfect
- Drawing pins or 'Blu Tac'
- Sheets of paper
- Crayons or colouring pencils
- An item of jewellery or something similar if you are planning on doing some psychometry.
- Photocopy the required number of the following handouts:
    Handout 2 - Body / Chakras outline

Extra tools if you want to do 'other things to try':
- A couple of different plants.
- A book or two on the metaphysical properties of crystals.
- Collection of crystals such as clear quartz, petalite and moonstone to enhance your sensitivity. Plus others in your collections to have a play with.

On the day of the meeting ensure that the room is prepared:
Are there enough seats for everyone and enough room for the work you are about to undertake?
Open the windows or burn some incense to freshen the air.
Cleanse the area.
Gather the required tools together. Call and remind anyone who has promised to bring something.
Set out some water and glasses.
Prepare some relaxing background music.
Ensure that the room isn't too cold or too warm.
Ensure that you're not going to be interrupted. Unplugging the phone and turning off mobiles are good ideas.

At the beginning of the meeting:
As people arrive ask them to add the names of anyone they know who needs some healing to the Healing Book. Remember that you don't need to put their full names and private information, first names, initials or nicknames will suffice. Whoever you intend to send the healing to, it will reach.

Once everyone has arrived and is comfortable then you can start.
Work your way through the script and exercises for this lesson as detailed on the following pages.

Read the following scripts out loud to the group. It's a time of meditation so keep your voice calm and relaxed, reading in a fairly slow and controlled manner. Instructions are in brackets and italics.

RELAXATION
- Ensure you're sitting or lying comfortably.
- Take your awareness to your hands, make a tight fist, hold for a count of 3, 2, 1, and release.
- Tense your lower arms, hold for 3, 2, 1, and release.
- Tense your upper arms, hold for 3, 2, 1, and release.
- Tense your shoulders, lifting them up towards your ears, hold for 3, 2, 1, and release.
- Take your awareness to your neck: pull your chin toward chest but keep it from touching chest, hold for 3, 2, 1, and then relax.
- Take your awareness to your lower face and jaw, bite hard and pull back the corners of your mouth, hold for 3, 2, 1, and then relax.
- Screw your eyes up and wrinkle your nose, hold for 3, 2, 1, and then relax.
- Move your awareness to your forehead, lift your eyebrows as high as possible, hold for 3, 2, 1, and then relax.
- Take your awareness to your upper torso, pull your shoulder blades together hold for 3, 2, 1, and then release.
- Tense your stomach muscles, pulling your bellybutton towards your spine, hold for 3, 2, 1, and then release.
- Taking your awareness to your legs tense your thigh muscles, hold for 3, 2, 1, and then release.
- Pull your toes towards your head tensing your calf muscles, hold for 3, 2, 1, and then release.
- Take your awareness to your feet, point and curl your toes downwards, hold for 3, 2, 1, and then release.
- Tense your whole body at once, hands, arms, face, neck, chest, stomach, thighs, calves and feet, screw your eyes up, hold for 3, 2, 1, and completely release.
- Now take your awareness to your breathing, preferably through your nose as this is more relaxing.
- Ensure that you're breathing slowly and deeply.
- As you inhale, your abdomen will gently rise. And as you exhale it will fall.
- If your mind drifts or you lose track during this exercise bring your attention back to refocus on your breathing.
- Take a long, slow, deep inhalation for a count of 1 - 2 - 3 - 4, hold for 1- 2 and exhale for 1 - 2 - 3 - 4.
- In 2 3 4, Hold (pause), Out 2 3 4
- In 2 3 4, Hold (pause), Out 2 3 4
- In 2 3 4, Hold (pause), Out 2 3 4
- In 2 3 4, Hold (pause), Out 2 3 4
- In 2 3 4, Hold (pause), Out 2 3 4
- Continue breathing slowly and deeply.
- *(Move on to the script below.)*

OPENING & PROTECTION
- Let us take a moment to close our eyes and calm our minds.
- Concentrate on your breathing, allowing the breath to become deeper and slower.
(Pause to allow everyone to take a couple of breaths in and out)
- Let us all mentally ask our Spirit Guides and Angels to draw close and create a circle around our own.
- We let it be known that we are happy to work with Spirit and that we only work in love and light. We ask that anyone from the spirit world who wishes to contact us only does so in love and light and with the highest intentions.
- We ask for your protection, guidance and wisdom as we blend our world with yours. *(Pause)*

- Let us blend and harmonise our energies as we sit together in circle.
- Let us send out a note of harmony to the person on our left. Visualise this as a pale pink mist coming from your heart area and moving towards the heart of the person sitting on your left. *(Pause)*
- As you continue to do this, become aware of receiving the same loving energy from the right.
- As we send and receive this energy, be aware of any changes in the atmosphere within the circle. *(Pause)*
- Have a sense of oneness with the group. *(Pause)*
- Now bring your attention back to yourself and the centre of your being, the lower abdominal area.
- Focus on your breathing; become aware of the rise and fall of your abdomen. As you inhale it will gently rise and as you exhale it will fall. *(Pause to allow everyone to take a few breaths in and out)*
- Have a sense of warmth here and in your mind's eye allow a symbol or shape to form. Imagine that this symbol or shape is sitting at and represents your centre. It may be a simple glow of light, a flame or a flower.
- With each in-breath visualise your symbol becoming larger, stronger or more open whichever is appropriate.
- With each out-breath, imagine that you are exhaling any negativity left from your day, or worries that you may have. *(Pause to allow everyone to take a few breaths in and out)*
- Now take your awareness to the soles of your feet, feeling their contact with the floor. Visualise lines of energy extending out from your feet and down into the ground. In your mind's eye, see these lines of energy as roots extending deep into the earth.
- Earth energy also travels back up through these roots revitalising and nourishing you.
- See this energy entering through the soles of your feet and travelling up through your legs to the base of your spine.
- At the base of the spine imagine that the energy becomes a sphere of deep red mist or light, as you visualise it, it becomes more vibrant in colour. *(Pause)*
- From this point a beam of energy leaves the red sphere and travels up towards the sacral area, just below the belly button. Here it forms a sphere of vibrant orange mist or light. As you focus on it, it becomes stronger in colour. *(Pause)*
- Gradually a beam of energy leaves the orange sphere and travels up towards the solar plexus, where it forms a sphere of clear yellow. With each breath, this yellow becomes stronger and brighter. *(Pause)*
- Once more a beam of energy leaves this sphere and continues its journey up to the heart area. Here a sphere of mist or light begins to form, which you may see as either green or pink. Focus on this area for a few breaths allowing the energy to grow stronger and clearer and to expand. *(Pause)*
- Gradually a beam of energy leaves the heart area and moves upwards to the throat. Here it forms a sphere of clear blue. Once more, as you focus on this area, allow the colour to expand and increase in strength. *(Pause)*
- Now, visualise a strand of energy leaving the throat area and linking with the third eye area, just between and slightly above the eyes. Here energy will begin to form as before. You may see this energy as either a rich indigo or violet, whichever you prefer. Concentrate on this energy and visualise it increasing in strength. *(Pause)*
- Again, a beam of light extends upwards from this area moving to the crown. As it does so, become aware of another beam of energy coming down from above to meet the first. As they meet at the crown a sphere of pure energy begins to form. You may see this energy as either violet or pure white light. This connects you with the higher realms of Spirit.
- As you hold this vision for a few breaths the light grows and strengthens. And as it does so, the beautiful pure light begins to overflow down and around you, surrounding you in its wonderful energy. It fills your aura, cleansing, balancing and strengthening it. You feel safe and comfortable. You feel relaxed and light. *(Longer pause before moving on to the script below.)*

CONSCIOUS CONNECTION
- Take your awareness back to the soles of your feet, feeling their contact with the floor. Visualise lines of energy extending out from your feet and down into the ground.
- In your mind's eye, see these lines of energy as roots extending deep into the earth. Maintain this feeling of energy at the feet and be aware of earth energy moving up through these roots entering your energy system, revitalising and nourishing you. It may help to see them beginning to glow with light as the energy travels up from the earth and enters your energy system.
- Now take your awareness to the crown of your head.
- Imagine that you are being suspended by a piece of string from this point. The piece of string hangs from a point far above you, so far above you that you are unable to see its origin.
- You should have a sense of being lifted upwards.
- In your mind's eye, the string is a brilliant white light, a magical connection with higher realms. Its brilliance and its power connects with and enters into your energy system.
- You can sense this energy entering your energy system through your crown chakra. It feels amazingly empowering.

HEALING
- Slowly open your eyes and join hands with those sitting to either side of you. This increases the flow of healing energy.
- We know that our Guides, Angels and loved ones in Spirit have come forward and that they surround us with their healing energies. We ask them to help us as we send out our healing today. *(Pause)*
- Visualise a pool of brilliant white light forming and growing in the middle of our circle. *(Pause)*
- This is a pool of healing energy from which we can all draw when we need to. Know that this universal healing energy will find its way to all of those for whom we request healing.
- We ask for healing for each of us here, for our minds, bodies and spirit.
(If there are absent members: We ask for healing for the members of our group who cannot be with us today.)
- We ask for healing for all of those on our Absent Healing List. Take a moment to visualise them standing in the healing pool.
- I would also like to ask for special healing for _____

(Mention anyone else that you feel healing is really important for today. Gently squeeze the hand of the person to your left to indicate that it's their turn. Let everyone have a turn at saying this part before continuing with the script.)
- We send our healing thoughts to Mother Earth and to the plant and animal kingdom. Thank you.
- Release your hands but keep your eyes closed so that you remain relaxed and peaceful as we go in to our meditation. *(Brief pause before moving on to the script below.)*

MEDITATION
- Ensure that you're sitting comfortably with your hands on your knees, palms facing upwards.
- Close your eyes.
- Take a deep inhalation, and breathe out slowly. Continue to breathe slowly and deeply.
- During this meditation you will always be safe and protected, you will feel relaxed and comfortable. If, however, there is anything that does make you feel uneasy, or you wish to come back out of the meditation, you can do so at any time by counting backwards from 3 to 1 and taking a deep breath in and out. You. Can then bring your awareness back to your physical body, particularly your feet and open your eyes.
- For now though, continue to breathe slowly and deeply, your body feels relaxed and your mind is clear
- As you breathe, images may begin to form in your mind's eye. Don't try to manipulate or analyse them, simply observe them. If you don't automatically see these images, simply imagine or sense them.
- Ahead of you lies a staircase or series of ten steps. Move towards them. At the bottom you can see a

LESSON THREE – INCREASING YOUR SENSITIVITY

doorway. We're going to slowly go down these steps towards the door feeling safe and confident at all times. So moving down the steps on my count,
- 10, 9, 8, with each step feeling lighter and lighter.
- 7, 6, 5, feeling calm and peaceful,
- 4, 3, relaxed and light
- 2 and 1, you find yourself standing in front of the door. Reaching out you open the door and as you do so, a wonderful, warm light shines through from the other side, bathing your whole being in its rays.
- As you stand in this light for a few moments, your physical body is warmed through and your energy body is nourished and energised. This gives you a sense of comfort and completeness and offers further protection on your journey. *(Pause for a short while.)*
- Today's journey is to help you tune in more to your senses, feelings and memories.
- The rays of light subside and you can now see through the doorway to the other side.
- As your eyes adjust to the change in light, colours begin to form shapes. You can see your sanctuary on the other side of the doorway.
- You step through, closing the door behind you .
- If your sanctuary is indoors move through it towards a door or window. Think about which season, time of year or weather is your absolute favourite.
- What does it sound like? Look like? Smell like? What would you do? Where would you go? What would you see?
- Looking outside, or around you, you see that very season, or type weather manifesting around you. Today you're going to enjoy your favourite type of weather or time of year.
- Feel free to go out, or stay in, and enjoy it.
- Savour the sights, sounds and smells.
- Walk in the snow, sun or rain.
- Enjoy the plant and animal life and see yourself taking part in the activities that you would love to do. It's up to you how you experience this day.
- Enjoy your time and I will return for you shortly.

(Pause 3-4 minutes)
- I hope you have enjoyed your season or weather and the sensations associated with it. It is now time to return to the physical world.
- So make you way back through your sanctuary to the doorway that leads to the stairwell.
- Open the door. Step through closing the door behind you.
- Know that your sanctuary is your own space that you can return to at any time for relaxation, guidance and healing.
- And keeping your sense of calm and wellbeing, it is time to head back up the stairs. So moving back up the stairs on my count,
- 1, 2, 3, breathing slowly and deeply,
- 4, 5, 6, your body is starting to feel heavier
- 7, 8, bringing your awareness back to your physical body,
- 9 and 10, on that top step now and when you're ready, step off the top step.
- **Bringing your awareness completely back to your physical body and this room, your contact with the chair, your feet with the floor. Slowly begin to move your fingers and toes, and in your own time, opening your eyes, fully awake and aware and in the physical world.**

(If you are reading this aloud for someone else, watch for them starting to wriggle fingers and toes. If they appear not want to come back to the room simply repeat the last paragraph, in bold, but raising your voice so that it's said slightly louder and firmer. Repeat a third time if necessary moving over to the person and at the end just saying their name and asking that they come back now into the room, placing your hand gently on their shoulder.)

Spend a few minutes sharing experiences of the meditation. Remember that it's okay if someone fell asleep, could see nothing or did their own thing. If you're keeping a personal journal, you may wish to take some time to record you experience. Don't forget to date the entry.

THEORY: INCREASING YOUR SENSITIVITY
The following 'theory' section should be read aloud to the group. You may want to get others to join in and take it in turns to read.

As you work more with energy and with the exercises in this book, you'll probably notice that you become more and more sensitive. You will be more aware of the moods and energies of other people around you and pick up on the 'vibes' of a place or situation more readily. This is good, and you can continue to build on it to progress your development further. Your awareness has altered so that instead of only being aware your physical body you're now progressively more aware of your energetic field. Now, as certain things pass through your energy field you can feel them more readily, just as though someone had brushed against your physical body. This could be another person's aura or a spirit presence.

To deliberately expand this awareness further you will need to practise opening and expanding your energy field. Other exercises that will help you to increase your sensitivity are psychometry and working with people's auras, so we're going to look at some practical work along those lines here before challenging you further by getting you out and about and using some other ways to tap into the information that's available around you.

Opening
'Opening' is a term used to describe the process by which you alter and expand your energies and your awareness beyond your physical bodies so that you're able to tap into the unseen energies that exist at a higher vibration. We do it at the beginning of each of our lessons to prepare for the work we are about to undertake. Opening consists of two elements. The first is elevating your energy. This means you're turning up its frequency, from a lower earthly level to a higher, more spiritual level. The second is expansion of your energy field. As mentioned, you are now highly sensitive to anything that comes into contact with your energy field; by expanding your energy field you basically increase the area from which you can pick up information. This is how you need to be when you're working with spiritual and psychic development exercises. .

Discuss any personal experiences or thoughts on the subject (but keep any eye on the time).

PRACTICAL WORK
Read out each exercise, one at a time to the group so that you are all clear as to what you are doing, then allocate a time to complete the exercise.

Step 1 - Elevating Your Energy
Before you begin, find a position that you feel comfortable in and can maintain for the duration of this exercise. It's best to be upright in a chair or cross-legged on the floor, perhaps supported by a cushion if required. Read out the following:

- Take your awareness to your feet and to the energy entering through your soles; imagine it travelling up through your legs to the base of your spine.
- At the base of the spine imagine that the energy becomes a sphere of deep red mist or light. As you visualise it, it becomes more vibrant in colour.
- From this point a beam of energy leaves the red sphere and travels up towards the sacral area, just below the belly button. Here it forms a sphere of vibrant orange mist or light. As you focus on it, it becomes stronger in colour.
- Gradually, a beam of energy leaves the orange sphere and travels up towards the solar plexus, where it forms a sphere of clear yellow. With each breath, this yellow becomes stronger and brighter.

- Once more a beam of energy leaves this sphere and continues its journey up to the heart area. Here a sphere of mist or light begins to form, which you may see as either green or pink. Focus on this area for a few breaths allowing the energy to grow stronger and clearer. It may begin to expand.
- Gradually, a beam of energy leaves the heart area and moves upwards to the throat. Here it forms a sphere of clear blue. Once more, as you focus on this area, allow the colour to expand and increase in strength.
- Now, visualise a strand of energy leaving the throat area and linking with the third eye area, just between and slightly above the eyes. Here energy will begin to form as before. You may see this energy as either a rich indigo or violet, whichever you prefer. Concentrate on this energy and visualise it increasing in strength and energy.
- Again, a beam of light extends upwards from this area moving up to the crown. As it does so, become aware of a beam of energy coming down from high above to meet the first at the crown, A sphere of pure energy begins to form in this area. You may see this energy as either violet or pure white light. This connects you with the higher realms of spirit.
- *(Continue on to stage 2.)*

Step 2 - Expanding Your Awareness
- As you hold this vision for a few breaths the light grows and strengthens. The sphere becomes larger and brighter and as it does so, the beautiful pure light begins to overflow down and around you, surrounding you in this wonderful energy.
- It fills your aura, cleansing, balancing and strengthening it. The light around your physical body grows stronger and brighter. It extends out in all directions around you.
- See in your mind's eye how far it extends.
- Now take a deep slow breath in and as you slowly exhale, imagine your aura expanding further as though you're blowing it up like a balloon but maintaining its strength and brightness.
- Continue to breathe in this way to expand your energy further. As you do so, you feel safe and comfortable. You feel relaxed and light. *(Pause for a few breaths)*
- *(Now try the exercises in step 3.)*

Step 3 - Interacting with others' energies
Read out: When you meet other people or go into places or situations, your auras are the first part of you that pick up on information in the form of energy. This is then filtered down to your conscious mind for interpretation and / or action. The exercises here will demonstrate how you can affect others and be affected by those around you.

Exercise 1: How you can affect your aura and others'
- Work in pairs for this exercise.
- One of you (the subject) should stand up or sit in a chair.
- You must focus on your own energy field. Visualise it surrounding you.
- When you feel that you're ready visualise or feel it changing shape in some way. You can pull it in close to you, or push it out so that it gets bigger and bigger or push it high above your head. You could also visualise it as a specific colour, as very bright or even moving around you in a particular direction. Once you've chosen what you are going to do, without telling your partner, focus on it completely until your partner notices the change.
- The second person can sit opposite, walk around or simply stand next to the subject. It's your role to pick up on any changes or fluctuations in the subject's aura. You can feel it with your hands, sense the changes or, if you're lucky, you may even see them. Sometimes you will 'see' in your mind's eye and sometimes you will just 'know' what has changed. Whichever way you find that you work, go with it.
- Tell your partner when you pick up on the change and see if you're correct.
- Try two or three different things before swapping over and repeating the exercise.

Exercise 2: How others can affect your aura and you
- One person (the subject) should stand up and close their eyes. Be aware of any sensations that you pick up on around you as the exercise progresses. You may find that you sway or feel as though you're going to fall in a particular direction. Keeping your eyes shut, tell the group about the sensations that you're experiencing or point to an area that starts to feel different.
- The rest of the group should all stand in a circle around the subject at about four feet away. Then one of you should step in slowly and quietly, standing nearer to them until the subject picks up on the energy change and says out loud where the person is or points to them.
- You can also use your hands to either push or pull the subject's aura in a specific direction. Work gently and slowly as the subject can be affected quite tangibly by this exercise.
- When the subject says or shows that they can feel the change, swap around and repeat the exercise with a different subject, taking it in turns to experience how others can affect your energy in this way.

Looking At Auras
Read out: It's possible with practice to learn to tune into a person's aura or that of a place or object, and pick up information about it, either visually or simply by 'knowing' or 'sensing'. Information that you may pick up could be the colours in the aura, its strength, any weak spots, imbalances or damaged areas. So let's have a practice.

'Looking at Auras' Exercise
- You can either work in pairs for this exercise or have one subject while the rest of the group works.
- Have some copies of the 'body/chakras outline' (Handout 2) and some pencils and crayons to hand.
- The subject should stand up or sit in a chair, preferably against a pale background. If this isn't possible attach a large sheet of white paper to the wall behind. (Sheets from a cheap flipchart pad are ideal.)
- The other(s) should be sitting opposite at least five feet away. Look past the subject at the air around or above them allowing your eyes to relax and go slightly out of focus.
- You may notice the air changing around the subject, perhaps appearing thicker. You may begin to see the etheric aura first, like a clear glow outlining the body.
- Eventually you may start to see colours or you may sense them in some way. Perhaps a colour, feeling or sensation pops into your head.
- Share what you pick up. If you're working in a group you may find that others are getting the same information as you.
- Or, you could use crayons or coloured pencils to draw what you 'see' on the 'body/chakras outline'.

Scanning
Read out: Scanning can be used to pick up energy fluctuations in the energies surrounding places, objects and people. Scanning works in two ways, firstly because you encourage and capitalise on the natural sensitivity in your palm chakras. Secondly the energy that you channel through your hands kind of 'bounces back' from the energy of the person or object, giving you a form of energetic feedback that you can feel and learn to interpret. Here you will focus on auras to help you get used to the method.

By feeling or 'scanning' someone's aura it's possible to find hot or cold spots, which can indicate an energetic imbalance or area of ill health within the physical body. Scanning is simple but may take practice, the more you do it, the more finely tuned your hands become to different sensations. That's what we're going to do now.

NOTE: You cannot use scanning to diagnose a medical condition, it's by no means a scientifically proven method and it's also against the law to do so. However it can be used to understand where a person may need more healing energy, and this very often turns out to be a point where there is a physical problem. Please never scare your friends by telling them that they have a problem. However, if you find an energy imbalance, do discuss it, perhaps you could say 'I am picking up a hotspot around your elbow, which would indicate an energy imbalance, can you think of any reason why this might be?' If your gut instinct is that there may be a physical condition that they aren't aware of it would be wise to gently suggest that they check it out with their doctor. Use your intuition but please be careful. With your increased sensitivity and intuition also comes responsibility.

Scanning Exercise
- Working in pairs one person should be seated or lying comfortably.
- The other should consciously connect with universal energy. Allow it to begin to flow through you. You may be able to feel it at your palms.
- Start from either the head or the feet if they're lying down. If they're seated then stand behind them and start at the back of their head. Place your hands a few inches above their body, in the aura.
- Move your hands slowly through their aura until you have covered the entire area of their body.
- You may feel heat, tingling, pulsing or cold areas or you may intuitively know at a certain point that there's an imbalance.
- Discuss your experiences and provide feedback to each other.
- Swap over and repeat.

Psychometry
Read out: Psychometry is sensing and interpreting energy emanations from objects. It could be likened to being able to feel and translate the fingerprints left by anyone who has touched an object. Objects can be 'read' like other tools such as tarot cards or used to connect with a loved one in spirit in order to receive messages for the owner.

As you hold an object in your hands you may find words or images popping into your head that have no meaning or relevance to you. It's important that you simply pass them onto the person whose object it is that you're reading. Typically items of jewellery are used for this type of work but anything that you regularly have around you can be used, including mobiles phone (although you should turn them off first or they may make you jump!). You can also try Psychometry with objects that belonged to a loved one that has passed to spirit.

When trying psychometry, whether you write down the information as you receive it and feedback to your partner later, or talk them through it straight away, it's a good idea to keep a written record of the messages. They may be validated later, by friends or family members. Your friend may have to check up on it to confirm the details or you may receive information about a future event. We've had a go before but we're going to do it again. It's a brilliant way to increase your sensitivity.

Psychometry Exercise
- Working in pairs each person should provide the other with an item of jewellery or a personal possession.
- You can both work at the same time or take it in turns. It's entirely up to you.
- Before you begin ask for protection and consciously connect with universal energy. You may also like to centre your energy.
- As you hold the item in your hands open up your energy field and focus on the energy of the object. Relax. Feel its memories, allow images to form in your mind's eye, take note of fragrances, feelings, sensations, words that pop into your head, sounds that you hear. Say the first thing you get. Don't try to analyse it too much.
- What are you doing with the object? How are you handling it? That can also mean something to or represent something about the person concerned. For example, twisting and turning an object in your hands could indicate that the person is restless, or feels that they are going round in circles with a problem. It may even have been a familiar action of a particular loved one.
- Sit quietly for a few minutes and tell your friend what you're sensing or seeing.

CLOSING & GROUNDING
Once you have completed the exercises everyone should sit comfortably and complete the following meditation to close and ground their energy. Read out the following:
- Sit in a comfortable position and close your eyes.
- Bring your attention to your breathing and focus on this for a few breaths. *(Pause)*
- Take your awareness to the invisible energy field surrounding you and visualise it drawing in close around your physical body. *(Pause)*
- Take your awareness to the area just above your crown and see a sphere of light sitting here.
- Imagine that sphere of light shrinking in size until it's tiny, then sinking down through the crown of your head.
- See it slowly descending down past the brow. *(Pause)*
- Into the throat. *(Pause)*
- Then following the line of the spine, down, through your body, towards your heart area. *(Pause)*
- Down to your solar plexus. *(Pause)*
- Through the abdominal area. *(Pause)*
- To the base of your spine. *(Pause)*
- Now visualise the sphere of energy either leaving through the base of your spine, or dividing in two and sinking down through your legs and leaving through the soles of your feet.
- Feel this energy leaving you and connecting with the earth.
- Have a sense of downward movement, deep in to the earth. *(Pause)*
- Become more aware of your feet and your physical body.
- Let us take a moment to thank our Spirit Guides, Angels and loved ones in Spirit for their presence, protection and wisdom whilst we've been working. Knowing that they will always be on hand should we need to call on them. *(Pause)*
- **Now bring your awareness back to your physical body, the chair you are sitting on and your contact with the floor.**
- **Begin to bring some movement back in to your fingers and toes.**
- **In your own time opening your eyes, fully awake and aware and in the physical world.**

(Watch for them starting to wriggle fingers and toes and keep an eye on anyone who doesn't do this. If a member of the group appears not to want to come back to the room simply repeat the last three points, in bold, but raising your voice so that it said slightly louder and firmer. Repeat a third time if necessary moving over to the person and at the end just saying their name and asking that they come back into the room now, placing a hand gently on their shoulder.)

Check to ensure that everyone feels grounded before you finish the session. If not, get them to walk around for a little while. Stamping your feet or jumping up and down helps to bring you back to the physical world. If these don't do the trick, you can ground your energy very readily by eating a small amount of food such as a biscuit.

OTHER THINGS TO TRY:
- You can observe the auras of plants and animals for some extra practice, but take it easy, it's a different type of exercise for your eyes than they're used to so don't do too much at any one time.
- Working with crystals - try holding different crystals, one at a time and seeing what information you can sense from them. What properties might they have? What does their energy feel like? For example, does the crystal appear to have a fast or slow vibration? What do you think you could use it for? Make notes and then compare these with information from books to see if you've found something that others have felt about the stones. Even if you've sensed something different, that's fine, crystals can work slightly differently for each person.
- Crystals that can help to improve your sensitivity include clear quartz, petalite and moonstone. Hold, carry or wear them while working to enhance your abilities.

AND ANOTHER THING...
- Put all of these skills in to practice by going out as a group. Try visiting a place of natural beauty, a river, lake, woodland or valley. Then go along to an historic building and see what you can pick up.
- Take time to sit quietly and put protection in place. Open and expand your energies and then see what you get. You may see in your mind's eye or hear words in your head. You may see auras or colours around certain objects or feel physical sensations. If you can, take some time to close your eyes and let your mind tune into the place. What comes to you? Write it down and discuss it with the group. You will probably be surprised at the similar things you pick up on. If you're at an historic building, don't do any research before you go. Do it afterwards and see if you get any validation for the things that you picked up.
- You could try using the 'sensing prompt' in Handout 3 to help you analyse what you're feeling or to prompt more information to come to you.
- Why not spend a day doing this as a group field trip? Make a list of 2 or 3 places to visit in one day and go along together. Compare notes and experiences.

FOR DISCUSSION
- What have we got from this lesson? Best bits? Tricky bits?
- Key Concepts - how are we getting on with patience, acceptance, faith?
- Healing - feedback from those in the healing book? Success stories?

Next Time...

The next lesson will be covering 3RD EYE CHAKRA DEVELOPMENT.

You will need to arrange for the following tools to be brought along:
- Ask each person to bring one or two drawings and / or pictures cut from magazines each placed in to an enevelope so that no-one else sees them.
- A selection of small to medium sized objects - you could ask each person to bring one.
- A shoe box.

Extra tools if you want to do 'other things to try':
- Item(s) to scry with such as a crystal ball, obsidian mirror, a bowl of water, maybe with with a small amount of oil, dark ink or wax dropped into, candle, or incense.
- A range of plants (include some flowering plants as well as evergreens, and you may also like to use a freshly picked flower).
- A selection of different crystals - they could include amethyst, jasper and haemetite.
- Large sheets of white paper – a cheap flipchart pad is perfect
- Drawing pins or 'Blu Tac'

LESSON FOUR
'3RD EYE' CHAKRA DEVELOPMENT

PREPARATION
Well in advance of your meeting ensure that you have all of the tools that you require for this lesson. If not, find out if another group member has access to what you need.

Regular tools:
- Healing book
- Pens and pencils
- Paper
- Candles & matches if desired
- Box of tissues

Tools for this lesson:
- Ask each person to bring one or two drawings and / or pictures cut from magazines each placed in to an enevelope so that no-one else sees them.
- A selection of small to medium sized objects - you could ask each person to bring one each.
- A shoe box

Extra tools if you want to do 'other things to try':
- Item(s) to scry with such as a crystal ball, obsidian mirror, bowl of water, maybe with a with a small amount of oil, dark ink or wax dropped into, candle, or incense.
- A range of plants (include some flowering plants as well as evergreens, and you may also like to use a freshly picked flower).
- A selection of different crystals - they could include amethyst, jasper and haemetite.
- Large sheets of white paper – a cheap flipchart pad is perfect
- Drawing pins or 'Blu Tac'

On the day of the meeting ensure that the room is prepared:
Are there enough seats for everyone and enough room for the work you are about to undertake?
Open the windows or burn some incense to freshen the air.
Cleanse the area.
Gather the required tools together. Call and remind anyone who has promised to bring something.
Set out some water and glasses.
Ensure that the room isn't too cold or too warm.
Ensure that you're not going to be interrupted. Unplugging the phone and turning off mobiles are good ideas.

At the beginning of the meeting:
As people arrive ask them to add the names of anyone they know who needs some healing to the Healing Book. Remember that you don't need to put their full names and private information, first names, initials or nicknames will suffice. Whoever you intend to send the healing to, it will reach.

Once everyone has arrived and is comfortable then you can start.
Work your way through the script and exercises for this lesson as detailed on the following pages.

Read the following scripts out loud to the group. It's a time of meditation so keep your voice calm and relaxed, reading in a fairly slow and controlled manner. Instructions are in brackets and italics.

RELAXATION
- Ensure you're sitting or lying comfortably.
- Take your awareness to your hands, make a tight fist, hold for a count of 3, 2, 1, and release.
- Tense your lower arms, hold for 3, 2, 1, and release.
- Tense your upper arms, hold for 3, 2, 1, and release.
- Tense your shoulders, lifting them up towards your ears, hold for 3, 2, 1, and release.
- Take your awareness to your neck: pull your chin toward chest but keep it from touching chest, hold for 3, 2, 1, and then relax.
- Take your awareness to your lower face and jaw, bite hard and pull back the corners of your mouth, hold for 3, 2, 1, and then relax.
- Screw your eyes up and wrinkle your nose, hold for 3, 2, 1, and then relax.
- Move your awareness to your forehead, lift your eyebrows as high as possible, hold for 3, 2, 1, and then relax.
- Take your awareness to your upper torso, pull your shoulder blades together hold for 3, 2, 1, and then release.
- Tense your stomach muscles, pulling your bellybutton towards your spine, hold for 3, 2, 1, and then release.
- Taking your awareness to your legs tense your thigh muscles, hold for 3, 2, 1, and then release.
- Pull your toes towards your head tensing your calf muscles, hold for 3, 2, 1, and then release.
- Take your awareness to your feet, point and curl your toes downwards, hold for 3, 2, 1, and then release.
- Tense your whole body at once, hands, arms, face, neck, chest, stomach, thighs, calves and feet, screw your eyes up, hold for 3, 2, 1, and completely release.
- Now take your awareness to your breathing, preferably through your nose as this is more relaxing.
- Ensure that you're breathing slowly and deeply.
- As you inhale, your abdomen will gently rise. And as you exhale it will fall.
- If your mind drifts or you lose track during this exercise bring your attention back to refocus on your breathing.
- Take a long, slow, deep inhalation for a count of 1 - 2 - 3 - 4, hold for 1- 2 and exhale for 1 - 2 - 3 - 4.
- In 2 3 4, Hold (pause), Out 2 3 4
- In 2 3 4, Hold (pause), Out 2 3 4
- In 2 3 4, Hold (pause), Out 2 3 4
- In 2 3 4, Hold (pause), Out 2 3 4
- In 2 3 4, Hold (pause), Out 2 3 4
- Continue breathing slowly and deeply.
- *(Move on to the script below.)*

OPENING & PROTECTION
- Let us take a moment to close our eyes and calm our minds.
- Concentrate on your breathing, allowing the breath to become deeper and slower.

(Pause to allow everyone to take a couple of breaths in and out)

- Let us all mentally ask our Spirit Guides and Angels to draw close and create a circle around our own.
- We let it be known that we are happy to work with Spirit and that we only work in love and light. We ask that anyone from the spirit world who wishes to contact us only does so in love and light and with the highest intentions.
- We ask for your protection, guidance and wisdom as we blend our world with yours. *(Pause)*
- Let us blend and harmonise our energies as we sit together in circle.
- Let us send out a note of harmony to the person on our left. Visualise this as a pale pink mist coming from your heart area and moving towards the heart of the person sitting on your left. *(Pause)*
- As you continue to do this, become aware of receiving the same loving energy from the right.

LESSON FOUR – '3RD EYE' CHAKRA DEVELOPMENT

- As we send and receive this energy, be aware of any changes in the atmosphere within the circle. *(Pause)*
- Have a sense of oneness with the group. *(Pause)*
- Now bring your attention back to yourself and the centre of your being, the lower abdominal area.
- Focus on your breathing; become aware of the rise and fall of your abdomen. As you inhale it will gently rise and as you exhale it will fall. *(Pause to allow everyone to take a few breaths in and out)*
- Have a sense of warmth here and in your mind's eye allow a symbol or shape to form. Imagine that this symbol or shape is sitting at and represents your centre. It may be a simple glow of light, a flame or a flower.
- With each in-breath visualise your symbol becoming larger, stronger or more open whichever is appropriate.
- With each out-breath, imagine that you are exhaling any negativity left from your day, or worries that you may have. *(Pause to allow everyone to take a few breaths in and out)*
- Now take your awareness to the soles of your feet, feeling their contact with the floor. Visualise lines of energy extending out from your feet and down into the ground. In your mind's eye, see these lines of energy as roots extending deep into the earth.
- Earth energy also travels back up through these roots revitalising and nourishing you.
- See this energy entering through the soles of your feet and travelling up through your legs to the base of your spine.
- At the base of the spine imagine that the energy becomes a sphere of deep red mist or light, as you visualise it, it becomes more vibrant in colour. *(Pause)*
- From this point a beam of energy leaves the red sphere and travels up towards the sacral area, just below the belly button. Here it forms a sphere of vibrant orange mist or light. As you focus on it, it becomes stronger in colour. *(Pause)*
- Gradually a beam of energy leaves the orange sphere and travels up towards the solar plexus, where it forms a sphere of clear yellow. With each breath, this yellow becomes stronger and brighter. *(Pause)*
- Once more a beam of energy leaves this sphere and continues its journey up to the heart area. Here a sphere of mist or light begins to form, which you may see as either green or pink. Focus on this area for a few breaths allowing the energy to grow stronger and clearer and to expand. *(Pause)*
- Gradually a beam of energy leaves the heart area and moves upwards to the throat. Here it forms a sphere of clear blue. Once more, as you focus on this area, allow the colour to expand and increase in strength. *(Pause)*
- Now, visualise a strand of energy leaving the throat area and linking with the third eye area, just between and slightly above the eyes. Here energy will begin to form as before. You may see this energy as either a rich indigo or violet, whichever you prefer. Concentrate on this energy and visualise it increasing in strength. *(Pause)*
- Again, a beam of light extends upwards from this area moving to the crown. As it does so, become aware of another beam of energy coming down from above to meet the first. As they meet at the crown a sphere of pure energy begins to form. You may see this energy as either violet or pure white light. This connects you with the higher realms of Spirit.
- As you hold this vision for a few breaths the light grows and strengthens. And as it does so, the beautiful pure light begins to overflow down and around you, surrounding you in its wonderful energy. It fills your aura, cleansing, balancing and strengthening it. You feel safe and comfortable. You feel relaxed and light. *(Longer pause before moving on to the script below.)*

CONSCIOUS CONNECTION

- Take your awareness back to the soles of your feet, feeling their contact with the floor. Visualise lines of energy extending out from your feet and down into the ground.
- In your mind's eye, see these lines of energy as roots extending deep into the earth. Maintain this feeling of energy at the feet and be aware of earth energy moving up through these roots entering your energy system, revitalising and nourishing you. It may help to see them beginning to glow with light as the energy travels up from the earth and enters your energy system.

- Now take your awareness to the crown of your head.
- Imagine that you are being suspended by a piece of string from this point. The piece of string hangs from a point far above you, so far above you that you are unable to see its origin.
- You should have a sense of being lifted upwards.
- In your mind's eye, the string is a brilliant white light, a magical connection with higher realms. Its brilliance and its power connects with and enters into your energy system.
- You can sense this energy entering your energy system through your crown chakra. It feels amazingly empowering.

HEALING

- Slowly open your eyes and join hands with those sitting to either side of you. This increases the flow of healing energy.
- We know that our Guides, Angels and loved ones in Spirit have come forward and that they surround us with their healing energies. We ask them to help us as we send out our healing today. *(Pause)*
- Visualise a pool of brilliant white light forming and growing in the middle of our circle. *(Pause)*
- This is a pool of healing energy from which we can all draw when we need to. Know that this universal healing energy will find its way to all of those for whom we request healing.
- We ask for healing for each of us here, for our minds, bodies and spirit.

(If there are absent members: We ask for healing for the members of our group who cannot be with us today.)

- We ask for healing for all of those on our Absent Healing List. Take a moment to visualise them standing in the healing pool.
- I would also like to ask for special healing for _____

(Mention anyone else that you feel healing is really important for today. Gently squeeze the hand of the person to your left to indicate that it's their turn. Let everyone have a turn at saying this part before continuing with the script.)

- We send our healing thoughts to Mother Earth and to the plant and animal kingdom. Thank you.
- Release your hands and slowly open your eyes.

THEORY: '3RD EYE' CHAKRA DEVELOPMENT

The following 'theory' section should be read aloud to the group. You may want to get others to join in and take it in turns to read.

The '3rd eye', or brow chakra is associated with all of your senses on all levels, perception, intuition, higher consciousness, visions, inner vision, pre-cognition, imagination, visualisation, concentration, self-mastery, dreams spiritual, universal and intellectual knowledge, E.S.P. and psychic abilities. It helps you with creation or manifestation, elevation of your own consciousness and spiritual awareness, to evaluate experiences and understand life's lessons. The 3rd eye chakra is said to connect you with all levels of creation and in what seems like a contradiction in terms, helps you not only to journey within but to connect with the higher consciousness too. It is an avenue to wisdom, to inner vision, and greater wisdom, seeing beyond what is physically or apparently occurring.

If there is disharmonious function of this chakra it's likely that the person is ruled by intellectual thought processes and analysis and does not consider the more intuitive methods of understanding. It's all about science, and proving through careful study, there is no room for spirituality. The person may try to influence the thoughts of others. In the case of an underactive brow chakra the person would be very materialistic and only see the material world, they would have no time for spiritual awareness or discussion.

This chakra is said to be linked to the pineal gland which is light sensitive. It's also associated with the colours indigo and violet.

Imagination, intuition, visualisation and intention are not only increased by working to activate this chakra further, but are also keys for you to do just that. The more you use these skills, the easier it is for you to use them and the more adept you become at them.

Certain crystals are ideal for developing the 3rd eye chakra including amethyst, lapis lazuli, purple fluorite, sodalite (which is also good for group work as it fosters a sense of trust and harmony), chevron amethyst, and if you can find it, an amethyst 'flower'. Helen found amethyst flowers to be very powerful and the first time that she placed one on her brow chakra, she had a spontaneous remote viewing session, which she could later corroborate with the people she had seen.

Amethyst is an excellent stone for this chakra, apart from its colour, because its qualities are to promote sleep and dreams, it's protective, opens you up to spiritual and psychic enlightenment and communication, encourages focus, is calming and enhances meditation. It also allows you to take that which you learn on a esoteric level and apply it in a practical, common-sense way on a physical level. It seems to embody a lot of what the brow chakra is about.

In 'The Chakra Handbook' by Shalila Sharaman and Bodo J. Baginski it's suggested that this chakra can also be stimulated by contemplating the night sky. Visualising it would be one way, but going out and spending time actually looking at the night sky would be even better. Meditating on its deep indigo blue, with pin pricks of starlight, the vastness of the universe stretching way beyond your limited vision and your place within it. Opening your eyes and your mind to the night sky makes a lot of sense when working with this chakra.

The element that is associated with this chakra in a lot of books and other sources is radium. Its association comes from its high vibrational rate, its ability to break down patterns and its association with power and light, all closely aligned with this chakra. Interestingly the areas of the UK that we have always been drawn to as very spiritual places, such as Devon, Cornwall, Somerset and South Shropshire are all areas which have higher levels of Radon, the gas produced by the decay of radium from the rocks beneath the surface of the earth. Is this because the natural occurrence of radium in the earth is stimulating the 3rd eye chakra causing greater spiritual awareness while at these locations?

Overwork or too much 3rd eye work can cause headaches. Conversely, a couple of members of our own development group have commented that pressure in the third eye area, which they frequently mistook for the onset of a headache or migraine, had been alleviated by work to unblock and develop this chakra. Funnily enough lapis lazuli, purple fluorite and amethyst crystals that all stimulate this chakra can also help to relieve these headaches. (However, please ensure that recurrent are unexplained headaches or migraines are looked into by your G.P.) Always remember to close and ground after working with this chakra.

It's quite common to 'see' eyes looking back at you during meditation and this can be a symbolic representation of your own third eye and its development, particularly if there is just one of them. This can also indicate a natural aptitude for clairvoyance and psychic work using the 3rd eye chakra.

Discuss any personal experiences or thoughts on the subject (but keep any eye on the time).

PRACTICAL WORK
Read out each exercise, one at a time to the group so that you are all clear as to what you are doing, then allocate a time to complete the exercise.

Exercise 1 - Meditation
- Ensure that you're sitting comfortably with your hands on your knees, palms facing upwards.
- Close your eyes.
- Take your awareness to your hands, make a tight fist, hold for a count of 3, 2, 1, and release.
- Tense your lower arms, hold for 3, 2, 1, and release.
- Tense your upper arms, hold for 3, 2, 1, and release.
- Tense your shoulders, lifting them up towards your ears, hold for 3, 2, 1, and release.
- Take your awareness to your neck: pull your chin toward chest but keep it from touching chest, hold for 3, 2, 1, and then relax.

- Take your awareness to your lower face and jaw, bite hard and pull back the corners of your mouth, hold for 3, 2, 1, and then relax.
- Screw your eyes up and wrinkle your nose, hold for 3, 2, 1, and then relax.
- Move your awareness to your forehead, lift your eyebrows as high as possible, hold for 3, 2, 1, and then relax.
- Take your awareness to your upper torso, pull your shoulder blades together, hold for 3, 2, 1, and then release.
- Tense your stomach muscles, pulling your bellybutton towards your spine, hold for 3, 2, 1, and then release.
- Take your awareness to your legs tense your thigh muscles, hold for 3, 2, 1, and then release.
- Pull your toes towards your head tensing your calf muscles, hold for 3, 2, 1, and then release.
- Taking your awareness to your feet, point and curl your toes downwards, hold for 3, 2, 1, and then release.
- Tense your whole body at once, hands, arms, face, neck, chest, stomach, thighs, calves and feet, screw your eyes up, hold for 3, 2, 1, and completely release.
- Now take your awareness to your breathing, preferably through your nose as this is more relaxing.
- Ensure that you are breathing slowly and deeply.
- As you inhale, your abdomen will gently rise. And as you exhale it will fall.
- If your mind drifts or you lose track during this exercise bring your attention back to refocus on your breathing.
- Take a long, slow, deep inhalation for a count of 1 - 2 - 3 - 4, hold for 1- 2 and exhale for 1 - 2 - 3 - 4.
- In 2 3 4, Hold (pause), Out 2 3 4
- In 2 3 4, Hold (pause), Out 2 3 4
- In 2 3 4, Hold (pause), Out 2 3 4
- In 2 3 4, Hold (pause), Out 2 3 4
- In 2 3 4, Hold (pause), Out 2 3 4
- Continue breathing slowly and deeply.
- During this meditation you will always be safe and protected, you will feel relaxed and comfortable. If, however, there is anything that does make you feel uneasy, or you wish to come back out of the meditation, you can do so at any time by counting backwards from 3 to 1 and taking a deep breath in and out. You can then bring your awareness back to your physical body, particularly your feet and open your eyes.
- For now though, continue to breathe slowly and deeply, your body feels relaxed and your mind is clear.
- As you breathe, images may begin to form in your mind's eye. Don't try to manipulate or analyse them, simply observe them. If you don't automatically see these images, simply imagine or sense them.
- Ahead of you lies a staircase or series of ten steps. Move towards them. At the bottom you can see a doorway. We're going to slowly go down these steps towards the door feeling safe and confident at all times. So moving down the steps on my count,
- 10, 9, 8, with each step feeling lighter and lighter.
- 7, 6, 5, feeling calm and peaceful,
- 4, 3, relaxed and light
- 2 and 1, you find yourself standing in front of the door. Reaching out you open the door and as you do so, a wonderful, warm light shines through from the other side, bathing your whole being in its rays.
- As you stand in this light for a few moments, your physical body is warmed through and your energy body is nourished and energised. This gives you a sense of comfort and completeness and offers further protection on your journey. *(Pause for a short while.)*
- Today's journey is to help you to develop your 3rd eye vision.
- The rays of light subside and you can now see through the doorway to the other side.
- As your eyes adjust to the change in light, colours begin to form shapes. You can see your sanctuary on the other side of the doorway.
- You step through, closing the door behind you.
- Look around your sanctuary. You will see a door, you may not even have noticed this door before.
- Head towards this door and when you're ready open it and step through. You find yourself in the

LESSON FOUR – '3RD EYE' CHAKRA DEVELOPMENT

- middle of a valley. A beautiful green valley with rolling hills to either side of you.
- You can hear the birds singing. You can hear the insects all around you. It's a warm summer's day, the sun shines above you and there's a gentle breeze to keep you cool.
- Look around you. Look at all the beautiful sights within the valley, the lush green of the grass, the bright blue of the summer sky, the bright white of the few fluffy clouds. The vivid leaves on the trees, their greenery like no other leaves you've seen. The beautiful wild flowers that grow all around the valley, from the purple foxgloves to the tiniest bright yellow buttercups. You are surrounded by beauty wherever you look.
- As you walk through this magnificent valley you find a sheltered spot, beneath you the grass feels soft and springy and is very comfortable to sit on. You sit down here in this sheltered spot. There's a large oak tree near you providing you with shade. There's no-one else around you, it's a place of beautiful peace and serenity.
- And as you sit down you're aware of a brook or stream babbling gently beside you. Sit in this beautiful place and look around you. And as you look around, you look up to the hills that surround you on all sides and you see, on top of the tallest hill, that there's a tree. A beautiful tree that stands alone, an ancient tree that has stood on the top of that hill for many, many centuries. Look carefully at that tree and as you do so, you are aware that your '3rd eye' or brow chakra begins to open wider and wider. *(Pause)*
- You look at that tree with your third eye, and as you do, you feel a connection between that distant tree and your inner being.
- A spiral reaches out from your 3rd eye and brings your vision right to the tree and so you find yourself transported to the top of the hill, and you're standing right by that tree. Close enough to touch it.
- Look at what else is around you next to the tree. There are more flowers, there may be animals and insects.
- You're aware of the fresh, clear air at the very top of this hill.
- Then you're aware that there are fantastic views all around . You can see far into the distance. You can see far away lands. Perhaps you can see the sea. Perhaps the clouds are within touching distance for you.
- You now have the ability, at the top of this hill, to look at anything you want to look at. Look at anything, or any place at all and use the vision from your 3rd eye to transport you to that place. So perhaps you want to visit a far off land, or you want to be by the sea or to float on the clouds. Or perhaps you can see someone in the distance you would like to go towards.
- Again, allowing the spiralling energy from your 3rd eye chakra to extend out ot the place you wish to go to and then to transport you there.
- I'm going to leave you here for a time while you explore and I will return for you shortly. *(Pause for a few minutes.)*
- And now it's time to begin your journey back. So focus all your attention completely on the top of the hill with the ancient tree.
- You find yourself back on top of the hill in the beautiful green valley. Take a moment to take a look around from this vantage point and make a note of anything that may have changed since you have been on your journey. *(Pause)*
- And then, remembering to open your 3rd eye wide again, focus your attention back on the spot in the valley where you were siitting by the babbling brook. Allow the spiralling energy of your 3rd eye to transport you back to that lovely place. Sitting in the shade of the oak tree. Make a note of significant changes here too. *(Pause)*
- Now, with gratitude to the universe, leave this shady area and make your way back to the doorway that led from your sanctuary. Enter your sanctuary and walk through to the doorway leading to your stairwell.
- Open the door. Step through closing the door behind you.
- Know that your sanctuary is your own space that you can return to at any time for relaxation, guidance and healing.
- And keeping your sense of calm and wellbeing, it is time to head back up the stairs. So moving back up the stairs on my count,

- 1, 2, 3, breathing slowly and deeply,
- 4, 5, 6, your body is starting to feel heavier,
- 7, 8, bringing your awareness back to your physical body,
- 9 and 10, on that top step now and when you're ready, step off the top step.
- **Bringing your awareness completely back to your physical body and this room, your contact with the chair, your feet with the floor. Slowly begin to move your fingers and toes, and in your own time, opening your eyes, fully awake and aware and in the physical world.**

(If you are reading this aloud for someone else, watch for them starting to wriggle fingers and toes. If they appear not want to come back to the room simply repeat the last paragraph, in bold, but raising your voice so that it's said slightly louder and firmer. Repeat a third time if necessary moving over to the person and at the end just saying their name and asking that they come back now into the room, placing your hand gently on their shoulder.)

Spend a few minutes sharing experiences of the meditation or making notes about it if you are keeping a personal journal. Don't forget to date the entry.

Exercise 2 - Preparation
Step 1 - Elevating Your Energy
- Ensure everyone is comfortable before reading out the following:
- Take your awareness to your feet and to the energy entering through your soles; imagine it travelling up through your legs to the base of your spine.
- At the base of the spine imagine that the energy becomes a sphere of deep red mist or light. As you visualise it, it becomes more vibrant in colour.
- From this point a beam of energy leaves the red sphere and travels up towards the sacral area, just below the belly button. Here it forms a sphere of vibrant orange mist or light. As you focus on it, it becomes stronger in colour.
- Gradually, a beam of energy leaves the orange sphere and travels up towards the solar plexus, where it forms a sphere of clear yellow. With each breath, this yellow becomes stronger and brighter.
- Once more a beam of energy leaves this sphere and continues its journey up to the heart area. Here a sphere of mist or light begins to form, which you may see as either green or pink. Focus on this area for a few breaths allowing the energy to grow stronger and clearer. It may begin to expand.
- Gradually, a beam of energy leaves the heart area and moves upwards to the throat. Here it forms a sphere of clear blue. Once more, as you focus on this area, allow the colour to expand and increase in strength.
- Now, visualise a strand of energy leaving the throat area and linking with the third eye area, just between and slightly above the eyes. Here energy will begin to form as before. You may see this energy as either a rich indigo or violet, whichever you prefer. Concentrate on this energy and visualise it increasing in strength and energy.
- Again, a beam of light extends upwards from this area moving up to the crown. As it does so, become aware of a beam of energy coming down from high above to meet the first at the crown, A sphere of pure energy begins to form in this area. You may see this energy as either violet or pure white light. This connects you with the higher realms of spirit.
- *(Move on to Step 2.)*

Step 2 - Expanding Your Awareness
- As you hold this vision for a few breaths the light grows and strengthens. The sphere becomes larger and brighter and as it does so, the beautiful pure light begins to overflow down and around you, surrounding you in this wonderful energy.
- It fills your aura, cleansing, balancing and strengthening it. The light around your physical body grows stronger and brighter. It extends out in all directions around you.
- See in your mind's eye how far it extends.

LESSON FOUR - '3RD EYE' CHAKRA DEVELOPMENT

- Now take a deep slow breath in and as you slowly exhale, imagine your aura expanding further as though you're blowing it up like a balloon but maintaining its strength and brightness.
- Continue to breathe in this way to expand your energy further. As you do so, you feel safe and comfortable. You feel relaxed and light.
- *(Move on to Exercise 3.)*

Exercise 3 - Opening the '3rd eye' chakra
- Read the following to the group:
- Concentrate on your breathing, allowing it to slow and steady. Visualise a closed eye in the centre of your forehead.
- As you visualise it, see it gently and easily beginning to open. Watch as it opens wider and wider until it's fully open.
- Now visualise a beam of light entering through your crown chakra and travelling down to your third eye. Watch the light diffuse through your third eye and extend outwards from it.
- Maintain this vision noticing how it progresses and changes. Notice any sensations or images that you may become aware of. *(Pause)*
- Imagine your 3rd eye gently closing.
- In your own time, slowly open your eyes. Fully awake and aware and in the physical world.
- *(Move straight on to Exercise 4.)*

Exercise 4 - Take a '3rd eye' look
- Collect up all the envelopes that people have bought (in sealed envelopes). Give them a good shuffle and number them. Place them in the middle of the group.
- Have some paper and pens on hand for notes to be made.
- Relax and visualise your third eye opening wide, allowing energy to flow to it and through it.
- As you become aware of your third eye opening, take one of the envelopes and hold it in your hands. Using your third eye visualise what's in the envelope. Allow pictures to form, noting down the envelope's number and what you are seeing. You may be aware of colours and shapes rather than, or as well as, definite images.
- Remember that this exercise is about seeing rather than sensing, so work on images and pictures rather than a sense of what is in the envelope.
- Repeat the exercise with the other envelopes. At the end open the envelopes and compare what everyone saw with the content of each envelope.
- Tip- Don't be tempted to open the envelopes as you go along as looking at the images with your normal vision will distract from visualising with your third eye!
- Alternatively (or as well as this exercise), place a number of small objects in a shoe box and close it, then work as a group, focussing your attention on it. Pass the box around and see if you can find out what the objects are.

CLOSING & GROUNDING
Once you have completed the exercises everyone should sit comfortably and complete the following meditation to close and ground their energy. Read out the following:
- Sit in a comfortable position and close your eyes.
- Bring your attention to your breathing and focus on this for a few breaths. *(Pause)*
- Take your awareness to the invisible energy field surrounding you and visualise it drawing in close around your physical body. *(Pause)*
- Take your awareness to the area just above your crown and see a sphere of light sitting here.
- Imagine that sphere of light shrinking in size until it's tiny, then sinking down through the crown of your head.

- See it slowly descending down past the brow. *(Pause)*
- Into the throat. *(Pause)*
- Then following the line of the spine, down, through your body, towards your heart area. (Pause)
- Down to your solar plexus. *(Pause)*
- Through the abdominal area. *(Pause)*
- To the base of your spine. *(Pause)*
- Now visualise the sphere of energy either leaving through the base of your spine, or dividing in two and sinking down through your legs and leaving through the soles of your feet.
- Feel this energy leaving you and connecting with the earth.
- Have a sense of downward movement, deep in to the earth. *(Pause)*
- Become more aware of your feet and your physical body.
- Let us take a moment to thank our Spirit Guides, Angels and loved ones in Spirit for their presence, protection and wisdom whilst we've been working. Knowing that they will always be on hand should we need to call on them. *(Pause)*
- **Now bring your awareness back to your physical body, the chair you are sitting on and your contact with the floor.**
- **Begin to bring some movement back in to your fingers and toes.**
- **In your own time opening your eyes, fully awake and aware and in the physical world.**

(Watch for them starting to wriggle fingers and toes and keep an eye on anyone who doesn't do this. If a member of the group appears not to want to come back to the room simply repeat the last three points, in bold, but raising your voice so that it said slightly louder and firmer. Repeat a third time if necessary moving over to the person and at the end just saying their name and asking that they come back into the room now, placing a hand gently on their shoulder.)

Check to ensure that everyone feels grounded before you finish the session. If not, get them to walk around for a little while. Stamping your feet or jumping up and down helps to bring you back to the physical world. If these don't do the trick, you can ground your energy very readily by eating a small amount of food such as a biscuit.

OTHER THINGS TO TRY:

Scrying

- For this exercise there are many things you can use to gaze in to: Crystal ball, obsidian mirror, bowl of water, a bowl of water with a small amount of oil, dark ink or wax dropped into, candle flame, incense smoke or flames.
- Use a room with dimmed lights, light a couple of candles only, placed low and behind you.
- Close your eyes and concentrate on your breathing. If you can, visualise yourself surrounded by white light. Allow yourself to relax and your breathing will slow.
- Focus your intention on reading for yourself, or for a friend.
- When you feel ready, slowly open your eyes and look upon the reflective surface. Relax your eyes – just like when looking at auras.
- Turn or move the item until you have as few reflections as possible and you can't see yourself, then allow your eyes to 'tune out', looking through it not at it.
- You may see a cloudiness forming (especially with the crystal ball). Let it form, then keep watching as it begins to clear. It may swirl around fast before it does so.
- It's natural when you first see something to jolt and lose your concentration. Just start again, you'll soon get used to it.
- Try not to stare or push things too much - allow things to happen slowly and be prepared to try a few times before you get results.
- If you're not successful with one tool try another. Just because a crystal ball doesn't work for you, doesn't mean that you can't scry at all.

LESSON FOUR – '3RD EYE' CHAKRA DEVELOPMENT

Looking at the auras of plants and crystals
- Collect together a range of plants and crystals-include some flowering plants as well as evergreens, and you may also like to use a freshly picked flower. For the crystals it's important to choose those which you're drawn to work with, but they could include amethyst, jasper and haemetite.
- You may find that it helps to place the object on a piece of white paper, or against a pale background.
- Relax, then look past the object at the air around or above it, allowing your eyes to relax and go slightly out of focus; this is the same technique used when looking at the auras of other people.
- You may notice the air changing around the object, perhaps appearing thicker. You may begin to see the etheric aura first, like a clear glow outlining it.
- Eventually you may start to see colours or you may sense them in some way. Perhaps a colour, feeling or sensation pops into your head.
- Take note of any differences in the energy fields around the objects-how does the picked flower compare to the evergreen plant for example? Are the auras of the crystals different in any way?
- Share what you pick up. You may find that others are getting the same information as you.

AND ANOTHER THING...
- Try working with the fragrances of mint and jasmine – try using mint to clear your mind and increase your focus. Jasmine opens your mind up to visions and images. (It's best to use essential oils rather than chemical synthetic fragrances.)
- Try meditating with a piece of amethyst or other relevant crystal, either gazing at it sat in front of you, holding it in your lap or placing it on your brow while lying down.
- Any form of scrying – you are using your eyes but activating the third eye. (Crystal gazing, fire gazing candle gazing etc.)
- Research and experiment with remote viewing exercises.
- Mirror gazing: This can be a useful tool for enhancing your 3rd eye chakra abilities. You may want to do this in the company of others as it can be a little disconcerting! In a relaxed state simply stare in to a mirror at your own reflection, allowing your gaze to soften and go slightly out of focus. You may see things in the mirror's reflection, or even see you own features altering.
- For extremely advanced work, try using the crystal moldavite. But use it with care (and don't carry it on or near you when driving, is Helen's advice). It's expensive but you only need a very small piece as it's extremely powerful if you're sensitive to crystals. Research the stone first, and try handling some before you buy it to judge your reactions to it.

FOR DISCUSSION
- What have we got from this lesson? Best bits? Tricky bits?
- Key Concepts - how are we getting on with patience, acceptance, faith?
- Healing - feedback from those in the healing book? Success stories?

Next Time...

The next lesson will be covering ANGELIC ENERGY.

You will need to arrange for the following tools to be brought along:
- Items to create and angelic environment: angelic pictures, statues, candles, pieces of angelite and celestite crystals, appropriate meditative music.
- Angel divination cards if you have access to some
- If you decide to spend some time during this lesson to make your own angel cards you will need to bring art material as appropriate and photocopy the required number of the angel card handouts (Handout 4) on to card.

LESSON FIVE
ANGELIC ENERGY

PREPARATION
Well in advance of your meeting ensure that you have all of the tools that you require for this lesson. If not, find out if another group member has access to what you need.

Regular tools:
- Healing book
- Pens and pencils
- Paper
- Candles & matches if desired
- Box of tissues

Tools for this lesson:
- Items to create and angelic environment: angelic pictures, statues, candles, pieces of angelite and celestite crystals, appropriate meditative music.
- Angel divination cards if you have access to some
- If you decide to spend some time during this lesson to make your own angel cards you will need to bring art material as appropriate and photocopy the required number of the angel card handouts (Handout 4) on to card.

On the day of the meeting ensure that the room is prepared:
Are there enough seats for everyone and enough room for the work you are about to undertake?
Open the windows or burn some incense to freshen the air.
Cleanse the area.
Gather the required tools together. Call and remind anyone who has promised to bring something.
Set out some water and glasses.
Prepare some relaxing background music.
Ensure that the room isn't too cold or too warm.
Ensure that you're not going to be interrupted. Unplugging the phone and turning off mobiles are good ideas.

At the beginning of the meeting:
As people arrive ask them to add the names of anyone they know who needs some healing to the Healing Book. Remember that you don't need to put their full names and private information, first names, initials or nicknames will suffice. Whoever you intend to send the healing to, it will reach.

Once everyone has arrived and is comfortable then you can start.
Work your way through the script and exercises for this lesson as detailed on the following pages.

Read the following scripts out loud to the group. It's a time of meditation so keep your voice calm and relaxed, reading in a fairly slow and controlled manner. Instructions are in brackets and italics.

RELAXATION
- Ensure you're sitting or lying comfortably.
- Take your awareness to your hands, make a tight fist, hold for a count of 3, 2, 1, and release.
- Tense your lower arms, hold for 3, 2, 1, and release.
- Tense your upper arms, hold for 3, 2, 1, and release.
- Tense your shoulders, lifting them up towards your ears, hold for 3, 2, 1, and release.
- Take your awareness to your neck: pull your chin toward chest but keep it from touching chest, hold for 3, 2, 1, and then relax.
- Take your awareness to your lower face and jaw, bite hard and pull back the corners of your mouth, hold for 3, 2, 1, and then relax.
- Screw your eyes up and wrinkle your nose, hold for 3, 2, 1, and then relax.
- Move your awareness to your forehead, lift your eyebrows as high as possible, hold for 3, 2, 1, and then relax.
- Take your awareness to your upper torso, pull your shoulder blades together hold for 3, 2, 1, and then release.
- Tense your stomach muscles, pulling your bellybutton towards your spine, hold for 3, 2, 1, and then release.
- Taking your awareness to your legs tense your thigh muscles, hold for 3, 2, 1, and then release.
- Pull your toes towards your head tensing your calf muscles, hold for 3, 2, 1, and then release.
- Take your awareness to your feet, point and curl your toes downwards, hold for 3, 2, 1, and then release.
- Tense your whole body at once, hands, arms, face, neck, chest, stomach, thighs, calves and feet, screw your eyes up, hold for 3, 2, 1, and completely release.
- Now take your awareness to your breathing, preferably through your nose as this is more relaxing.
- Ensure that you're breathing slowly and deeply.
- As you inhale, your abdomen will gently rise. And as you exhale it will fall.
- If your mind drifts or you lose track during this exercise bring your attention back to refocus on your breathing.
- Take a long, slow, deep inhalation for a count of 1 - 2 - 3 - 4, hold for 1- 2 and exhale for 1 - 2 - 3 - 4.
- In 2 3 4, Hold (pause), Out 2 3 4
- In 2 3 4, Hold (pause), Out 2 3 4
- In 2 3 4, Hold (pause), Out 2 3 4
- In 2 3 4, Hold (pause), Out 2 3 4
- In 2 3 4, Hold (pause), Out 2 3 4
- Continue breathing slowly and deeply.
- *(Move on to the script below.)*

OPENING & PROTECTION
- Let us take a moment to close our eyes and calm our minds.
- Concentrate on your breathing, allowing the breath to become deeper and slower.

(Pause to allow everyone to take a couple of breaths in and out)

- Let us all mentally ask our Spirit Guides and Angels to draw close and create a circle around our own.
- We let it be known that we are happy to work with Spirit and that we only work in love and light. We ask that anyone from the spirit world who wishes to contact us only does so in love and light and with the highest intentions.
- We ask for your protection, guidance and wisdom as we blend our world with yours. *(Pause)*
- Let us blend and harmonise our energies as we sit together in circle.
- Let us send out a note of harmony to the person on our left. Visualise this as a pale pink mist coming from your heart area and moving towards the heart of the person sitting on your left. *(Pause)*

LESSON FIVE - ANGELIC ENERGY

- As you continue to do this, become aware of receiving the same loving energy from the right.
- As we send and receive this energy, be aware of any changes in the atmosphere within the circle. *(Pause)*
- Have a sense of oneness with the group. *(Pause)*
- Now bring your attention back to yourself and the centre of your being, the lower abdominal area.
- Focus on your breathing; become aware of the rise and fall of your abdomen. As you inhale it will gently rise and as you exhale it will fall. *(Pause to allow everyone to take a few breaths in and out)*
- Have a sense of warmth here and in your mind's eye allow a symbol or shape to form. Imagine that this symbol or shape is sitting at and represents your centre. It may be a simple glow of light, a flame or a flower.
- With each in-breath visualise your symbol becoming larger, stronger or more open whichever is appropriate.
- With each out-breath, imagine that you are exhaling any negativity left from your day, or worries that you may have. *(Pause to allow everyone to take a few breaths in and out)*
- Now take your awareness to the soles of your feet, feeling their contact with the floor. Visualise lines of energy extending out from your feet and down into the ground. In your mind's eye, see these lines of energy as roots extending deep into the earth.
- Earth energy also travels back up through these roots revitalising and nourishing you.
- See this energy entering through the soles of your feet and travelling up through your legs to the base of your spine.
- At the base of the spine imagine that the energy becomes a sphere of deep red mist or light, as you visualise it, it becomes more vibrant in colour. *(Pause)*
- From this point a beam of energy leaves the red sphere and travels up towards the sacral area, just below the belly button. Here it forms a sphere of vibrant orange mist or light. As you focus on it, it becomes stronger in colour. *(Pause)*
- Gradually a beam of energy leaves the orange sphere and travels up towards the solar plexus, where it forms a sphere of clear yellow. With each breath, this yellow becomes stronger and brighter. *(Pause)*
- Once more a beam of energy leaves this sphere and continues its journey up to the heart area. Here a sphere of mist or light begins to form, which you may see as either green or pink. Focus on this area for a few breaths allowing the energy to grow stronger and clearer and to expand. *(Pause)*
- Gradually a beam of energy leaves the heart area and moves upwards to the throat. Here it forms a sphere of clear blue. Once more, as you focus on this area, allow the colour to expand and increase in strength. *(Pause)*
- Now, visualise a strand of energy leaving the throat area and linking with the third eye area, just between and slightly above the eyes. Here energy will begin to form as before. You may see this energy as either a rich indigo or violet, whichever you prefer. Concentrate on this energy and visualise it increasing in strength. *(Pause)*
- Again, a beam of light extends upwards from this area moving to the crown. As it does so, become aware of another beam of energy coming down from above to meet the first. As they meet at the crown a sphere of pure energy begins to form. You may see this energy as either violet or pure white light. This connects you with the higher realms of Spirit.
- As you hold this vision for a few breaths the light grows and strengthens. And as it does so, the beautiful pure light begins to overflow down and around you, surrounding you in its wonderful energy. It fills your aura, cleansing, balancing and strengthening it. You feel safe and comfortable. You feel relaxed and light. *(Longer pause before moving on to the script below.)*

CONSCIOUS CONNECTION

- Take your awareness back to the soles of your feet, feeling their contact with the floor. Visualise lines of energy extending out from your feet and down into the ground.
- In your mind's eye, see these lines of energy as roots extending deep into the earth. Maintain this

feeling of energy at the feet and be aware of earth energy moving up through these roots entering your energy system, revitalising and nourishing you. It may help to see them beginning to glow with light as the energy travels up from the earth and enters your energy system.
- Now take your awareness to the crown of your head.
- Imagine that you are being suspended by a piece of string from this point. The piece of string hangs from a point far above you, so far above you that you are unable to see its origin.
- You should have a sense of being lifted upwards.
- In your mind's eye, the string is a brilliant white light, a magical connection with higher realms. Its brilliance and its power connects with and enters into your energy system.
- You can sense this energy entering your energy system through your crown chakra. It feels amazingly empowering.

HEALING
- Slowly open your eyes and join hands with those sitting to either side of you. This increases the flow of healing energy.
- We know that our Guides, Angels and loved ones in Spirit have come forward and that they surround us with their healing energies. We ask them to help us as we send out our healing today. *(Pause)*
- Visualise a pool of brilliant white light forming and growing in the middle of our circle. *(Pause)*
- This is a pool of healing energy from which we can all draw when we need to. Know that this universal healing energy will find its way to all of those for whom we request healing.
- We ask for healing for each of us here, for our minds, bodies and spirit.

(If there are absent members: We ask for healing for the members of our group who cannot be with us today.)
- We ask for healing for all of those on our Absent Healing List. Take a moment to visualise them standing the healing pool.
- I would also like to ask for special healing for _____

(Mention anyone else that you feel healing is really important for today. Gently squeeze the hand of the person to your left to indicate that it's their turn. Let everyone have a turn at saying this part before continuing with the script.)
- We send our healing thoughts to Mother Earth and to the plant and animal kingdom. Thank you.
- Release your hands but keep your eyes closed so that you remain relaxed and peaceful as we go in to our meditation.

THEORY: ANGELIC ENERGY
The following 'theory' section should be read aloud to the group. You may want to get others to join in and take it in turns to read.

In recent years there's been an increased interest in working with angels, in a variety of ways. What does this mean and how is it different to the spiritual and psychic development you have looked at so far?

Perhaps we should start by defining what an angel is. Variously an angel can be described as a celestial body, a heavenly messenger, agents of pure unconditional love or a religious being set apart from humankind. However many people believe that angels also walk amongst us and can be identified by the random acts of kindness that they do. Clearly definitions can and do vary. In our experience the most important thing to remember about angels is that they're always willing to assist you when you ask for their help. Here's some angel theory for you:

The word 'angel' is believed to have come from a Greek word for messenger, 'angelos'.

Many believe that existence occurs on many levels, similar to the differing levels of your own energy bodies that we covered in the Beginner's Guide. So if there are different levels of creation, beyond that of the physical world, spirit beings and angels could be classed as those that inhabit them and bring messages back and forth between these realms of existence. In this belief system when someone passes over, after physical death, they may move on to the next level of existence, spirit guides could reside in the one beyond that, as they appear to have a more advanced level of consciousness. The angelic hierachy of existence is beyond these dimensions at an even higher vibratory level and consists of, in ascending order of development: Elementals – Devas – Angels – Archangels.

Angelic Realms	archangels angels devas elementals	More highly evolved spiritual beings
Spirit World	spirit guides ghosts/spirits	
Physical World	human beings plants & animals all physical things	

Diagram to illustrate the idea of an ascending hierachy of evolvement.

Elementals are the essence or spirit of something within the plant and animal kingdom and may appear as fairies, elves, sprites etc. Elementals evolve into devas, and have a greater jurisdiction. For example a dryad (or tree spirit) may evolve to become a deva (or the guardian) of a forest. Others devas may protect sacred sites, shrines and places with magical or mystical qualities. With development, devas evolve to become angels. Archangels exist at a higher level still and are great beings of light, the most highly evolved of all beings, as far as we know! It's believed that they watch over groups of angels, a bit like a team leader. Some of these archangels are widely written about and have certain attributes associated with them:
- Michael – blue / gold, protection, courage, strength, truth, integrity.
- Gabriel – indigo / white, guidance, vision, inspiration, prophecy, purification.
- Raphael – green / deep pink, healing, wholeness, unity.

These archangels can be called on should you need any of the 'gifts' that they bring. By aligning yourself with their energies you will bring more of their qualities into your life and your own being.

Other angel mythology states that angels are actually a completely different life form to humans and that they have never incarnated in physical form. (Except Archangels Metatron and Sandalphon who, legend states were elevated to these ranks to reward them for their good works on earth.)

Some also say that angels are genderless, possessing what you would call, male and female qualities in one being.

It's entirely possible that the term angel is simply more socially acceptable (or more acceptable to the individual given their faith, upbringing or frame of reference) than saying that you're working with spirit. It's something that's more readily understood by the majority and has no negative associations.

Whether you believe in angels or not, you'll find that as you work on your development and the more that you meditate, you'll begin to experience the presence of increasingly higher levels of spiritual energies. You will find that they are obviously different and of a higher level of being than the spirits that contact you ordinarily through your work. Some sense these energies so tangibly that it's almost as if there's a physical presence. Some see or sense them and refer to them as angelic or higher evolved beings as that is how their conscious mind translates their high frequency. It's almost as if you're tapping into the collective consciousness of the universe at the highest level. Creating a connection to angels is often a very powerful and emotional experience.

Other types of angels
There are certain people who we like to describe as 'angels that walk among us'. These are the truly kind, loving human beings who are of a more spiritual way of thinking and being. They perform acts of kindness, and often bravery, without thought for themselves or of recompense. These are not the types of angels that you would be working and connecting with, but we feel they should be mentioned and

recognised in some way. We're sure that you know someone who would fall into this category.

Guardian angels: Much anecdotal evidence about angels describes ways in which they've helped people in times of great danger or fear. From the person who is comforted at the side of a road following an accident to those who have been physically pulled from a wreck by someone who has later inexplicably vanished. Sometimes these guardian angels are recognised as deceased loved ones, although often only after the event, and sometimes they're completely unknown to the person concerned. Many others tell of being miraculously kept or steered away from danger. Although referred to as guardian angels these can be loved ones in spirit, spirit guides, or any being from the angelic hierarchy.

Why bother connecting with angels?
By the very nature that you're seeking spiritual and psychic development you will come into contact with, or at least be more aware of different levels of being, including the highly evolved beings, or angels.

By creating a connection with angels you can benefit from their assistance in a myriad of ways. Angels can help protect, guide and inspire you. They're great for assisting in finding lost items, even acquiring car parking spaces and helping with trouble free journeys, They can come through during readings, healing and other types of psychic and spiritual work, they help to repair things (vehicles and IT equipment) and in finding direction – in life and literally if you are lost!

'Angels' may be perceived as a Christian term. Whether you use this phrase or not is up to you. Working with this higher level or angel energy is not dependent on religious beliefs, so, if you believe in an existence beyond our own physical world you will have someone from the higher realms looking out for you, and you can most certainly work with them.

Some signs that may indicate that angels are around you:
- a rush of warmth.
- sparks or shafts of light. (These will only occur very occasionally and for short periods, if you regularly see lights at the edge of your vision, or have disturbed vision you should consult your G.P. or optician.)
- pure white feathers laying on the path in front of you or floating down from above or appearing in unexpected places.
- having a sense of a large comforting presence especially behind you but often enveloping you in their wings. (They seem to be 9-10 feet tall.)
- and of course, if you're lucky, you may actually see one!

Leave a discussion on Angelic theories until step 2 of the practical work.

PRACTICAL WORK
Read out each exercise, one at a time to the group so that you are all clear as to what you are doing, then allocate a time to complete the exercise.

Step 1 - Attracting the angels
Create an angelic environment by surrounding yourself with angelic pictures, statues, candles etc. as this helps you to draw angels close to you. Use crystals like celestite, also known as 'stone of heaven', or angelite. Angels also love music so ensure that you play gentle, meditative music to help open the communication channels between you. Some people like to have a crystal dedicated to working with angels and to hold the crystal whilst meditating and attempting contact with their angels.

Step 2 - Angelic Experiences
If anyone has had angelic experiences, take some time to discuss them, how they helped and how they made you feel.

Step 3 - Meditation to meet your guardian angel
- Ensure that you're sitting comfortably with your hands on your knees, palms facing upwards.
- Close your eyes.
- Take your awareness to your hands, make a tight fist, hold for a count of 3, 2, 1, and release.
- Tense your lower arms, hold for 3, 2, 1, and release.
- Tense your upper arms, hold for 3, 2, 1, and release.
- Tense your shoulders, lifting them up towards your ears, hold for 3, 2, 1, and release.
- Take your awareness to your neck: pull your chin toward chest but keep it from touching chest, hold for 3, 2, 1, and then relax.
- Take your awareness to your lower face and jaw, bite hard and pull back the corners of your mouth hold for 3, 2, 1, and then relax.
- Screw your eyes up and wrinkle your nose, hold for 3, 2, 1, and then relax.
- Move your awareness to your forehead, lift your eyebrows as high as possible, hold for 3, 2, 1, and then relax.
- Take your awareness to your upper torso, pull your shoulder blades together hold for 3, 2, 1, and then release.
- Tense your stomach muscles, pulling your bellybutton towards your spine, hold for 3, 2, 1, and then release.
- Taking your awareness to your legs tense your thigh muscles, hold for 3, 2, 1, and then release.
- Pull your toes towards your head tensing your calf muscles, hold for 3, 2, 1, and then release.
- Taking your awareness to your feet, point and curl your toes downwards, hold for 3, 2, 1, and then release.
- Tense your whole body at once, hands, arms, face, neck, chest, stomach, thighs, calves and feet, screw your eyes up, hold for 3, 2, 1, and completely release.
- Now take your awareness to your breathing, preferably through your nose, as this is more relaxing.
- Ensure that you are breathing slowly and deeply.
- As you inhale, your abdomen will gently rise. And as you exhale it will fall.
- If your mind drifts or you lose track during this exercise bring your attention back to refocus on your breathing.
- Take a long, slow, deep inhalation for a count of 1 - 2 - 3 - 4, hold for 1- 2 and exhale for 1 - 2 - 3 - 4.
- In 2 3 4, Hold (pause), Out 2 3 4
- In 2 3 4, Hold (pause), Out 2 3 4
- In 2 3 4, Hold (pause), Out 2 3 4
- In 2 3 4, Hold (pause), Out 2 3 4
- In 2 3 4, Hold (pause), Out 2 3 4
- Continue breathing slowly and deeply.
- During this meditation you will always be safe and protected, you will feel relaxed and comfortable. If, however, there is anything that does make you feel uneasy, or you wish to come back out of the meditation, you can do so at any time by counting backwards from 3 to 1 and taking a deep breath in and out. You can then bring your awareness back to the physical body, particularly your feet and open your eyes.
- For now though, continue to breathe slowly and deeply, your body feels relaxed and your mind is clear.
- As you breathe images may begin to form in your mind's eye. Don't try to manipulate or analyse them, simply observe them. If you do not automatically see these images, simply imagine or sense them.
- Ahead of you lies a staircase or series of ten steps. Move towards them. At the bottom you can see a doorway. We're going to slowly go down these steps towards the door feeling safe and confident at all times. So moving down the steps on my count:
- 10, 9, 8, with each step feeling lighter and lighter.
- 7, 6, 5, feeling calm and peaceful,
- 4, 3, relaxed and light
- 2 and 1, you find yourself standing in front of the door. Reaching out you open the door and as you do

so, a wonderful, warm light shines through from the other side, bathing your whole being in its rays.
- As you stand in this light for a few moments, your physical body is warmed through and your energy body is nourished and energised. This gives you a sense of comfort and completeness and offers further protection on your journey. *(Pause for a short while)*
- Today's journey is to help you connect with your guardian angel, or other angelic beings who wish to communicate with you at this point in your spiritual journey.
- The rays of light subside and you can now see through the doorway to the other side.
- As your eyes adjust to the change in light, colours begin to form shapes. You can see your sanctuary on the other side of the doorway.
- You step through, closing the door behind you.
- Find a place in your sanctuary that you can sit comfortably.
- Make yourself at home in this safe place. *(Pause)*
- Ask that your guardian angel, or other relevant angelic being, draw close to you. You may begin to feel their warmth and love in the area around you.
- Pure bright light fills the room as they draw near. Unconditional love pours forth enveloping every part of your being.
- Allow your heart chakra to open wide and connect with this wonderful angelic energy. *(Pause for 20-30 seconds.)*
- Gradually you begin to see the outline of your angelic visitor appearing before you. They are surrounded by an extraordinary cloak of light, the colour of it more vivid and beautiful than any earthly colour you have ever seen before.
- The colour begins to swirl around you too, bringing love, healing and energy. It restores and revives you.
- Enjoy this most wonderful energy. As you do so, you may be aware of celestial singing or other sound or music coming through that resonates with your heart, mind, body and soul. *(Pause for 20-30 seconds.)*
- Now you are ready to communicate with your angel. You can ask their name. And whether they have a message or any advice for you. Spend some time communicating with your angel now. *(Pause for a couple of minutes.)*
- Now you have had some time to communicate with your angel, it is time to begin your journey back. Before you do so, your angel has a gift for you, perhaps symbolic, but one which has great relevance to you and the path which you are on. Open your hands and receive the gift from your angel. If you are unsure why you have been given this gift, ask your angel to explain it to you. *(Pause for 30 seconds.)*
- Bid your angel farewell, knowing that they always remain close to you and will work with you whenever you ask them to.
- Gradually the images fade and a mist falls over them. You are in your sanctuary. You are safe and warm. Thank your angel for allowing you this insight today.
- You may wish to place your angelic gift in a special place in your sanctuary where you will be able to return to it whenever you like. You will bring the essence of this gift back with you as you return to the physical world.
- Now make your way to the doorway leading to your stairwell.
- Open the door. Step through closing the door behind you.
- Know that your sanctuary is your own space that you can return to at any time for relaxation, guidance and healing.
- And keeping your sense of calm and wellbeing, it is time to head back up the stairs. So moving back up the stairs on my count,
- 1, 2, 3, breathing slowly and deeply,
- 4, 5, 6, your body is starting to feel heavier,
- 7, 8, bringing your awareness back to your physical body,
- 9 and 10, on that top step now and when you're ready, step off the top step.

- Bringing your awareness completely back to your physical body and this room, your contact with the chair, your feet with the floor. Slowly begin to move your fingers and toes, and in your own time, opening your eyes, fully awake and aware and in the physical world.

(If you are reading this aloud for someone else, watch for them starting to wriggle fingers and toes. If they appear not want to come back to the room simply repeat the last paragraph, in bold, but raising your voice so that it's said slightly louder and firmer. Repeat a third time if necessary moving over to the person and at the end just saying their name and asking that they come back now into the room, placing your hand gently on their shoulder.)

- Spend a few minutes sharing experiences of the meditation or making notes about it if you are keeping a personal journal. Don't forget to date the entry.

Step 4 - Exercise 1 - An angel's touch
- Read out the following:
- Sit comfortably in your chair. Close your eyes and concentrate on your breathing, allowing yourself to relax.
- With each breath, find yourself becoming calmer and more relaxed.
- Take your awareness to your crown chakra and visualise a sphere of pure energy in this area. You may see this energy as any colour that comes to mind.
- As you hold this vision for a few breaths the light grows and strengthens. The sphere becomes larger and brighter and as it does so, the beautiful pure light begins to overflow down and around you, surrounding you in this wonderful energy.
- It fills your aura, cleansing, balancing and strengthening it. The light around your physical body grows stronger and brighter. It extends out in all directions around you. *(Pause)*
- See in your mind's eye how far it extends.
- Now take a deep slow breath in and as you slowly exhale, imagine your aura expanding further as though you're blowing it up like a balloon but maintaining its strength and brightness.
- Continue to breathe in this way to expand your energy further. As you do so, you feel safe and comfortable. You feel relaxed and light. *(Pause)*
- Now mentally ask your guardian angel to approach you. *(Pause)*
- Be aware of any changes in the energy field around you, of any sensations you may feel. *(Pause for 30 - 60 seconds.)*
- Take a deep slow breath and relax.
- Next ask your angel to touch you. *(Pause for 20 - 30 seconds.)*
- Thank your angel for their contact. *(Pause) (*)*
- Maintaining your sense of peace and calm, bring your awareness back to the room and in your own time open your eyes.
- *(This exercise can be repeated as often as you like. It can take several attempts until you feel or sense your angel as it can take time to become used to the subtle energy changes the angel creates.)*

Exercise 2 - Listening for your angel's name
Repeat exercise 1 up to and including requesting a touch from your angel. (*) Then read out the following:
- Ask your angel to tell you their name.
- Allow yourself to trust in the first name that comes into your head, however strange or unusual, or perhaps even ordinary, it may seem. *(Pause)*
- Now ask your angel to give you a sign, signal or sound that you can use to request their presence. Or that will indicate them being close by. *(Pause for 30 - 60 seconds.)*
- Thank your angel for this information. *(Pause) (*)*
- Maintaining your sense of peace and calm, bring your awareness back to the room and in your own time open your eyes.
- *(Again this exercise can take several attempts before you gain the desired result: allowing yourself to fully relax, and perseverance, will help you to be successful.)*

Angel divination cards
- Read out the following: If you have access to angel cards, ask your angels to connect with you and pass messages to you or to others through the cards. Using cards that depict angelic beings can give very powerful and profound results. They help you to connect into this high level of universal knowledge, wisdom and understanding very quickly. There are a multitude of angel card packs available if you wish to buy some. As we always say, be guided by your intuition and buy the cards that you feel drawn to.
- Alternatively, you could photocopy Handout 4 - Angel cards, on to a reasonable thickness of A4 card, cut out the cards and decorate them with angelic images and colours that you feel are appropriate to the words. It might be a good idea to do this all together in the group while you're in the right frame of mind and environment to tune in to the angelic energies.
- If you want to try making your own cards from scratch, you may find that you're able to channel the appropriate words or phrases for them if you've already established a connection to your angels. Decorate the cards with angelic images and different colours if you wish.
- Use the cards in the way that feels right to you, for example, you may choose to give single card readings, a three card reading, a five card reading, or it may vary depending on who you're reading for.
- Working in pairs, take it in turns to read for each other.
- Ask your angels to connect with you and pass messages for your partner during the angel card reading. Use the words and images on the cards, just as with any card reading. (See our Beginners Course Companion for more on card readings.)
- As with any reading remember that you have a responsibility to the person that you are reading for, please ensure that you pass on any information that you receive in a sensible and sensitive way. Allow yourself to be guided as to whether certain parts of the message should be left unsaid if necessary.

CLOSING & GROUNDING
Once you have completed the exercises everyone should sit comfortably and complete the following meditation to close and ground their energy. Read out the following:
- Sit in a comfortable position and close your eyes.
- Bring your attention to your breathing and focus on this for a few breaths. *(Pause)*
- Take your awareness to the invisible energy field surrounding you and visualise it drawing in close around your physical body. *(Pause)*
- Take your awareness to the area just above your crown and see a sphere of light sitting here.
- Imagine that sphere of light shrinking in size until it's tiny, then sinking down through the crown of your head.
- See it slowly descending down past the brow. *(Pause)*
- Into the throat. *(Pause)*
- Then following the line of the spine, down, through your body, towards your heart area. *(Pause)*
- Down to your solar plexus. *(Pause)*
- Through the abdominal area. *(Pause)*
- To the base of your spine. *(Pause)*
- Now visualise the sphere of energy either leaving through the base of your spine, or dividing in two and sinking down through your legs and leaving through the soles of your feet.
- Feel this energy leaving you and connecting with the earth.
- Have a sense of downward movement, deep in to the earth. *(Pause)*
- Become more aware of your feet and your physical body.
- Let us take a moment to thank our Spirit Guides, Angels and loved ones in Spirit for their presence, protection and wisdom whilst we've been working. Knowing that they will always be on hand should we need to call on them. *(Pause)*
- **Now bring your awareness back to your physical body, the chair you are sitting on and your contact with the floor.**

- **Begin to bring some movement back in to your fingers and toes.**
- **In your own time opening your eyes, fully awake and aware and in the physical world.**

(Watch for them starting to wriggle fingers and toes and keep an eye on anyone who doesn't do this. If a member of the group appears not to want to come back to the room simply repeat the last three points, in bold, but raising your voice so that it said slightly louder and firmer. Repeat a third time if necessary moving over to the person and at the end just saying their name and asking that they come back into the room now, placing a hand gently on their shoulder.)

Check to ensure that everyone feels grounded before you finish the session. If not, get them to walk around for a little while. Stamping your feet or jumping up and down helps to bring you back to the physical world. If these don't do the trick, you can ground your energy very readily by eating a small amount of food such as a biscuit.

OTHER THINGS TO TRY:

- Either: Pick a random angel card each morning taking special note of its message - this may be the words that are on the card, or a message which is channelled to you through the card - trust your intuition to guide you. You can carry the card around with you during the day, looking at it every so often to remind you of the message and of the angelic energy that's with you on that day. You may like to keep a diary noting the cards you have drawn and the events during the day that related to them. Doing this exercise daily will help you to establish a strong connection to angelic energy.
- Or: Select twelve angel cards, one for each of the next twelve months. Each card will give you a theme for the given month. Again it's good to keep a record of which card relates to which month, and to note down any events related to it. When Diane did this one January, she drew the 'Study' card for October and during that month joined the Open University-something that had certainly not been in her conscious plan at the beginning of that year.

AND ANOTHER THING:

- Setting the scene - as we have done in the practical section, create an angelic environment at home by surrounding yourself with angelic pictures, statues, candles etc. as this helps you to draw angelic energy close to you. Use crystals like celestite, also known as 'stone of heaven', or angelite. Play gentle, meditative music when you wish to open the communication channels between you. Some people like to have a crystal dedicated to working with angels and to hold the crystal whilst meditating and attempting contact with their angels.
- Keep an eye out for repeating number sequences, for example you may see the time of 11.11 on a digital clock and soon after see a door number 111. You may also see repeating number combinations such as 5s and 3s, for example a number 53 bus followed by 53 on a number plate. If such synchronicities occur, many believe that they hold messages from your angels. There are several books that explain the meanings of such number patterns such as Doreen Virtue's 'Angel Numbers'. Both of us number sequences, and their messages via this book highly useful and profound.
- Once you've begun to communicate with your angel in the ways described above, you will find that there are indicators of their presence around you in your everyday life. Look out for white feathers in unexpected places; these are commonly believed to be angelic 'calling cards'. You may find that they suddenly appear when you are feeling vulnerable, upset and in need of your angel's help. Remember to thank your angel for their love and assistance whenever they provide you with a physical sign or their presence.
- Whenever you need help from your angels - ask! Try asking for a parking space when you set off to the shops, or help to retain important facts for exams or work presentations. The more you communicate with your angels in this way, the more you will be aware of their presence in your life.
- Make a note of any angelic experiences that you have. This serves as a personal reminder of your angelic communications and of how the angels are always willing to help when asked.

- You may want to read up on the subject, try 'Angel Therapy' by Denise Whichello Brown - a good beginner's book on the subject. Or any books on angels by Doreen Virtue for more advanced information. Also look out for her angel cards.

FOR DISCUSSION
- What have we got from this lesson? Best bits? Tricky bits?
- Key Concepts - how are we getting on with patience, acceptance, faith?
- Healing - feedback from those in the healing book? Success stories?

Next Time...

The next lesson will be covering PSYCHOKINESIS.

You will need to arrange for the following tools to be brought along:
- A number of pens (with rounded barrels so that they roll easily)
- One or more clean dry glass jars
- A small feather to go in each jar
- One or more pendulum (either a crystal pendulum on a chain or a small object, such as a ring, on a length of string).
- Something to suspend the pendulum from such as a wine bottle holder or a banana holder with a hook.

Extra tools if you want to do 'other things to try':
- Crystals to help with this lesson are agate, aventurine, carnelian, citrine, haematite, clear quartz and smokey quartz.
- One or more candles in a large upright jar or storm lantern (and some matches).
- A selection of cheap, 2nd hand or unwanted spoons.

LESSON SIX
PSYCHOKINESIS

PREPARATION
Well in advance of your meeting ensure that you have all of the tools that you require for this lesson. If not, find out if another group member has access to what you need.

Regular tools:
- Healing book
- Pens and pencils
- Paper
- Candles & matches if desired
- Box of tissues

Tools for this lesson:
- A number of pens (with rounded barrels so that they roll easily)
- One or more clean dry glass jars
- A small feather to go in each jar
- One or more pendulum (either a crystal pendulum on a chain or a small object, such as a ring, on a length of string).
- Something to suspend the pendulum from such as a wine bottle holder or a banana holder with a hook.

Extra tools if you want to do 'other things to try':
- Crystals to help with this lesson are agate, aventurine, carnelian, citrine, haematite, clear quartz and smokey quartz.
- One or more candles in a large upright jar or storm lantern (and some matches).
- A selection of cheap, 2nd hand or unwanted spoons.

On the day of the meeting ensure that the room is prepared:
Are there enough seats for everyone and enough room for the work you are about to undertake?
Open the windows or burn some incense to freshen the air.
Cleanse the area.
Gather the required tools together. Call and remind anyone who has promised to bring something.
Set out some water and glasses.
Prepare some relaxing background music.
Ensure that the room isn't too cold or too warm.
Ensure that you're not going to be interrupted. Unplugging the phone and turning off mobiles are good ideas.

At the beginning of the meeting:
As people arrive ask them to add the names of anyone they know who needs some healing to the Healing Book. Remember that you don't need to put their full names and private information, first names, initials or nicknames will suffice. Whoever you intend to send the healing to, it will reach.

Once everyone has arrived and is comfortable then you can start.
Work your way through the script and exercises for this lesson as detailed on the following pages.

Read the following scripts out loud to the group. It's a time of meditation so keep your voice calm and relaxed, reading in a fairly slow and controlled manner. Instructions are in brackets and italics.

RELAXATION
- Ensure you're sitting or lying comfortably.
- Take your awareness to your hands, make a tight fist, hold for a count of 3, 2, 1, and release.
- Tense your lower arms, hold for 3, 2, 1, and release.
- Tense your upper arms, hold for 3, 2, 1, and release.
- Tense your shoulders, lifting them up towards your ears, hold for 3, 2, 1, and release.
- Take your awareness to your neck: pull your chin toward chest but keep it from touching chest, hold for 3, 2, 1, and then relax.
- Take your awareness to your lower face and jaw, bite hard and pull back the corners of your mouth, hold for 3, 2, 1, and then relax.
- Screw your eyes up and wrinkle your nose, hold for 3, 2, 1, and then relax.
- Move your awareness to your forehead, lift your eyebrows as high as possible, hold for 3, 2, 1, and then relax.
- Take your awareness to your upper torso, pull your shoulder blades together hold for 3, 2, 1, and then release.
- Tense your stomach muscles, pulling your bellybutton towards your spine, hold for 3, 2, 1, and then release.
- Taking your awareness to your legs tense your thigh muscles, hold for 3, 2, 1, and then release.
- Pull your toes towards your head tensing your calf muscles, hold for 3, 2, 1, and then release.
- Take your awareness to your feet, point and curl your toes downwards, hold for 3, 2, 1, and then release.
- Tense your whole body at once, hands, arms, face, neck, chest, stomach, thighs, calves and feet, screw your eyes up, hold for 3, 2, 1, and completely release.
- Now take your awareness to your breathing, preferably through your nose as this is more relaxing.
- Ensure that you're breathing slowly and deeply.
- As you inhale, your abdomen will gently rise. And as you exhale it will fall.
- If your mind drifts or you lose track during this exercise bring your attention back to refocus on your breathing.
- Take a long, slow, deep inhalation for a count of 1 - 2 - 3 - 4, hold for 1- 2 and exhale for 1 - 2 - 3 - 4.
- In 2 3 4, Hold (pause), Out 2 3 4
- In 2 3 4, Hold (pause), Out 2 3 4
- In 2 3 4, Hold (pause), Out 2 3 4
- In 2 3 4, Hold (pause), Out 2 3 4
- In 2 3 4, Hold (pause), Out 2 3 4
- Continue breathing slowly and deeply.
- *(Move on to the script below.)*

OPENING & PROTECTION
- Let us take a moment to close our eyes and calm our minds.
- Concentrate on your breathing, allowing the breath to become deeper and slower.

(Pause to allow everyone to take a couple of breaths in and out)

- Let us all mentally ask our Spirit Guides and Angels to draw close and create a circle around our own.
- We let it be known that we are happy to work with Spirit and that we only work in love and light. We ask that anyone from the spirit world who wishes to contact us only does so in love and light and with the highest intentions.
- We ask for your protection, guidance and wisdom as we blend our world with yours. *(Pause)*
- Let us blend and harmonise our energies as we sit together in circle.
- Let us send out a note of harmony to the person on our left. Visualise this as a pale pink mist coming from your heart area and moving towards the heart of the person sitting on your left. *(Pause)*

LESSON SIX - PSYCHOKINESIS

- As you continue to do this, become aware of receiving the same loving energy from the right.
- As we send and receive this energy, be aware of any changes in the atmosphere within the circle. *(Pause)*
- Have a sense of oneness with the group. *(Pause)*
- Now bring your attention back to yourself and the centre of your being, the lower abdominal area.
- Focus on your breathing; become aware of the rise and fall of your abdomen. As you inhale it will gently rise and as you exhale it will fall. *(Pause to allow everyone to take a few breaths in and out)*
- Have a sense of warmth here and in your mind's eye allow a symbol or shape to form. Imagine that this symbol or shape is sitting at and represents your centre. It may be a simple glow of light, a flame or a flower.
- With each in-breath visualise your symbol becoming larger, stronger or more open whichever is appropriate.
- With each out-breath, imagine that you are exhaling any negativity left from your day, or worries that you may have. *(Pause to allow everyone to take a few breaths in and out)*
- Now take your awareness to the soles of your feet, feeling their contact with the floor. Visualise lines of energy extending out from your feet and down into the ground. In your mind's eye, see these lines of energy as roots extending deep into the earth.
- Earth energy also travels back up through these roots revitalising and nourishing you.
- See this energy entering through the soles of your feet and travelling up through your legs to the base of your spine.
- At the base of the spine imagine that the energy becomes a sphere of deep red mist or light, as you visualise it, it becomes more vibrant in colour. *(Pause)*
- From this point a beam of energy leaves the red sphere and travels up towards the sacral area, just below the belly button. Here it forms a sphere of vibrant orange mist or light. As you focus on it, it becomes stronger in colour. *(Pause)*
- Gradually a beam of energy leaves the orange sphere and travels up towards the solar plexus, where it forms a sphere of clear yellow. With each breath, this yellow becomes stronger and brighter. *(Pause)*
- Once more a beam of energy leaves this sphere and continues its journey up to the heart area. Here a sphere of mist or light begins to form, which you may see as either green or pink. Focus on this area for a few breaths allowing the energy to grow stronger and clearer and to expand. *(Pause)*
- Gradually a beam of energy leaves the heart area and moves upwards to the throat. Here it forms a sphere of clear blue. Once more, as you focus on this area, allow the colour to expand and increase in strength. *(Pause)*
- Now, visualise a strand of energy leaving the throat area and linking with the third eye area, just between and slightly above the eyes. Here energy will begin to form as before. You may see this energy as either a rich indigo or violet, whichever you prefer. Concentrate on this energy and visualise it increasing in strength. *(Pause)*
- Again, a beam of light extends upwards from this area moving to the crown. As it does so, become aware of another beam of energy coming down from above to meet the first. As they meet at the crown a sphere of pure energy begins to form. You may see this energy as either violet or pure white light. This connects you with the higher realms of Spirit.
- As you hold this vision for a few breaths the light grows and strengthens. And as it does so, the beautiful pure light begins to overflow down and around you, surrounding you in its wonderful energy. It fills your aura, cleansing, balancing and strengthening it. You feel safe and comfortable. You feel relaxed and light. *(Longer pause before moving on to the script below.)*

CONSCIOUS CONNECTION

- Take your awareness back to the soles of your feet, feeling their contact with the floor. Visualise lines of energy extending out from your feet and down into the ground.
- In your mind's eye, see these lines of energy as roots extending deep into the earth. Maintain this

feeling of energy at the feet and be aware of earth energy moving up through these roots entering your energy system, revitalising and nourishing you. It may help to see them beginning to glow with light as the energy travels up from the earth and enters your energy system.
- Now take your awareness to the crown of your head.
- Imagine that you are being suspended by a piece of string from this point. The piece of string hangs from a point far above you, so far above you that you are unable to see its origin.
- You should have a sense of being lifted upwards.
- In your mind's eye, the string is a brilliant white light, a magical connection with higher realms. Its brilliance and its power connects with and enters into your energy system.
- You can sense this energy entering your energy system through your crown chakra. It feels amazingly empowering.

HEALING
- Slowly open your eyes and join hands with those sitting to either side of you. This increases the flow of healing energy.
- We know that our Guides, Angels and loved ones in Spirit have come forward and that they surround us with their healing energies. We ask them to help us as we send out our healing today. *(Pause)*
- Visualise a pool of brilliant white light forming and growing in the middle of our circle. *(Pause)*
- This is a pool of healing energy from which we can all draw when we need to. Know that this universal healing energy will find its way to all of those for whom we request healing.
- We ask for healing for each of us here, for our minds, bodies and spirit.

(If there are absent members: We ask for healing for the members of our group who cannot be with us today.)
- We ask for healing for all of those on our Absent Healing List. Take a moment to visualise them standing in the healing pool.
- I would also like to ask for special healing for _____

(Mention anyone else that you feel healing is really important for today. Gently squeeze the hand of the person to your left to indicate that it's their turn. Let everyone have a turn at saying this part before continuing with the script.)
- We send our healing thoughts to Mother Earth and to the plant and animal kingdom. Thank you.
- Release your hands but keep your eyes closed so that you remain relaxed and peaceful as we go in to our meditation. *(Brief pause before moving on to the Meditation script.)*

MEDITATION
- Ensure that you're sitting comfortably with your hands on your knees, palms facing upwards.
- Close your eyes.
- Take a deep inhalation, and breathe out slowly. Continue to breathe slowly and deeply.
- During this meditation you will always be safe and protected, you will feel relaxed and comfortable. If, however, there is anything that does make you feel uneasy, or you wish to come back out of the meditation, you can do so at any time by counting backwards from 3 to 1 and taking a deep breath in and out. You can then bring your awareness back to the physical body, particularly your feet and open your eyes.
- For now though, continue to breathe slowly and deeply, your body feels relaxed and your mind is clear.
- As you breathe images may begin to form in your mind's eye. Don't try to manipulate or analyse them, simply observe them. If you do not automatically see these images, simply imagine or sense them.
- Ahead of you lies a staircase or series of ten steps. Move towards them. At the bottom you can see a doorway. We're going to slowly go down these steps towards the door feeling safe and confident at all times. So moving down the steps on my count:
- 10, 9, 8, with each step feeling lighter and lighter.
- 7, 6, 5, feeling calm and peaceful,

LESSON SIX - PSYCHOKINESIS

- 4, 3, relaxed and light
- 2 and 1, you find yourself standing in front of the door. Reaching out you open the door and as you do so, a wonderful, warm light shines through from the other side, bathing your whole being in its rays.
- As you stand in this light for a few moments, your physical body is warmed through and your energy body is nourished and energised. This gives you a sense of comfort and completeness and offers further protection on your journey. *(Pause for a short while)*
- Today's journey is to inspire a sense of openness and potential for transformation.
- The rays of light subside and you can now see through the doorway to the other side.
- As your eyes adjust to the change in light, colours begin to form shapes. You can see your sanctuary on the other side of the doorway.
- You step through, closing the door behind you
- Move through your sanctuary towards your outside space, or your sanctuary may already be an outside space.
- Wander through your outside space or open sanctuary, it is an area of peace and retreat just for you.
- Although you may come here often it's always unveiling new images and places to explore.
- Today you notice a doorway hidden away in this outside space. It is old and shabby and may have ivy or other plants covering it. It's handle and hinges are rusted.
- You step closer to it, drawn by an inner wonder and curiosity.
- You reach out your hand and as you place it against the solid old door it glows with a gentle light and the door transforms.
- It's no longer old and worn, it's clean and clear of obstacles. You try the handle and the door opens easily for you.
- Feeling safe and unworried you step through to explore what the doorway will reveal to you.
- You hear a gentle voice on the breeze welcoming you to this place.
- You have entered a magical world. Take time to look around you and take it all in, the plants, the animals, the landscape. Pathways lead to wherever you wish to go and you will see whatever you wish to see in this mystical place. Here you can explore your full potential, you can be whoever or whatever you desire. It's a place of transformation. If you wish to know what it is to soar with the eagles or swim with ocean creatures you can, Whatever you see here, you can transform into. Simply reach out and touch the creature, plant or item that you wish to be, close your eyes and open your mind. You will be transformed. Your whole being will experience that new existence. If you wish to return to your own form, simply say 'thank you, I must return' and you will do so swiftly and safely.
- Go now and explore, be whatever you want to be, learn what you need to learn, absorb the essence of the experience that you desire, and I will return for you shortly. *(Pause for 3-4 minutes)*
- It will shortly be time to return to your sanctuary. If you're not back to your own self, say 'thank you, I must return' *(Brief pause)*
- Remember these feelings of wonder, know that you have within you the potential to transform and be free. Return with these feelings now as you move back, passing through the magical doorway to your sanctuary.
- Move through your sanctuary and find you way back to the doorway that leads to the stairwell.
- Open the door that leads to the stairwell. Step through closing the door behind you.
- Know that your sanctuary is your own space that you can return to at any time for relaxation, guidance and healing.
- And keeping that sense of calm and wellbeing, it is time to head back up the stairs. So moving back up the stairs on my count,
- 1, 2, 3, breathing slowly and deeply,
- 4, 5, 6, your body is starting to feel heavier
- 7, 8, bringing your awareness back to your physical body,
- 9 and 10, on that top step now and when you're ready, step off the top step.

- **Bringing your awareness completely back to your physical body and this room, your contact with the chair, your feet with the floor. Slowly begin to move your fingers and toes, and in your own time, opening your eyes, fully awake and aware and in the physical world.**

(Watch for them starting to wriggle fingers and toes and keep an eye on anyone who doesn't do this. If a member of the group appears not to want to come back to the room simply repeat the last paragraph, in bold, but raising your voice so that it said slightly louder and firmer. Repeat a third time if necessary moving over to the person and at the end just saying their name and asking that they come back now in to the room, placing your hand gently on their shoulder.)

Spend a few minutes sharing experiences of the meditation. Remember that it's okay if someone fell asleep, could see nothing or did their own thing. If you're keeping a personal journal, you may wish to take some time to record you experience. Don't forget to date the entry.

THEORY: PSYCHOKINESIS
The following 'theory' section should be read aloud to the group. You may want to get others to join in and take it in turns to read.

Psychokinesis (or telekinesis, as it's sometimes known) is the ability to move physical objects with the power of the mind, or other unexplained force. The movement occurs without the person having any physical contact with the object. There's no definitive explanation of how this works, or 100% scientific proof that it can, or for that matter, that it can't be done. We believe it can as we have seen it in action. But you only have our word for that.

Could it be that you have untapped brain potential that allows you to move and control objects? Is it that you can 'become one' with the object and project your consciousness in to it, willing it to move? Or is there another explanation? Here are some things to think about:

From previous exercises in this book you should already have seen and felt how you can affect people and be affected through your auras. So, if you're able to extend your energetic body out powerfully enough, maybe you can exert a force (small or otherwise) on a physical object causing it to move. Or, if you can channel energy and focus it towards an object, then you can exert a force on that object causing it to move. We believe that spirit beings are able to use an individual's or group's energy to get their attention, through the creation of sound or movement of objects, so why can't we manipulate this energy too? If, as many spiritual philosophies suggest, everything that exists is all one, made of and linked by the same universal energy but appearing as separate parts, then we simply must be able to cause movement to these other parts through our invisible connections.

Practising psychokinesis has a number of benefits to your development, although some may just wish to do it for its own sake to prove that it can be done. The discipline of energy creation, visualisation, sustained focus and the opening up of the mind to new possibilities are all good reasons to pursue the challenge that this subject brings. You need a deep understanding of energy work and to be able to work with it practically too. You also need a lot of patience, at first movement may be so miniscule, occurring at a molecular level, that you're unable to see it with your eyes. The effect may need to build to a critical point before visible movement occurs to confirm that you've succeeded. Why not just give it a go and see how you get on with it?

However entertaining these exercises might be once you master them, please don't be tempted to use them as party trick to show off. Remember they are part of your personal development.

Discuss any personal experiences or thoughts on the subject (but keep any eye on the time).

LESSON SIX - PSYCHOKINESIS

PRACTICAL WORK
Read out each exercise, one at a time to the group so that you are all clear as to what you are doing, then allocate a time to complete the exercise.

Read out: We have included a number of different ways to attempt psychokinesis, give them all a go (although maybe not all in one session) and see which way you prefer to work, then persevere with it. Psychokinesis isn't something you will learn in one session, it will probably take some time. Have a go on a regular basis, interspersed with other development exercises to stretch and improve all of your skills. Quite often, improvement in other aspects of psychic work will encourage the skills that you don't take to immediately so that one day, something just clicks and you can do it.

It's really important to get the hang of opening up, so we are going to repeat two exercises from a previous chapter first.

Step 1 - Elevating Your Energy
Before you begin, find a seated position that you feel comfortable in and can maintain for the duration of this exercise. It's best to be upright in a chair or cross-legged on the floor, perhaps supported by a cushion if required. Once everyone is comfortable, read out the following:
- Take your awareness to your feet and to the energy entering through your soles, imagine it travelling up through your legs to the base of your spine.
- At the base of the spine imagine that the energy becomes a sphere of deep red mist or light. As you visualise it, it becomes more vibrant in colour.
- From this point a beam of energy leaves the red sphere and travels up towards the sacral area, just below the belly button. Here it forms a sphere of vibrant orange mist or light. As you focus on it, it becomes stronger in colour.
- Gradually, a beam of energy leaves the orange sphere and travels up towards the solar plexus, where it forms a sphere of clear yellow. With each breath, this yellow becomes stronger and brighter.
- Once more a beam of energy leaves this sphere and continues its journey up to the heart area. Here a sphere of mist or light begins to form, which you may see as either green or pink. Focus on this area for a few breaths allowing the energy to grow stronger and clearer. It may begin to expand.
- Gradually, a beam of energy leaves the heart area and moves upwards to the throat. Here it forms a sphere of clear blue. Once more, as you focus on this area, allow the colour to expand and increase in strength.
- Now, visualise a strand of energy leaving the throat area and linking with the third eye area, just between and slightly above the eyes. Here energy will begin to form as before. You may see this energy as either a rich indigo or violet, whichever you prefer. Concentrate on this energy and visualise it increasing in strength and energy.
- Again, a beam of light extends upwards from this area moving up to the crown. As it does so, become aware of a beam of energy coming down from high above to meet the first at the crown. A sphere of pure energy begins to form in this area. You may see this energy as either violet or pure white light. This connects you with the higher realms of spirit.
- *(Continue on to step 2.)*

Step 2 - Expanding Your Awareness:
- As you hold this vision for a few breaths the light grows and strengthens. The sphere becomes larger and brighter and as it does so, the beautiful pure light begins to overflow down and around you, surrounding you in this wonderful energy.
- It fills your aura, cleansing, balancing and strengthening it. The light around your physical body grows stronger and brighter. It extends out in all directions around you. See in your mind's eye how far it extends.
- Now take a deep slow breath in and as you slowly exhale, imagine your aura expanding further as

though you're blowing it up with each breath like a balloon but maintaining its strength and brightness. Continue to breathe in this way to expand your energy further. As you do so, you feel safe and comfortable. You feel relaxed and light.
- *(Continue on to step 3.)*

Step 3 - Energy build up
- Slowly open your eyes. Place your hands together in prayer position, palm-to-palm in front of your face, about one fist distance between the fingers and the tip of the nose.
- Your fingers are straight and the palms are pressed slightly together.
- Your elbows are raised and aren't touching the body and the forearms are almost but not quite parallel with the floor.
- Keep your eyes focussed on the tips of the middle fingers.
- Maintain this position for a few minutes, breathing slowly and deeply.
- Keep your shoulders relaxed and don't allow tension to creep into your body.
- Keep the focus of your attention on the palms of your hands, and their contact with each other. You may become aware of heat building up.
- After a minute or so separate your hands very slightly. Take your focus and, if necessary, your eyes to the space between your palms. Very slowly move your hands slightly away from and then towards each other, as though gently pumping the air between the palms. You should become aware of some resistance here.
- Very gradually take your hands further apart and as they come back towards each other, still with that pumping action, make the gap between your palms larger and larger.
- Move your hands around as though you are holding a ball of energy between your palms. That is exactly what you 've created.
- If you're more of a visual person you may see this build up of energy as light or colour. If not, try closing your eyes for a short while to see if you can 'see' it in your mind's eye.
- Continue to allow energy to flow through you, adding to this ball of energy, but now turn your hands slightly as though you are gently pushing or passing the ball towards someone else.
- Feel the energy flowing from your hands and streaming outwards. If you can, visualise it too.
- Hold this focus and flow for a few minutes before bringing your palms back together.
- Place your hands in your lap and bring your awareness back to the room.
- Slowly open your eyes.

Step 4 - Move it!
Read out: Read through the different methods and options listed and discuss which one each of you will try. You don't all have to do the same thing, just ensure that you each have what you need. You may want to work in pairs and take it in turns to create movement and observe the object (in case one of you miss it when you're eyes are shut). Only work in short bursts to begin with (1-2 minutes at a time) and see what happens. If you're observing your partners attempts DO NOT try to join in. You could counteract their work.

Method 1 - Directing energy
Following on from our previous exercises focus on channelling energy from your aura towards the object causing it to move. Much like a breeze or draught would. You may need to hold your palms up facing the object, although don't get too close. Or you could visualise the energy being channelled from a specific chakra. Alternatively imagine that your whole being is directing a blast of energy towards the object. You must maintain this for a few minutes so you may need to build up the time that you spend on this exercise from 1-2 minutes to 5, 10, maybe eventually 15 minutes in order to have an effect.

Method 2 - Visualisation

Focus your attention on the object for a minute or so. Then close your eyes and continue to hold the vision of the object in your mind. Once you have the vision clear, 'see' it start to move, and then 'watch' it in your mind's eye as it continues to do so, as though you're playing a movie in your mind. After a short while, slowly open your eyes, the object may have, or may still be moving, but if not, attempt to combine this visualisation of movement with having your eyes open and looking at the object. This is very advanced. If you're unable to do this, return to the visualisation with your eyes closed and repeat the exercise a few times. Always 'see' the movement in the same direction so as not to send out mixed signals. As before, you may need to build up the length of time you spend on this exercise.

Method 3 - Become one

Have you seen 'The Matrix'? If not, it's worth a watch. If you have you'll be familiar with the term, 'there is no spoon'. That is what this method is based on. We are all one, so you must project your consciousness into the object that you're trying to move. Try to feel yourself becoming the object and then moving as the object. The theory being that there is no spoon because you are the spoon, and the spoon is you. Again, this is a very advanced technique. You'll probably need to do this with your eyes closed.

Try to find which method works for you. Stick to one method for a while rather than switching back and forth between methods. It can take many attempts to see results or you may find it works straight away for you.

Options

a) Pen Rolling

- Find a pen that is completely rounded so that it rolls easily across a table if you blow hard on it.
- Close any doors and windows and turn off any fans or heaters.
- Sit comfortably at a table with the pen in the middle of it. Ensure that it doesn't roll initially - the table may be on a slope!
- Relax and focus on the pen, use your chosen method from above to attempt to cause the pen to roll.
- You may see the pen start to vibrate, this is the beginning, movement will follow given enough focus and practice.

b) Feather Floating

- You will need a clean dry glass or jar and a small feather
- Place the feather on the table and turn the jar or glass over to cover it. Or you could use a lidded jar to trap the feather and exclude draughts.
- Sit comfortably at the table and relax.
- Now focus on the feather and use your chosen method to attempt to move, or float it.
- You may see small vibrations of the feather, this is the beginning, movement will follow given enough focus and practice.

c) Pendulum swinging

- Use a weight on a length of string or cord. Try a wedding ring, a DIY plumb line, a dowsing pendulum or crystal on a chain.
- Hang the pendulum from something and place it where you can comfortably sit in front of it, and so that it can swing freely. Try a wine bottle holder or a banana holder with a hook.
- Close any doors and windows and turn off any fans or heaters.
- Ensure that the pendulum is at a complete stop before starting this exercise.
- Relax and focus on the pendulum, use your chosen method from Step 4 to attempt to cause it to swing.
- You may see the pendulum start to vibrate, this is the beginning. Movement will follow given enough focus and practice.

CLOSING & GROUNDING
Once you have completed the exercises everyone should sit comfortably and complete the following meditation to close and ground their energy. Read out the following:
- Sit in a comfortable position and close your eyes.
- Bring your attention to your breathing and focus on this for a few breaths. *(Pause)*
- Take your awareness to the invisible energy field surrounding you and visualise it drawing in close around your physical body. *(Pause)*
- Take your awareness to the area just above your crown and see a sphere of light sitting here.
- Imagine that sphere of light shrinking in size until it's tiny, then sinking down through the crown of your head.
- See it slowly descending down past the brow. *(Pause)*
- Into the throat. *(Pause)*
- Then following the line of the spine, down, through your body, towards your heart area. (Pause)
- Down to your solar plexus. *(Pause)*
- Through the abdominal area. *(Pause)*
- To the base of your spine. *(Pause)*
- Now visualise the sphere of energy either leaving through the base of your spine, or dividing in two and sinking down through your legs and leaving through the soles of your feet.
- Feel this energy leaving you and connecting with the earth.
- Have a sense of downward movement, deep in to the earth. *(Pause)*
- Become more aware of your feet and your physical body.
- Let us take a moment to thank our Spirit Guides, Angels and loved ones in Spirit for their presence, protection and wisdom whilst we've been working. Knowing that they will always be on hand should we need to call on them. *(Pause)*
- **Now bring your awareness back to your physical body, the chair you are sitting on and your contact with the floor.**
- **Begin to bring some movement back in to your fingers and toes.**
- **In your own time opening your eyes, fully awake and aware and in the physical world.**

(Watch for them starting to wriggle fingers and toes and keep an eye on anyone who doesn't do this. If a member of the group appears not to want to come back to the room simply repeat the last three points, in bold, but raising your voice so that it said slightly louder and firmer. Repeat a third time if necessary moving over to the person and at the end just saying their name and asking that they come back into the room now, placing a hand gently on their shoulder.)

Check to ensure that everyone feels grounded before you finish the session. If not, get them to walk around for a little while. Stamping your feet or jumping up and down helps to bring you back to the physical world. If these don't do the trick, you can ground your energy very readily by eating a small amount of food such as a biscuit.
of food such as a biscuit.

OTHER THINGS TO TRY:
- Crystals to help focus your concentration are agate, aventurine, carnelian, citrine, haematite, clear quartz and smokey quartz.
- Flame bending - Attempt to affect the movement of a candle flame. You must place the candle in a large upright jar or storm lantern to prevent draughts from influencing it. Try to bend the flame on one side as a solid flame rather than a flickering one.
- Spoon Bending - Spend 10 to 15 minutes practising your chosen method on a metal spoon to see if you can bend it. Or you could try something referred to sometimes as 'warm forming'.
    Warm forming
    - Hold the spoon in one hand and place your thumb and index finger of your other hand either side

of the thin neck area of its stem.
- Rub it gently and focus on the metal softening, you could use method 3 to do this, or visualise the molecules of the metal moving faster and further apart.
- You should feel a slight sensation in your fingers as the metal becomes ready, stop rubbing and with a stroke of your finger the spoon will bend out of shape.

AND ANOTHER THING...
- Cut out a small square of paper or foil and fold it in half diagonally. Unfold it and fold it again diagonally the other way so that when you unfold it, the creases make an 'x' corner to corner. This makes a pyramid shape. Take a cork and push a needle or pin in to the end of it. Hang the pyramid on the top of the pin or needle, so that it looks like an umbrella. Place a glass or jar over the top to prevent draughts, or even warm air from your hands (if held close) causing movement. Now try to move it.
- Try moving a cocktail stick clockwise and anticlockwise as it floats in a glass of water.
- Any exercises that focus your mind will help you to develop your psychokinesis abilities, including regular meditation.
- Practise regularly, and keep notes of your attempts in a journal. Many people say that practising for 5 or 10 minutes every day rather than hours at a time is best.
- Don't make this the only thing you do, try lots of other things from this book and others.
- Alternate the exercises and don't be afraid to tweak them. For instance, if you think that channelling and beaming energy from your heart chakra, or any other, might work, try it a few times and see how it feels.

FOR DISCUSSION
- What have we got from this lesson? Best bits? Tricky bits?
- Key Concepts - how are we getting on with patience, acceptance, faith?
- Healing - feedback from those in the healing book? Success stories?

Next Time...
The next lesson will be covering AUTOMATIC WRITING.
You will need to arrange for the following tools to be brought along:
- A planchette if you are going to try it. (You can buy them from quite few websites and Ebay sellers.)
- A lot of pencils & a sharpener.
- Lots of large sheets of white paper – a cheap flipchart pad is perfect but A4 works just as well.

LESSON SEVEN
AUTOMATIC WRITING

PREPARATION
Well in advance of your meeting ensure that you have all of the tools that you require for this lesson. If not, find out if another group member has access to what you need.

Regular tools:
- Healing book
- Pens and pencils
- Paper
- Candles & matches if desired
- Box of tissues

Tools for this lesson:
- A planchette if you are going to try it. (You can buy them from quite few websites and Ebay sellers.)
- A lot of pencils & a sharpener.
- Lots of large sheets of white paper – a cheap flipchart pad is perfect but A4 works just as well.

On the day of the meeting ensure that the room is prepared:
Are there enough seats for everyone and enough room for the work you are about to undertake?
Open the windows or burn some incense to freshen the air.
Cleanse the area.
Gather the required tools together. Call and remind anyone who has promised to bring something.
Set out some water and glasses.
Prepare some relaxing background music.
Ensure that the room isn't too cold or too warm.
Ensure that you're not going to be interrupted. Unplugging the phone and turning off mobiles are good ideas.

At the beginning of the meeting:
As people arrive ask them to add the names of anyone they know who needs some healing to the Healing Book. Remember that you don't need to put their full names and private information, first names, initials or nicknames will suffice. Whoever you intend to send the healing to, it will reach.

Once everyone has arrived and is comfortable then you can start.
Work your way through the script and exercises for this lesson as detailed on the following pages.

Read the following scripts out loud to the group. It's a time of meditation so keep your voice calm and relaxed, reading in a fairly slow and controlled manner. Instructions are in brackets and italics.

RELAXATION
- Ensure you're sitting or lying comfortably.
- Take your awareness to your hands, make a tight fist, hold for a count of 3, 2, 1, and release.
- Tense your lower arms, hold for 3, 2, 1, and release.
- Tense your upper arms, hold for 3, 2, 1, and release.
- Tense your shoulders, lifting them up towards your ears, hold for 3, 2, 1, and release.

- Take your awareness to your neck: pull your chin toward chest but keep it from touching chest, hold for 3, 2, 1, and then relax.
- Take your awareness to your lower face and jaw, bite hard and pull back the corners of your mouth, hold for 3, 2, 1, and then relax.
- Screw your eyes up and wrinkle your nose, hold for 3, 2, 1, and then relax.
- Move your awareness to your forehead, lift your eyebrows as high as possible, hold for 3, 2, 1, and then relax.
- Take your awareness to your upper torso, pull your shoulder blades together hold for 3, 2, 1, and then release.
- Tense your stomach muscles, pulling your bellybutton towards your spine, hold for 3, 2, 1, and then release.
- Taking your awareness to your legs tense your thigh muscles, hold for 3, 2, 1, and then release.
- Pull your toes towards your head tensing your calf muscles, hold for 3, 2, 1, and then release.
- Take your awareness to your feet, point and curl your toes downwards, hold for 3, 2, 1, and then release.
- Tense your whole body at once, hands, arms, face, neck, chest, stomach, thighs, calves and feet, screw your eyes up, hold for 3, 2, 1, and completely release.
- Now take your awareness to your breathing, preferably through your nose as this is more relaxing.
- Ensure that you're breathing slowly and deeply.
- As you inhale, your abdomen will gently rise. And as you exhale it will fall.
- If your mind drifts or you lose track during this exercise bring your attention back to refocus on your breathing.
- Take a long, slow, deep inhalation for a count of 1 - 2 - 3 - 4, hold for 1- 2 and exhale for 1 - 2 - 3 - 4.
- In 2 3 4, Hold (pause), Out 2 3 4
- In 2 3 4, Hold (pause), Out 2 3 4
- In 2 3 4, Hold (pause), Out 2 3 4
- In 2 3 4, Hold (pause), Out 2 3 4
- In 2 3 4, Hold (pause), Out 2 3 4
- Continue breathing slowly and deeply.
- *(Move on to the script below.)*

OPENING & PROTECTION
- Let us take a moment to close our eyes and calm our minds.
- Concentrate on your breathing, allowing the breath to become deeper and slower.

(Pause to allow everyone to take a couple of breaths in and out)
- Let us all mentally ask our Spirit Guides and Angels to draw close and create a circle around our own.
- We let it be known that we are happy to work with Spirit and that we only work in love and light. We ask that anyone from the spirit world who wishes to contact us only does so in love and light and with the highest intentions.
- We ask for your protection, guidance and wisdom as we blend our world with yours. *(Pause)*
- Let us blend and harmonise our energies as we sit together in circle.
- Let us send out a note of harmony to the person on our left. Visualise this as a pale pink mist coming from your heart area and moving towards the heart of the person sitting on your left. *(Pause)*
- As you continue to do this, become aware of receiving the same loving energy from the right.
- As we send and receive this energy, be aware of any changes in the atmosphere within the circle. *(Pause)*
- Have a sense of oneness with the group. *(Pause)*
- Now bring your attention back to yourself and the centre of your being, the lower abdominal area.
- Focus on your breathing; become aware of the rise and fall of your abdomen. As you inhale it will gently rise and as you exhale it will fall. *(Pause to allow everyone to take a few breaths in and out)*
- Have a sense of warmth here and in your mind's eye allow a symbol or shape to form. Imagine that this symbol or shape is sitting at and represents your centre. It may be a simple glow of light, a flame or a flower.
- With each in-breath visualise your symbol becoming larger, stronger or more open whichever is appropriate.

- With each out-breath, imagine that you are exhaling any negativity left from your day, or worries that you may have. *(Pause to allow everyone to take a few breaths in and out)*
- Now take your awareness to the soles of your feet, feeling their contact with the floor. Visualise lines of energy extending out from your feet and down into the ground. In your mind's eye, see these lines of energy as roots extending deep into the earth.
- Earth energy also travels back up through these roots revitalising and nourishing you.
- See this energy entering through the soles of your feet and travelling up through your legs to the base of your spine.
- At the base of the spine imagine that the energy becomes a sphere of deep red mist or light, as you visualise it, it becomes more vibrant in colour. *(Pause)*
- From this point a beam of energy leaves the red sphere and travels up towards the sacral area, just below the belly button. Here it forms a sphere of vibrant orange mist or light. As you focus on it, it becomes stronger in colour. *(Pause)*
- Gradually a beam of energy leaves the orange sphere and travels up towards the solar plexus, where it forms a sphere of clear yellow. With each breath, this yellow becomes stronger and brighter. *(Pause)*
- Once more a beam of energy leaves this sphere and continues its journey up to the heart area. Here a sphere of mist or light begins to form, which you may see as either green or pink. Focus on this area for a few breaths allowing the energy to grow stronger and clearer and to expand. *(Pause)*
- Gradually a beam of energy leaves the heart area and moves upwards to the throat. Here it forms a sphere of clear blue. Once more, as you focus on this area, allow the colour to expand and increase in strength. *(Pause)*
- Now, visualise a strand of energy leaving the throat area and linking with the third eye area, just between and slightly above the eyes. Here energy will begin to form as before. You may see this energy as either a rich indigo or violet, whichever you prefer. Concentrate on this energy and visualise it increasing in strength. *(Pause)*
- Again, a beam of light extends upwards from this area moving to the crown. As it does so, become aware of another beam of energy coming down from above to meet the first. As they meet at the crown a sphere of pure energy begins to form. You may see this energy as either violet or pure white light. This connects you with the higher realms of Spirit.
- As you hold this vision for a few breaths the light grows and strengthens. And as it does so, the beautiful pure light begins to overflow down and around you, surrounding you in its wonderful energy. It fills your aura, cleansing, balancing and strengthening it. You feel safe and comfortable. You feel relaxed and light. *(Longer pause before moving on to the script below.)*

CONSCIOUS CONNECTION
- Take your awareness back to the soles of your feet, feeling their contact with the floor. Visualise lines of energy extending out from your feet and down into the ground.
- In your mind's eye, see these lines of energy as roots extending deep into the earth. Maintain this feeling of energy at the feet and be aware of earth energy moving up through these roots entering your energy system, revitalising and nourishing you. It may help to see them beginning to glow with light as the energy travels up from the earth and enters your energy system.
- Now take your awareness to the crown of your head.
- Imagine that you are being suspended by a piece of string from this point. The piece of string hangs from a point far above you, so far above you that you are unable to see its origin.
- You should have a sense of being lifted upwards.
- In your mind's eye, the string is a brilliant white light, a magical connection with higher realms. Its brilliance and its power connects with and enters into your energy system.
- You can sense this energy entering your energy system through your crown chakra. It feels amazingly empowering.

HEALING

- Slowly open your eyes and join hands with those sitting to either side of you. This increases the flow of healing energy.
- We know that our Guides, Angels and loved ones in Spirit have come forward and that they surround us with their healing energies. We ask them to help us as we send out our healing today. *(Pause)*
- Visualise a pool of brilliant white light forming and growing in the middle of our circle. *(Pause)*
- This is a pool of healing energy from which we can all draw when we need to. Know that this universal healing energy will find its way to all of those for whom we request healing.
- We ask for healing for each of us here, for our minds, bodies and spirit.

(If there are absent members: We ask for healing for the members of our group who cannot be with us today.)

- We ask for healing for all of those on our Absent Healing List. Take a moment to visualise them standing in the healing pool.
- I would also like to ask for special healing for _____

(Mention anyone else that you feel healing is really important for today. Gently squeeze the hand of the person to your left to indicate that it's their turn. Let everyone have a turn at saying this part before continuing with the script.)

- We send our healing thoughts to Mother Earth and to the plant and animal kingdom. Thank you.
- Release your hands but keep your eyes closed so that you remain relaxed and peaceful as we go in to our meditation. *(Brief pause before moving on to the Meditation script.)*

MEDITATION

- Ensure that you're sitting comfortably with your hands on your knees, palms facing upwards.
- Close your eyes.
- Take a deep inhalation, and breathe out slowly. Continue to breathe slowly and deeply.
- During this meditation you will always be safe and protected, you will feel relaxed and comfortable. If, however, there is anything that does make you feel uneasy, or you wish to come back out of the meditation, you can do so at any time by counting backwards from 3 to 1 and taking a deep breath in and out. You can then bring your awareness back to the physical body, particularly your feet and open your eyes.
- For now though, continue to breathe slowly and deeply, your body feels relaxed and your mind is clear.
- As you breathe images may begin to form in your mind's eye. Don't try to manipulate or analyse them, simply observe them. If you do not automatically see these images, simply imagine or sense them.
- Ahead of you lies a staircase or series of ten steps. Move towards them. At the bottom you can see a doorway. We're going to slowly go down these steps towards the door feeling safe and confident at all times. So moving down the steps on my count:
- 10, 9, 8, with each step feeling lighter and lighter.
- 7, 6, 5, feeling calm and peaceful,
- 4, 3, relaxed and light
- 2 and 1, you find yourself standing in front of the door. Reaching out you open the door and as you do so, a wonderful, warm light shines through from the other side, bathing your whole being in its rays.
- As you stand in this light for a few moments, your physical body is warmed through and your energy body is nourished and energised. This gives you a sense of comfort and completeness and offers further protection on your journey. *(Pause for a short while)*
- Today's journey is to help you to connect with the power of symbols and words.
- The rays of light subside and you can now see through the doorway to the other side.
- As your eyes adjust to the change in light, colours begin to form shapes. You can see your sanctuary on the other side of the doorway.
- You step through, closing the door behind you.
- Find a place in your sanctuary that you can sit comfortably,
- As you sit comfortably, allow your third eye chakra to open wide. *(Pause)*

LESSON SEVEN - AUTOMATIC WRITING

- As it opens pictures and symbols begin to dance in front of you. Allow the images to flow, don't worry about trying to remember them all. As you watch, you see that words appear too. Again allow the words to flow before your eyes. *(Pause for 20 - 30 seconds.)*
- As you continue to watch, ask that your guide for automatic writing draws close to you. Feel their presence and ask them to show you words, pictures and symbols which have special meaning and relevance to you. The images begin to slow down, allowing you the chance to see them all clearly, one by one.
- One image in particular will hover in front of your eyes. Take a special note of it and the message that it brings. *(Pause)*
- What is it telling you? What emotions or feelings does it evoke within you?
- Your guide can help you to decipher the image if you need them to. Simply ask for their assistance in your understanding of this message. *(Pause for 20 - 30 seconds.)*
- Look at every line and detail of the image so that it imprints in to your subconscious mind. You may wish to touch it, and trace it out with your finger. *(Pause for 20 - 30 seconds.)*
- The symbols stop and you're aware of your sanctuary once more.
- You see a table in front of you with a scroll of parchment on it. Sit comfortably at the table. Your guide hands you a quill and ink. You take the quill in your hand as though you are about to write. Allow the quill to rest against the parchment. You may feel the quill begin to move. Allow it to do so. Allow it to flow across the surface of the page. Don't force it merely allow it to move freely wherever it wants, forming shapes, pictures or words. *(Pause for 30-60 seconds)*
- Once the quill stops moving see what it has drawn or written for you. Again take note of any special message for you asking your guide for help if required. *(Pause for 20 - 30 seconds)*
- Know that everything you have experienced here will remain with you and that your message, or at least the essence of it will come back with you to the physical world. You may return to this place and this exercise any time that you wish to communicate with a guide or loved one in spirit in this way. Or to receive guidance on your life journey.
- Thank your guide for their assistance and ask them to work with you when practising automatic writing in the physical world also.
- It is now time to leave your sanctuary so make your way towards the doorway that leads to the stairwell.
- Open the door that leads to the stairwell. Step through closing the door behind you.
- Know that your sanctuary is your own space that you can return to at any time for relaxation, guidance and healing.
- And keeping that sense of calm and wellbeing, it is time to head back up the stairs. So moving back up the stairs on my count,
- 1, 2, 3, breathing slowly and deeply,
- 4, 5, 6, your body is starting to feel heavier
- 7, 8, bringing your awareness back to your physical body,
- 9 and 10, on that top step now and when you're ready, step off the top step.
- **Bringing your awareness completely back to your physical body and this room, your contact with the chair, your feet with the floor. Slowly begin to move your fingers and toes, and in your own time, opening your eyes, fully awake and aware and in the physical world.**

(Watch for them starting to wriggle fingers and toes and keep an eye on anyone who doesn't do this. If a member of the group appears not to want to come back to the room simply repeat the last paragraph, in bold, but raising your voice so that it said slightly louder and firmer. Repeat a third time if necessary moving over to the person and at the end just saying their name and asking that they come back now in to the room, placing your hand gently on their shoulder.)

Spend a few minutes sharing experiences of the meditation. Remember that it's okay if someone fell asleep, could see nothing or did their own thing. If you're keeping a personal journal, you may wish to take some time to record you experience. Don't forget to date the entry.

THEORY: AUTOMATIC WRITING

The following 'theory' section should be read aloud to the group. You may want to get others to join in and take it in turns to read.

Automatic writing is a method whereby information is channelled from other sources through the recipient, using a pen and paper, while in an altered state of consciousness. Commonly this is performed by an individual medium working on their own. However, we're going to describe two alternative ways in which you can do automatic writing in a group with fantastic results. Working on your own is slightly different to working in a group. Both can be very effective, but we prefer the group work and find we get the best results from it.

How does it work?

Automatic writing is a form of divination like any other that we've covered previously. One thought about how it works is that through an altered state of consciousness you're able to tap into the pool of information about everyone and everything, referred to as the 'collective unconscious.' Information is channelled via your physical body and written down as a result of tiny imperceptible muscular movement in your fingers, as we described for dowsing in 'A Beginner's Guide.' Your own consciousness is not involved in the process.

When you work as a group however, we believe that the additional energy that's built up can be channelled into the object you're using. This can allow spirit to manifest movement and quite literally spell out their messages.

There are many reason for using automatic writing as a method of spirit communication but there are also some downsides, or reasons not to rely on it solely.

Pros
- With practice it can give very accurate messages that will allow you to get validation from those concerned.
- It's easy to understand; not so dependant on or open to interpretation of feelings symbols or sensations.
- You can do it anywhere. It's a very flexible method of working as you can just use pen and paper.

Cons
- It can be easy to think that you're doing it yourself and let doubt creep in about the messages you're receiving.
- Absolute trust is required in those you work with.
- It can be quite addictive, because of its accuracy and can cause you to become lazy, forgetting other work that could develop your abilities further.
- It is best for established groups who have well developed skills and have worked with each other for a long time.
- It can seem a little disconcerting to the inexperienced, and this can allow fear to creep in.

The first and most common method of automatic writing is to work on your own. You sit holding a pen or pencil over a blank sheet of paper. You enter into an altered state and allow yourself to be a channel for the messages that will come through you. Your hand will move of its own volition (with practice) and the writing may or may not be your own. The information could be from your higher self, spirit guides, loved ones in spirit or more highly evolved beings. We've found that our own work while writing our books is quite often channelled in this way. Often we sit down to write (Helen always starts off with her with a pen and paper, Diane with her computer; either way works well.) and what is written is quite different to what we set out to say or write about. When we read it back we don't always recognise it as our own and are often surprised at the revelations and ideas that transpire. Sometimes we can tell which part of our writing is channelled because of the distinct change in style of language.

The second method is the one we like to use most in our group, and that is automatic writing in a group. For this we use slightly different methods and don't actually need to enter into a lowered brainwave pattern. There are two tools you can try. Decide which works best for you and your group.

Automatic writing using a planchette
A planchette is a piece of wood on small wheels with a hole in through which a pencil is placed. The planchette is placed on a blank sheet of paper, ensuring the pencil is in contact with the paper. Each person places a couple of fingers on the planchette, and a spokeperson requests that a message from the spirit world is written using the planchette. The planchette moves around and draws or writes on the paper underneath it. This was a traditional parlour game from the Victorian era and can be quite tricky to master, but it takes away a lot of the scepticsm surrounding automatic writing as it's very hard for anyone to 'cheat' (knowingly or not).

'The pencil'
This was a term coined by our own circle and we've found that it effectively produces profound messages from spirit, many of which can be validated by members of the group. It simply involves taking some paper and a pencil, each group member loosely places their fingers around the pencil as though they're holding it. With enough energy the pencil soon begins to move; writing and drawing of its own volition. We've had wonderful messages through this method from our guides, loved ones in spirit, angels and other highly evolved beings. Being a naturally sceptical bunch (which is quite healthy by the way) we've tried all sorts of ways to ensure that it's channelled work, not one of us, however well intentioned. We've worked with our left (or non-writing) hand, tried only lightly touching the pencil with one finger each (although that's a bit tricky), we've each taken it in turns to remove our contact with the pencil completely while it's writing, and so on. The pencil has always carried on, unless it's run out of energy.

This type of mediumship requires a lot of energy in order for it to be done effectively. It also takes practice for all present to be confident and positive, and to absolutely trust one another. You have to know 100 percent that one person is not manipulating the instrument that you're using.

Connection with your spirit guide is essential and must be strong when using automatic writing. This is because your guide will quite often act as the 'medium' on the other side bringing the messages through on behalf of deceased loved ones.

It should be noted that while writing is occurring (especially when working as a group) other things can happen such as changes in pressure or temperature around you, sensing spirit presences, physical activity, sounds, knocks etc. This is spirit communication too. They're using the group's energy to make themselves known in ways other than through the writing. Tell each other what you sense, and maybe have someone who isn't doing the automatic writing taking notes.

It's absolutely essential to understand that this method of spirit communication is advanced and should only be used by experienced individuals. It should go without saying, although we will say it anyway, that protection is vital, as is closing and grounding. The energy exercises will help to ensure that enough energy can be created and maintained to use these methods. However, you may find that both the planchette and the pencil make swift circular movements which we've found is a method of spirit helping the energy to builld up. Additionally the pencil will sometimes move up and down and bang on the table, this has the same effect.

Please remember that advice you receive from automatic writing should always be tempered with common sense and your own intuition about whether it feels right for you. Don't shift responsibility for your actions because 'spirit told me to'!

People sometimes ask if it's safe to use automatic writing in this way. The answer is yes, as long as you follow our methods, rules and guidelines. Remember you're in control in the physical world because it's your domain so there's nothing to fear with this type of work.

Rules and guidelines:
- Always put protection in place before you start.
- Ask your guides to mediate.
- Stop if anyone feels uncomfortable.
- Stop if messages are strange, disturbing or contain violent, aggressive language.
- Stop if you're being asked to do something that makes you feel uncomfortable.
- If messages are jumbled or confused it may be that the energy link isn't strong enough. Perhaps you are tired and can't build enough energy up to channel the messages correctly. Stop, close down and do something different if this happens.
- Remember spirit should always visit in love and light.
- Have a laugh and don't take yourselves too seriously!
- When you're learning it's best not to perform this type of activity at a venue with a history of paranormal activity or where any one feels uncomfortable.
- Use your normal venue and remember to cleanse the room and put protection up before you start.
- Open your energy fields before you start.
- Close and ground at the end.

Tips:
- Dim lighting with candles burning is preferable. Candlelight seems to help increase or focus the energy that's available, making it easier for spirit to move the object you're using.
- Before you begin, get your equipment together. Although any writing implement can be used, in our experience pencils are best. (Carpenter's pencils are thicker and easier to hold if doing group work.) As the volume of writing can be quite large once you get going, have a stock of pencils to hand, so that you can quickly swap them over as they blunt. Lots of paper is also needed!
- If you are working as individuals and the automatic writing isn't happening there are two schools of thought to help trigger it. The first is to doodle, the other is to write words in your normal handwriting, even if it is just the word 'write' or you could try 'I am writing these words to see if it will trigger the automatic writing'.
- If working with a planchette or pencil and it begins making circles (as described before) or, in the case of the pencil, banging up and down on the table, just go with it. Let it happen, once the energy levels are enough the writing will begin.
- Sometimes spirit will stop writing or gently tap the pencil on the paper if they want a fresh piece. You'll get used to their signs, it's often a case of trial and error until you discover what they want.

As a word of caution, in our experience, sometimes this kind of work can attract earthbound spirits who have not crossed over into the spirit world completely on their death. They can be mischievous or rude. Always ensure that you work in love and light, put protection in place and ask your spirit guides to be close and provide assistance and protection while you work. If you suspect or know that an earthbound spirit is making contact with you, you should break the communication with them by telling them quite firmly that you're going to say 'goodbye and god bless.' Then put the pencil down and take a short break before resuming, or close and ground your energies and cleanse the room again. If you're going to continue working, you may want to reinforce your protection and ask your guides to block the earthbound spirit from you. Then thank them for their help. If you need any further assistance with this type of occurrence, contact a well renowned medium, spiritualist church or rescue circle for advice.

Discuss any personal experiences or thoughts on the subject (but keep any eye on the time).

LESSON SEVEN - AUTOMATIC WRITING

PRACTICAL WORK
Read out each exercise, one at a time to the group so that you are all clear as to what you are doing, then allocate a time to complete the exercise.

Sit around a table with paper, pencils (and a planchette if you're using one) all ready in the middle. Before you start you may want to prepare some questions to ask during the writing. The 'Trance Mediumship script' - Handout 9, will help.

Once you're ready steps 1-4 should be read aloud before progressing to writing in step 5.

Step 1 - Conscious Connection Visualisation
- Take your awareness to the soles of your feet, feeling their contact with the floor. Visualise lines of energy extending out from your feet and down into the ground.
- In your mind's eye, see these lines of energy as roots extending deep into the earth. Maintain this feeling of energy at the feet and be aware of earth energy moving up through these roots entering your energy system, revitalising and nourishing you. It may help to see them beginning to glow with light as the energy travels up from the earth and enters your energy system.
- Now take your awareness to the crown of your head.
- Imagine that you're being suspended by a piece of string from this point. The piece of string hangs from a point far above you, so far above you that you are unable to see its origin.
- You should have a sense of being lifted upwards.
- In your mind's eye, the string is a brilliant white light, a magical connection with higher realms. Its brilliance and its power connects with and enters into your energy system.
- You can sense this energy entering your energy system through your crown chakra. It feels amazingly empowering.

Step 2 - Harmonising
- "Let us blend and harmonise our energies as we sit together in circle. Let us send out a note of harmony to the person on our left by visualising this a pale pink mist or light coming from our heart area and moving towards the heart of the person sitting on our left. As we continue to do this, become aware of receiving the same loving energy from the right. As we send and receive this, an energy circle is formed that encompasses all of us. Be aware of any changes in the atmosphere within the circle. Have a sense of oneness with the group."

Step 3 - Creating an energy source as a group
- Join hands in order to focus and build up the energy.
- Close your eyes and take your awareness to either your feet. Imagine roots extending out through this point and down deep into the earth.
- See these roots glowing with a bright white light. This is the powerful earth energy that nourishes all living things. The roots glow so bright and carry this energy all the way up to you and your contact with the ground. This wonderful energy enters your energetic system at this point. And moves up through your body and along the line of the spine to the centre of your being, just below the belly button. *(Pause)*
- Once you feel the energy here, take your awareness to a point just above the crown. Visualise a beam or funnel of pure white light coming down from the heavens. This is heavenly energy from the spirit realms. It enters your energetic body through the crown chakra and streams down through your head and neck towards your centre.
- As these two streams meet and become one at your centre, feel the energy building up, a powerful warmth may be felt. *(Pause)*
- Become aware of the palms of your hands and the connection you have with the group. You should feel warmth or tingling as your focus encourages the energy to be pulled from your centre to your hands.

- Maintain your contact and simply let the energy flow around the circle, passing from hand to hand. You may get a sense of it moving round in a particular direction. You may also experience different sensations such as your arms wanting to 'float' or move, or 'power surges' where your body, arms or hands shudder slightly. This is quite normal, just let the energy flow.
- *(Let the energy flow for a couple of minutes before moving on to step 4.)*

Step 4 - Intention and protection
- "Once again we ask our spirit guides and angels to draw close to us and create a circle around our own. We let it be known that we intend to act as channels for spirit during this time, to enable them to communicate with us by writing through us. We do this only in love and light and with the highest intentions, for the highest good. We ask that anyone in the realms of spirit that wishes to communicate do so with the same high intentions and that our spirit guides and angels enforce this on our behalf. We welcome our guides acting as intermediaries on behalf of spirit and thank them for their help."

Step 5 - Writing
- Each person should place a couple of fingers on the planchette or pencil.
- Focus your attention on the object allowing the energy to flow through your hands in to it.
- The pencil or planchette should begin to move of its own volition. Commonly it will move in circles to build up some energy before beginning to write coherently.
- One person who has been chosen should ask the questions. You may want to have one person not participating in the writing who will record the answers.)
- When you've finished (either because the writing has stopped, you have the answer to your question or it's not working), remove your contact from the object and thank your guides for their assistance.
- Bring your awareness to your centre and then close and ground.
- Record and discuss your experiences.

CLOSING & GROUNDING
Once you have completed the exercises everyone should sit comfortably and complete the following meditation to close and ground their energy. Read out the following:
- Sit in a comfortable position and close your eyes.
- Bring your attention to your breathing and focus on this for a few breaths. *(Pause)*
- Take your awareness to the invisible energy field surrounding you and visualise it drawing in close around your physical body. *(Pause)*
- Take your awareness to the area just above your crown and see a sphere of light sitting here.
- Imagine that sphere of light shrinking in size until it's tiny, then sinking down through the crown of your head.
- See it slowly descending down past the brow. *(Pause)*
- Into the throat. *(Pause)*
- Then following the line of the spine, down, through your body, towards your heart area. *(Pause)*
- Down to your solar plexus. *(Pause)*
- Through the abdominal area. *(Pause)*
- To the base of your spine. *(Pause)*
- Now visualise the sphere of energy either leaving through the base of your spine, or dividing in two and sinking down through your legs and leaving through the soles of your feet.
- Feel this energy leaving you and connecting with the earth.
- Have a sense of downward movement, deep in to the earth. *(Pause)*
- Become more aware of your feet and your physical body.
- Let us take a moment to thank our Spirit Guides, Angels and loved ones in Spirit for their presence, protection and wisdom whilst we've been working. Knowing that they will always be on hand should

LESSON SEVEN - AUTOMATIC WRITING

we need to call on them. *(Pause)*
- **Now bring your awareness back to your physical body, the chair you are sitting on and your contact with the floor.**
- **Begin to bring some movement back in to your fingers and toes.**
- **In your own time opening your eyes, fully awake and aware and in the physical world.**

(Watch for them starting to wriggle fingers and toes and keep an eye on anyone who doesn't do this. If a member of the group appears not to want to come back to the room simply repeat the last three points, in bold, but raising your voice so that it said slightly louder and firmer. Repeat a third time if necessary moving over to the person and at the end just saying their name and asking that they come back into the room now, placing a hand gently on their shoulder.)

Check to ensure that everyone feels grounded before you finish the session. If not, get them to walk around for a little while. Stamping your feet or jumping up and down helps to bring you back to the physical world. If these don't do the trick, you can ground your energy very readily by eating a small amount of food such as a biscuit.

OTHER THINGS TO TRY:
- Sit as individuals rather than a group. Have paper and a pencil on your lap, perhaps with a folder or book underneath to lean on. After performing the conscious connection exercise, each person should connect with their spirit guide while holding the pencil over the paper. Taking your focus to the palms of your hands should start the energy building up at this point. You could start to doodle or write a question that you would like to know the answer to. Or ask your guide for a message (rather than answers to questions) for yourself, a friends or your group. Eventually you may find that you start to write with the guidance of spirit and get answers to your questions. You can try this with your non-dominant hand. (Left if you're right handed and vice versa.)
- Try inspired writing such as poetry on your own but while in the company of the group. The energy and harmonious environment may well trigger something for you. One of our group regularly channels wonderful poems in this way.

AND ANOTHER THING...
- Get into the habit of recording dreams and meditations. You may find that other words and images flow through you as you write.
- Crystals that may help to encourage automatic writing are angelite, petalite and sugilite.
- You may find that inspirational writing flows well when you're out in nature, so next time you go for a walk in the woods or by the sea, arm yourself with pen and paper. Or plan a trip out with the group and see what you get.

FOR DISCUSSION
- What have we got from this lesson? Best bits? Tricky bits?
- Key Concepts - how are we getting on with patience, acceptance, faith?
- Healing - feedback from those in the healing book? Success stories?

Next Time...
The next lesson will be covering PSYCHIC ART.
You will need to arrange for the following tools to be brought along:
- Sheets of plain paper
- A selection of drawing materials e.g. pencils, pastels, crayons

LESSON EIGHT
PSYCHIC ART

PREPARATION
Well in advance of your meeting ensure that you have all of the tools that you require for this lesson. If not, find out if another group member has access to what you need.

Regular tools:
- Healing book
- Pens and pencils
- Paper
- Candles & matches if desired
- Box of tissues

Tools for this lesson:
- Sheets of plain paper
- A selection of drawing materials e.g. pencils, pastels, crayons
- Photocopy the required number of:
    - Handout 2 - Body / chakras outline
    - Handout 6 - Face outline &
    - Handout 7 - Basic colour information

On the day of the meeting ensure that the room is prepared:
Are there enough seats for everyone and enough room for the work you are about to undertake?
Open the windows or burn some incense to freshen the air.
Cleanse the area.
Gather the required tools together. Call and remind anyone who has promised to bring something.
Set out some water and glasses.
Prepare some relaxing background music.
Ensure that the room isn't too cold or too warm.
Ensure that you're not going to be interrupted. Unplugging the phone and turning off mobiles are good ideas.

At the beginning of the meeting:
As people arrive ask them to add the names of anyone they know who needs some healing to the Healing Book. Remember that you don't need to put their full names and private information, first names, initials or nicknames will suffice. Whoever you intend to send the healing to, it will reach.

Once everyone has arrived and is comfortable then you can start.
Work your way through the script and exercises for this lesson as detailed on the following pages.

Read the following scripts out loud to the group. It's a time of meditation so keep your voice calm and relaxed, reading in a fairly slow and controlled manner. Instructions are in brackets and italics.

RELAXATION
- Ensure you're sitting or lying comfortably.
- Take your awareness to your hands, make a tight fist, hold for a count of 3, 2, 1, and release.
- Tense your lower arms, hold for 3, 2, 1, and release.
- Tense your upper arms, hold for 3, 2, 1, and release.
- Tense your shoulders, lifting them up towards your ears, hold for 3, 2, 1, and release.
- Take your awareness to your neck: pull your chin toward chest but keep it from touching chest, hold for 3, 2, 1, and then relax.
- Take your awareness to your lower face and jaw, bite hard and pull back the corners of your mouth, hold for 3, 2, 1, and then relax.
- Screw your eyes up and wrinkle your nose, hold for 3, 2, 1, and then relax.
- Move your awareness to your forehead, lift your eyebrows as high as possible, hold for 3, 2, 1, and then relax.
- Take your awareness to your upper torso, pull your shoulder blades together hold for 3, 2, 1, and then release.
- Tense your stomach muscles, pulling your bellybutton towards your spine, hold for 3, 2, 1, and then release.
- Taking your awareness to your legs tense your thigh muscles, hold for 3, 2, 1, and then release.
- Pull your toes towards your head tensing your calf muscles, hold for 3, 2, 1, and then release.
- Take your awareness to your feet, point and curl your toes downwards, hold for 3, 2, 1, and then release.
- Tense your whole body at once, hands, arms, face, neck, chest, stomach, thighs, calves and feet, screw your eyes up, hold for 3, 2, 1, and completely release.
- Now take your awareness to your breathing, preferably through your nose as this is more relaxing.
- Ensure that you're breathing slowly and deeply.
- As you inhale, your abdomen will gently rise. And as you exhale it will fall.
- If your mind drifts or you lose track during this exercise bring your attention back to refocus on your breathing.
- Take a long, slow, deep inhalation for a count of 1 - 2 - 3 - 4, hold for 1- 2 and exhale for 1 - 2 - 3 - 4.
- In 2 3 4, Hold (pause), Out 2 3 4
- In 2 3 4, Hold (pause), Out 2 3 4
- In 2 3 4, Hold (pause), Out 2 3 4
- In 2 3 4, Hold (pause), Out 2 3 4
- In 2 3 4, Hold (pause), Out 2 3 4
- Continue breathing slowly and deeply.
- *(Move on to the script below.)*

OPENING & PROTECTION
- Let us take a moment to close our eyes and calm our minds.
- Concentrate on your breathing, allowing the breath to become deeper and slower.

(Pause to allow everyone to take a couple of breaths in and out)
- Let us all mentally ask our Spirit Guides and Angels to draw close and create a circle around our own.
- We let it be known that we are happy to work with Spirit and that we only work in love and light. We ask that anyone from the spirit world who wishes to contact us only does so in love and light and with the highest intentions.
- We ask for your protection, guidance and wisdom as we blend our world with yours. *(Pause)*
- Let us blend and harmonise our energies as we sit together in circle.
- Let us send out a note of harmony to the person on our left. Visualise this as a pale pink mist coming from your heart area and moving towards the heart of the person sitting on your left. *(Pause)*
- As you continue to do this, become aware of receiving the same loving energy from the right.
- As we send and receive this energy, be aware of any changes in the atmosphere within the circle. *(Pause)*
- Have a sense of oneness with the group. *(Pause)*

- Now bring your attention back to yourself and the centre of your being, the lower abdominal area.
- Focus on your breathing; become aware of the rise and fall of your abdomen. As you inhale it will gently rise and as you exhale it will fall. *(Pause to allow everyone to take a few breaths in and out)*
- Have a sense of warmth here and in your mind's eye allow a symbol or shape to form. Imagine that this symbol or shape is sitting at and represents your centre. It may be a simple glow of light, a flame or a flower.
- With each in-breath visualise your symbol becoming larger, stronger or more open whichever is appropriate.
- With each out-breath, imagine that you are exhaling any negativity left from your day, or worries that you may have. *(Pause to allow everyone to take a few breaths in and out)*
- Now take your awareness to the soles of your feet, feeling their contact with the floor. Visualise lines of energy extending out from your feet and down into the ground. In your mind's eye, see these lines of energy as roots extending deep into the earth.
- Earth energy also travels back up through these roots revitalising and nourishing you.
- See this energy entering through the soles of your feet and travelling up through your legs to the base of your spine.
- At the base of the spine imagine that the energy becomes a sphere of deep red mist or light, as you visualise it, it becomes more vibrant in colour. *(Pause)*
- From this point a beam of energy leaves the red sphere and travels up towards the sacral area, just below the belly button. Here it forms a sphere of vibrant orange mist or light. As you focus on it, it becomes stronger in colour. *(Pause)*
- Gradually a beam of energy leaves the orange sphere and travels up towards the solar plexus, where it forms a sphere of clear yellow. With each breath, this yellow becomes stronger and brighter. *(Pause)*
- Once more a beam of energy leaves this sphere and continues its journey up to the heart area. Here a sphere of mist or light begins to form, which you may see as either green or pink. Focus on this area for a few breaths allowing the energy to grow stronger and clearer and to expand. *(Pause)*
- Gradually a beam of energy leaves the heart area and moves upwards to the throat. Here it forms a sphere of clear blue. Once more, as you focus on this area, allow the colour to expand and increase in strength. *(Pause)*
- Now, visualise a strand of energy leaving the throat area and linking with the third eye area, just between and slightly above the eyes. Here energy will begin to form as before. You may see this energy as either a rich indigo or violet, whichever you prefer. Concentrate on this energy and visualise it increasing in strength. *(Pause)*
- Again, a beam of light extends upwards from this area moving to the crown. As it does so, become aware of another beam of energy coming down from above to meet the first. As they meet at the crown a sphere of pure energy begins to form. You may see this energy as either violet or pure white light. This connects you with the higher realms of Spirit.
- As you hold this vision for a few breaths the light grows and strengthens. And as it does so, the beautiful pure light begins to overflow down and around you, surrounding you in its wonderful energy. It fills your aura, cleansing, balancing and strengthening it. You feel safe and comfortable. You feel relaxed and light. *(Longer pause before moving on to the script below.)*

CONSCIOUS CONNECTION

- Take your awareness back to the soles of your feet, feeling their contact with the floor. Visualise lines of energy extending out from your feet and down into the ground.
- In your mind's eye, see these lines of energy as roots extending deep into the earth. Maintain this feeling of energy at the feet and be aware of earth energy moving up through these roots entering your energy system, revitalising and nourishing you. It may help to see them beginning to glow with light as the energy travels up from the earth and enters your energy system.

- Now take your awareness to the crown of your head.
- Imagine that you are being suspended by a piece of string from this point. The piece of string hangs from a point far above you, so far above you that you are unable to see its origin.
- You should have a sense of being lifted upwards.
- In your mind's eye, the string is a brilliant white light, a magical connection with higher realms. Its brilliance and its power connects with and enters into your energy system.
- You can sense this energy entering your energy system through your crown chakra. It feels amazingly empowering.

HEALING
- Slowly open your eyes and join hands with those sitting to either side of you. This increases the flow of healing energy.
- We know that our Guides, Angels and loved ones in Spirit have come forward and that they surround us with their healing energies. We ask them to help us as we send out our healing today. *(Pause)*
- Visualise a pool of brilliant white light forming and growing in the middle of our circle. *(Pause)*
- This is a pool of healing energy from which we can all draw when we need to. Know that this universal healing energy will find its way to all of those for whom we request healing.
- We ask for healing for each of us here, for our minds, bodies and spirit.

(If there are absent members: We ask for healing for the members of our group who cannot be with us today.)
- We ask for healing for all of those on our Absent Healing List. Take a moment to visualise them standing in the healing pool.
- I would also like to ask for special healing for _____

(Mention anyone else that you feel healing is really important for today. Gently squeeze the hand of the person to your left to indicate that it's their turn. Let everyone have a turn at saying this part before continuing with the script.)
- We send our healing thoughts to Mother Earth and to the plant and animal kingdom. Thank you.
- Release your hands but keep your eyes closed so that you remain relaxed and peaceful as we go in to our meditation. *(Brief pause before moving on to the Meditation script.)*

MEDITATION
- Ensure that you're sitting comfortably with your hands on your knees, palms facing upwards.
- Close your eyes.
- Take a deep inhalation, and breathe out slowly. Continue to breathe slowly and deeply.
- During this meditation you will always be safe and protected, you will feel relaxed and comfortable. If, however, there is anything that does make you feel uneasy, or you wish to come back out of the meditation, you can do so at any time by counting backwards from 3 to 1 and taking a deep breath in and out. You can then bring your awareness back to the physical body, particularly your feet and open your eyes.
- For now though, continue to breathe slowly and deeply, your body feels relaxed and your mind is clear.
- As you breathe images may begin to form in your mind's eye. Don't try to manipulate or analyse them, simply observe them. If you do not automatically see these images, simply imagine or sense them.
- Ahead of you lies a staircase or series of ten steps. Move towards them. At the bottom you can see a doorway. We're going to slowly go down these steps towards the door feeling safe and confident at all times. So moving down the steps on my count:
- 10, 9, 8, with each step feeling lighter and lighter.
- 7, 6, 5, feeling calm and peaceful,
- 4, 3, relaxed and light
- 2 and 1, you find yourself standing in front of the door. Reaching out you open the door, and as you do so a wonderful, warm light shines through from the other side, bathing your whole being in its rays.

LESSON EIGHT - PSYCHIC ART

- As you stand in this light for a few moments, your physical body is warmed through and your energy body is nourished and energised. This gives you a sense of comfort and completeness and offers further protection on your journey. *(Pause for a short while)*
- Today's journey is to help you to connect with the creativity inside your soul.
- The rays of light subside and you can now see through the doorway to the other side.
- As your eyes adjust to the change in light, colours begin to form shapes. You can see your sanctuary on the other side of the doorway.
- You step through, closing the door behind you.
- Look around you until you see a huge oak door with brass handle. Walk to this door, and, feeling safe and protected at all times, open the door.
- As you step through the door, you find yourself in a large spacious room.
- Ahead of you is a window with beautiful drapes either side of it.
- Go over to the drapes and touch them. Feel the texture of them in your hand, perhaps soft and silky, or heavy and velvety. See the exquisite colour of them and any patterns they might have. *(Pause)*
- Now look around the room. You see a desk, made of the finest wood. Move over to the desk, touch it, feel the intricate carvings, feel the texture of the wood beneath your hands.
- You see a chair, a huge, comfortable leather chair with a table by it. Go over to the chair, perhaps there are cushions or a blanket on the chair to help you to feel even more relaxed and comfortable as you sit in it.
- Look at the table in front of you. You will see there is a paint palette on the table. Each section of the palette full of paints of every colour of the rainbow and more. The colours glow with a vibrancy like no other colours you've seen before. Next to the palette is a paint brush and a large sheet of paper.
- Take the brush and dip it into the colour of your choice.
- Swirl the brush around on the paper, relaxing and allowing the brush to paint where and what it wants to.
- Now choose another colour and again let the brush flow over the paper.
- Do this as many times as you wish, using as many different colours as you choose. It doesn't matter what you paint, simply relax and enjoy the freedom of letting the brush flow, just as a little child might when they create art.
- See how the colours seem to dance on the page as you paint them and blend them together creating your own beautiful work of art. *(Pause for 30 - 60 seconds.)*
- As you paint you may be aware of someone coming into the room and sitting by your side. This is a special guide who comes to connect with you every time you follow a creative pursuit.
- Acknowledge their presence with thanks, and allow them to communicate with you as you paint.
- Take some time for this communication, or, if your guide has not made their presence known on this occasion, simply to paint and to have the freedom to express your creativity. *(Pause for a couple of minutes.)*
- It's nearly time to begin your journey back now.
- Lay down your paint brush and spend a few moments looking at the wonderful picture that you've created.
- Examine every detail of it as the painting may contain a message for you.
- Perhaps you can see a clear image or a symbol, or maybe the colours have special significance for you.
- Thank your creativity guide, whether present or not, for helping you to create such a beautiful work of art and for any insights you may have had. *(Pause)*
- It's now time to leave the room.
- Walk towards the oak door that leads back to your sanctuary until gradually the images that you have been observing start to fade.
- You're in your sanctuary. You're safe and warm.
- It's time to leave your sanctuary but know that what you have seen will stay with you as you return.
- Open the door that leads to the stairwell. Step through closing the door behind you.
- Know that your sanctuary is your own space that you can return to at any time for relaxation, guidance and healing.

- And keeping that sense of calm and wellbeing, it is time to head back up the stairs. So moving back up the stairs on my count,
- 1, 2, 3, breathing slowly and deeply,
- 4, 5, 6, your body is starting to feel heavier
- 7, 8, bringing your awareness back to your physical body,
- 9 and 10, on that top step now and when you're ready, step off the top step.
- **Bringing your awareness completely back to your physical body and this room, your contact with the chair, your feet with the floor. Slowly begin to move your fingers and toes, and in your own time, opening your eyes, fully awake and aware and in the physical world.**

(Watch for them starting to wriggle fingers and toes and keep an eye on anyone who doesn't do this. If a member of the group appears not to want to come back to the room simply repeat the last paragraph, in bold, but raising your voice so that it said slightly louder and firmer. Repeat a third time if necessary moving over to the person and at the end just saying their name and asking that they come back now in to the room, placing your hand gently on their shoulder.)

Spend a few minutes sharing experiences of the meditation. Remember that it's okay if someone fell asleep, could see nothing or did their own thing. If you're keeping a personal journal, you may wish to take some time to record you experience. Don't forget to date the entry.

THEORY: PSYCHIC ART
The following 'theory' section should be read aloud to the group. You may want to get others to join in and take it in turns to read.

Psychic art is a form of mediumship where the artist, usually in an altered state of consciousness, can produce an image of a person who is in the spirit world. Tuning in to the energy of the person they are drawing for, the artist draws someone who is linked to them. This may be a loved one, distant relative, or a spirit guide. As the spirit being is drawn, the medium/artist may also get other information about them that they can make notes on, a name, hobbies, messages etc. Occasionally a medium and a psychic artist will team up for an event or to provide personal readings and this can produce very interesting messages along with pictures as further evidence of spirit communication.

Sometimes psychic artists draw portraits of people still in the physical world whom the communicating spirit wishes to draw attention to, or send a message to. Some also draw pictures of animals that have passed into the spirit world.

Psychic art is also known as spirit art or spirit imaging because the drawings are channelled mediumstically rather than psychically. Sometimes psychic artists link to spirit before they attend a meeting or demonstration and channel a picture to take with them. This is known as pre-cognitive psychic art. We've seen psychic artists who work in this way and the results can be very impressive. Some people may also find that they have pre-cognitive psychic art skills which manifest in them drawing images of future events. Additionally, those who are drawn to past life work may find that they draw pictures or images connected to their own past lives, or those of their sitter when drawing for others.

As well as drawing portraits of spirit, guides and loved ones, psychic artists often produce auragrams. These are sketched pictures depicting a person's aura field and when interpreted can reveal a wealth of information about the sitter, just as an aura photograph can. This is something that we've included in previous exercises and is a great starting place to develop psychic art skills from.

Psychic artists use a range of different materials, from a basic HB pencil, to colourful pastels, and even biros! As always, we'd recommend using the material that you feel most comfortable with when undertaking this work. Many psychic artists experiment and find the materials they use change over time as their artistic abilities improve. For example they may be guided to move from black and white pictures to coloured portraits.

LESSON EIGHT - PSYCHIC ART

Psychic art can lend itself well to remote work. Many artists ask for a photograph or handwritten note from the person who requires a portrait, and then the're able to remotely link with the person's guides, and/or their own guides, to produce a piece of psychic art.

Before you begin drawing tell your spirit guide that you wish to develop your psychic art skills and request their assistance. Your regular guide may bring forward an artistic guide to help you with this type of work.

Psychic art can be a natural progression from automatic writing or your third eye work. However, for the less artistic among you (ourselves included) it may seem like a daunting prospect. It's our belief, and experience, that whatever your artistic ability, everyone is capable of producing psychic art. After all, you do have the advantage of help from above! Many well known psychic artists have had little or no formal artistic training and some even claim that they're only able to draw when working in this way with spirit's help. If you do lack confidence in your artistic talents, you may like to practise drawing in your spare time before you tackle the exercises below, although this isn't essential. If you do want to, we would advise drawing faces; perhaps copy faces from magazines or photographs for example. This will help you to get the proportions right, something that can be tricky and feel like a barrier in the beginning.

Alternatively you could use the face template in Handout 6. Place it under a blank piece of paper and use it to show you the correct proportions of the features as you draw. Remember it's only a guide; you should change the shape of the nose, mouth etc for each individual picture. This can be a good way of getting started if you're not a very confident artist. Diane was taught this technique by psychic artist Janette Oakman and found that for the first time ever she was able to produce a psychic portrait.

However you may just prefer to begin working through the exercises below and not get too hung up on perfectly drawn pictures at first. Relax and let the energy flow, with time, patience and your guide's help you will quickly improve as you go along.

Crystals which may facilitate psychic art are lapis lazuli and iolite.

Discuss any personal experiences or thoughts on the subject (but keep any eye on the time).

PRACTICAL WORK
Read out each exercise, one at a time to the group so that you are all clear as to what you are doing, then allocate a time to complete the exercise.

For these exercises you will need: Plenty of sheets of plain paper and a selection of drawing materials of your choice, e.g. pencils, pastels, crayons.

Exercise 1 - Doodle-bug!
- Sit in a comfortable space.
- Take long, slow deep breaths and relax.
- Ask your spirit guide to work with you and send you images or doodles that have a relevant message for you.
- As you did for the automatic writing exercises, allow the pencil to move across the paper. You may find that you're drawn to use specific colours, or change colours part way through.
- If the picture doesn't look like anything discernible don't be disheartened. Keep the flow of the pencil going until you feel the need to stop.
- When you have finished, analyse your drawing or doodle. You may see symbolic images within it, or may note the predominance of a particular colour. If you're unsure as to what it represents, ask your guide for some further information.
- Only ask for this information at the end as initially, you need simply to practise drawing/doodling. In later exercises you can combine the drawing with channelling information about the pictures or sitter you're working with.
- If you're struggling, try the conscious connection exercise again to encourage the flow of universal energy through you.

Exercise 2 - Auragrams
- Decide whether you will do an auragram of the area around the person's head, or a full body auragram. You could use Handout 6 or 2 as outlines. Remember for an auragram it isn't necessary to draw a detailed picture of the sitter. You're simply drawing in the details of their auric field.
- Working in pairs, one of you (the subject) should stand up or sit in a chair, preferably against a pale background. If this isn't possible attach a large sheet of white paper to the wall behind. (Sheets from a cheap flipchart pad are ideal.)
- The other should sit opposite at least five feet away. Look past the subject at the air around or above them allowing your eyes to relax and go slightly out of focus.
- As you tune in to their auric energy, you may notice the air changing around the subject, perhaps appearing thicker. You may begin to see the etheric aura, like a clear glow outlining the body.
- If you're good at this, you may start to see colours or you may sense them in some way. Put pen to paper and begin to create a picture of your friend's aura.
- Note the different colours that are around the person, as well as the relative proportions of their aura.
- When you have finished, use your knowledge of auras to interpret the colours you have drawn around your friend (see Handout 7 'Basic Colour Information'), but as always, please be careful to convey this information in a sensible and sensitive way.

Exercise 3 - Portraits and mediumship
- Work in pairs for this exercise, both drawing at the same time. Use the face outline in Handout 6 if you wish.
- Link with your guide, asking them to provide you with a portrait of someone relevant to your partner. You may see the image in its entirety at first, or you may be guided to begin drawing and see the image develop as you go along. As you draw, take note of any information that your guide is giving you about either the person you're drawing, or about your partner.
- Note that sometimes the person you're drawing may chose to present themselves looking younger, or healthier than they were before they passed. Again this is very normal, but can cause some confusion. Things like facial hair, glasses and so on can dramatically alter the way someone looks, so if your portrait cannot easily be identified, try asking your partner to imagine the picture with glasses on or so on. Some psychic artists have images of glasses, moustaches etc which they can overlay on portraits to help with identification. This is something you might consider if you wish to develop your psychic artistry over time.
- The information that you're given as you draw can also help the sitter to identify the portrait and should be passed onto them as necessary. (Remember that you may be drawing someone who is still in the physical world.) Also remember that often psychic artists will channel portraits of guides or even angels that the sitter may not find as easy to identify. This is where the mediumistic information you channel will become especially important.

CLOSING & GROUNDING
Once you have completed the exercises everyone should sit comfortably and complete the following meditation to close and ground their energy. Read out the following:
- Sit in a comfortable position and close your eyes.
- Bring your attention to your breathing and focus on this for a few breaths. *(Pause)*
- Take your awareness to the invisible energy field surrounding you and visualise it drawing in close around your physical body. *(Pause)*
- Take your awareness to the area just above your crown and see a sphere of light sitting here.
- Imagine that sphere of light shrinking in size until it's tiny, then sinking down through the crown of your head.
- See it slowly descending down past the brow. *(Pause)*

- Into the throat. *(Pause)*
- Then following the line of the spine, down, through your body, towards your heart area. *(Pause)*
- Down to your solar plexus. *(Pause)*
- Through the abdominal area. *(Pause)*
- To the base of your spine. *(Pause)*
- Now visualise the sphere of energy either leaving through the base of your spine, or dividing in two and sinking down through your legs and leaving through the soles of your feet.
- Feel this energy leaving you and connecting with the earth.
- Have a sense of downward movement, deep in to the earth. *(Pause)*
- Become more aware of your feet and your physical body.
- Let us take a moment to thank our Spirit Guides, Angels and loved ones in Spirit for their presence, protection and wisdom whilst we've been working. Knowing that they will always be on hand should we need to call on them. *(Pause)*
- **Now bring your awareness back to your physical body, the chair you are sitting on and your contact with the floor.**
- **Begin to bring some movement back in to your fingers and toes.**
- **In your own time opening your eyes, fully awake and aware and in the physical world.**

(Watch for them starting to wriggle fingers and toes and keep an eye on anyone who doesn't do this. If a member of the group appears not to want to come back to the room simply repeat the last three points, in bold, but raising your voice so that it said slightly louder and firmer. Repeat a third time if necessary moving over to the person and at the end just saying their name and asking that they come back into the room now, placing a hand gently on their shoulder.)

Check to ensure that everyone feels grounded before you finish the session. If not, get them to walk around for a little while. Stamping your feet or jumping up and down helps to bring you back to the physical world. If these don't do the trick, you can ground your energy very readily by eating a small amount of food such as a biscuit.

OTHER THINGS YOU CAN TRY:
- Attempt to draw a portrait remotely by following the above exercise for 'Portraits and mediumship', but instead of your sitter being with you, work remotely. However, be sure to ask before you draw a portrait for someone.

AND ANOTHER THING...
- If you think that it's something you may wish to pursue, you may want to practise drawing faces to get used to proportions etc.
- Pencils, charcoal and pastels are commonly used and can be smudged to create shading and other effects. Try experimenting with these different types of materials to find the ones that work best for you.

FOR DISCUSSION
- What have we got from this lesson? Best bits? Tricky bits?
- Key Concepts - how are we getting on with patience, acceptance, faith?
- Healing - feedback from those in the healing book? Success stories?

Next Time...
The next lesson will be covering MANIFESTATION.

You will need to arrange for the following tools to be brought along:
- Writing paper & envelopes

Extra tools if you want to do 'other things to try':
- Each person could bring a new notebook which they have chosen specially to begin a 'gratitude book'.

LESSON NINE
MANIFESTATION

PREPARATION
Well in advance of your meeting ensure that you have all of the tools that you require for this lesson. If not, find out if another group member has access to what you need.

Regular tools:
- Healing book
- Pens and pencils
- Paper
- Candles & matches if desired
- Box of tissues

Tools for this lesson:
- Writing paper & envelopes

Extra tools if you want to do 'other things to try':
- Each person could bring a new notebook which they have chosen specially to begin a 'gratitude book'.

On the day of the meeting ensure that the room is prepared:
Are there enough seats for everyone and enough room for the work you are about to undertake?
Open the windows or burn some incense to freshen the air.
Cleanse the area.
Gather the required tools together. Call and remind anyone who has promised to bring something.
Set out some water and glasses.
Prepare some relaxing background music.
Ensure that the room isn't too cold or too warm.
Ensure that you're not going to be interrupted. Unplugging the phone and turning off mobiles are good ideas.

At the beginning of the meeting:
As people arrive ask them to add the names of anyone they know who needs some healing to the Healing Book. Remember that you don't need to put their full names and private information, first names, initials or nicknames will suffice. Whoever you intend to send the healing to, it will reach.

Once everyone has arrived and is comfortable then you can start.
Work your way through the script and exercises for this lesson as detailed on the following pages.

Read the following scripts out loud to the group. It's a time of meditation so keep your voice calm and relaxed, reading in a fairly slow and controlled manner. Instructions are in brackets and italics.

RELAXATION
- Ensure you're sitting or lying comfortably.
- Take your awareness to your hands, make a tight fist, hold for a count of 3, 2, 1, and release.
- Tense your lower arms, hold for 3, 2, 1, and release.

- Tense your upper arms, hold for 3, 2, 1, and release.
- Tense your shoulders, lifting them up towards your ears, hold for 3, 2, 1, and release.
- Take your awareness to your neck: pull your chin toward chest but keep it from touching chest, hold for 3, 2, 1, and then relax.
- Take your awareness to your lower face and jaw, bite hard and pull back the corners of your mouth, hold for 3, 2, 1, and then relax.
- Screw your eyes up and wrinkle your nose, hold for 3, 2, 1, and then relax.
- Move your awareness to your forehead, lift your eyebrows as high as possible, hold for 3, 2, 1, and then relax.
- Take your awareness to your upper torso, pull your shoulder blades together hold for 3, 2, 1, and then release.
- Tense your stomach muscles, pulling your bellybutton towards your spine, hold for 3, 2, 1, and then release.
- Taking your awareness to your legs tense your thigh muscles, hold for 3, 2, 1, and then release.
- Pull your toes towards your head tensing your calf muscles, hold for 3, 2, 1, and then release.
- Take your awareness to your feet, point and curl your toes downwards, hold for 3, 2, 1, and then release.
- Tense your whole body at once, hands, arms, face, neck, chest, stomach, thighs, calves and feet, screw your eyes up, hold for 3, 2, 1, and completely release.
- Now take your awareness to your breathing, preferably through your nose as this is more relaxing.
- Ensure that you're breathing slowly and deeply.
- As you inhale, your abdomen will gently rise. And as you exhale it will fall.
- If your mind drifts or you lose track during this exercise bring your attention back to refocus on your breathing.
- Take a long, slow, deep inhalation for a count of 1 - 2 - 3 - 4, hold for 1- 2 and exhale for 1 - 2 - 3 - 4.
- In 2 3 4, Hold (pause), Out 2 3 4
- In 2 3 4, Hold (pause), Out 2 3 4
- In 2 3 4, Hold (pause), Out 2 3 4
- In 2 3 4, Hold (pause), Out 2 3 4
- In 2 3 4, Hold (pause), Out 2 3 4
- Continue breathing slowly and deeply.
- *(Move on to the script below.)*

OPENING & PROTECTION
- Let us take a moment to close our eyes and calm our minds.
- Concentrate on your breathing, allowing the breath to become deeper and slower.

(Pause to allow everyone to take a couple of breaths in and out)
- Let us all mentally ask our Spirit Guides and Angels to draw close and create a circle around our own.
- We let it be known that we are happy to work with Spirit and that we only work in love and light. We ask that anyone from the spirit world who wishes to contact us only does so in love and light and with the highest intentions.
- We ask for your protection, guidance and wisdom as we blend our world with yours. *(Pause)*
- Let us blend and harmonise our energies as we sit together in circle.
- Let us send out a note of harmony to the person on our left. Visualise this as a pale pink mist coming from your heart area and moving towards the heart of the person sitting on your left. *(Pause)*
- As you continue to do this, become aware of receiving the same loving energy from the right.
- As we send and receive this energy, be aware of any changes in the atmosphere within the circle. *(Pause)*
- Have a sense of oneness with the group. *(Pause)*
- Now bring your attention back to yourself and the centre of your being, the lower abdominal area.
- Focus on your breathing; become aware of the rise and fall of your abdomen. As you inhale it will gently rise and as you exhale it will fall. *(Pause to allow everyone to take a few breaths in and out)*
- Have a sense of warmth here and in your mind's eye allow a symbol or shape to form. Imagine that

this symbol or shape is sitting at and represents your centre. It may be a simple glow of light, a flame or a flower.
- With each in-breath visualise your symbol becoming larger, stronger or more open whichever is appropriate.
- With each out-breath, imagine that you are exhaling any negativity left from your day, or worries that you may have. *(Pause to allow everyone to take a few breaths in and out)*
- Now take your awareness to the soles of your feet, feeling their contact with the floor. Visualise lines of energy extending out from your feet and down into the ground. In your mind's eye, see these lines of energy as roots extending deep into the earth.
- Earth energy also travels back up through these roots revitalising and nourishing you.
- See this energy entering through the soles of your feet and travelling up through your legs to the base of your spine.
- At the base of the spine imagine that the energy becomes a sphere of deep red mist or light, as you visualise it, it becomes more vibrant in colour. *(Pause)*
- From this point a beam of energy leaves the red sphere and travels up towards the sacral area, just below the belly button. Here it forms a sphere of vibrant orange mist or light. As you focus on it, it becomes stronger in colour. *(Pause)*
- Gradually a beam of energy leaves the orange sphere and travels up towards the solar plexus, where it forms a sphere of clear yellow. With each breath, this yellow becomes stronger and brighter. *(Pause)*
- Once more a beam of energy leaves this sphere and continues its journey up to the heart area. Here a sphere of mist or light begins to form, which you may see as either green or pink. Focus on this area for a few breaths allowing the energy to grow stronger and clearer and to expand. *(Pause)*
- Gradually a beam of energy leaves the heart area and moves upwards to the throat. Here it forms a sphere of clear blue. Once more, as you focus on this area, allow the colour to expand and increase in strength. *(Pause)*
- Now, visualise a strand of energy leaving the throat area and linking with the third eye area, just between and slightly above the eyes. Here energy will begin to form as before. You may see this energy as either a rich indigo or violet, whichever you prefer. Concentrate on this energy and visualise it increasing in strength. *(Pause)*
- Again, a beam of light extends upwards from this area moving to the crown. As it does so, become aware of another beam of energy coming down from above to meet the first. As they meet at the crown a sphere of pure energy begins to form. You may see this energy as either violet or pure white light. This connects you with the higher realms of Spirit.
- As you hold this vision for a few breaths the light grows and strengthens. And as it does so, the beautiful pure light begins to overflow down and around you, surrounding you in its wonderful energy. It fills your aura, cleansing, balancing and strengthening it. You feel safe and comfortable. You feel relaxed and light. *(Longer pause before moving on to the script below.)*

CONSCIOUS CONNECTION
- Take your awareness back to the soles of your feet, feeling their contact with the floor. Visualise lines of energy extending out from your feet and down into the ground.
- In your mind's eye, see these lines of energy as roots extending deep into the earth. Maintain this feeling of energy at the feet and be aware of earth energy moving up through these roots entering your energy system, revitalising and nourishing you. It may help to see them beginning to glow with light as the energy travels up from the earth and enters your energy system.
- Now take your awareness to the crown of your head.
- Imagine that you are being suspended by a piece of string from this point. The piece of string hangs from a point far above you, so far above you that you are unable to see its origin.
- You should have a sense of being lifted upwards.

- In your mind's eye, the string is a brilliant white light, a magical connection with higher realms. Its brilliance and its power connects with and enters into your energy system.
- You can sense this energy entering your energy system through your crown chakra. It feels amazingly empowering.

HEALING

- Slowly open your eyes and join hands with those sitting to either side of you. This increases the flow of healing energy.
- We know that our Guides, Angels and loved ones in Spirit have come forward and that they surround us with their healing energies. We ask them to help us as we send out our healing today. *(Pause)*
- Visualise a pool of brilliant white light forming and growing in the middle of our circle. *(Pause)*
- This is a pool of healing energy from which we can all draw when we need to. Know that this universal healing energy will find its way to all of those for whom we request healing.
- We ask for healing for each of us here, for our minds, bodies and spirit.

(If there are absent members: We ask for healing for the members of our group who cannot be with us today.)

- We ask for healing for all of those on our Absent Healing List. Take a moment to visualise them standing in the healing pool.
- I would also like to ask for special healing for _____

(Mention anyone else that you feel healing is really important for today. Gently squeeze the hand of the person to your left to indicate that it's their turn. Let everyone have a turn at saying this part before continuing with the script.)

- We send our healing thoughts to Mother Earth and to the plant and animal kingdom. Thank you.
- Release your hands but keep your eyes closed so that you remain relaxed and peaceful as we go in to our meditation. *(Brief pause before moving on to the Meditation script.)*

MEDITATION

- Ensure that you're sitting comfortably with your hands on your knees, palms facing upwards.
- Close your eyes.
- Take a deep inhalation, and breathe out slowly. Continue to breathe slowly and deeply.
- During this meditation you will always be safe and protected, you will feel relaxed and comfortable. If, however, there is anything that does make you feel uneasy, or you wish to come back out of the meditation, you can do so at any time by counting backwards from 3 to 1 and taking a deep breath in and out. You can then bring your awareness back to the physical body, particularly your feet and open your eyes.
- For now though, continue to breathe slowly and deeply, your body feels relaxed and your mind is clear.
- As you breathe images may begin to form in your mind's eye. Don't try to manipulate or analyse them, simply observe them. If you do not automatically see these images, simply imagine or sense them.
- Ahead of you lies a staircase or series of ten steps. Move towards them. At the bottom you can see a doorway. We're going to slowly go down these steps towards the door feeling safe and confident at all times. So moving down the steps on my count:
- 10, 9, 8, with each step feeling lighter and lighter.
- 7, 6, 5, feeling calm and peaceful,
- 4, 3, relaxed and light
- 2 and 1, you find yourself standing in front of the door. Reaching out you open the door and as you do so, a wonderful, warm light shines through from the other side, bathing your whole being in its rays.
- As you stand in this light for a few moments, your physical body is warmed through and your energy body is nourished and energised. This gives you a sense of comfort and completeness and offers further protection on your journey. *(Pause for a short while)*
- Today's journey is to show you the nature of the abundant universe.

LESSON NINE - MANIFESTATION

- The rays of light subside and you can now see through the doorway to the other side.
- As your eyes adjust to the change in light, colours begin to form shapes. You can see your sanctuary on the other side of the doorway.
- You step through, closing the door behind you
- You see a set of doors that open up in to a garden area. Feeling safe and protected at all times, go through these doors.
- You step through the doors, in to the garden.
- Feel the soft springy grass underfoot and the warmth of the summer sun.
- All around you are an abundance of flowers of every variety, vibrantly coloured, their wonderful scent drifting towards you.
- The garden is also full of trees, many different trees, some in full blossom, some of them heavy with fruit.
- The whole garden is a garden of magical abundance.
- As you look around you find yourself drawn towards a flower or some fruit. Pick the flower or the fruit and hold it in your hand. Sense its energy, it feels almost alive in your hand.
- Notice that another flower or fruit has immediately grown to replace the one you picked. The garden constantly regenerates, replenishing itself.
- There's an abundance of beauty within the garden, enough for everyone to share.
- Take time to walk through the garden, see what other gifts it offers you. Perhaps there's a special crystal waiting for you on your pathway, an animal who wishes to communicate a message to you, or water to cleanse and heal you. Perhaps you see all of these, indeed there is no limit to the gifts that the garden of abundance bestows upon you. Enjoy its abundant offerings. *(Pause for a couple of minutes.)*
- Now it's time to begin your journey back through the garden of abundance, back to your sanctuary.
- As you walk back, soft grass underfoot, you notice ahead of you a single flower, of intense beauty and colour. This flower is for you and symbolises a gift from the universe for you.
- Touch or pick the flower, feeling its silky petals in your fingertips, Another flower has already begun to grow in its place. Remember as you observe this flower that the universe is a vast place, abundant with every possibility for you. *(Pause)*
- Focus on your heart's desire as you hold the flower, see your dream unfurl in your mind just as the petals of your flower once unfurled. *(Pause)*
- Give thanks for the abundance of the universe and the gifts it brings forth to you.
- Now continue walking until gradually the images that you have been observing start to fade and you find yourself at the doors leading back in to your sanctuary. Step through. You are in your sanctuary. You are safe and warm.
- Thank the universe for allowing you this insight today. *(Pause)*
- It's time to leave your sanctuary but know that what you have seen will stay with you as you return.
- Make your way towards the doorway leading to the stairs.
- Open the door that leads to the stairwell. Step through closing the door behind you.
- Know that your sanctuary is your own space that you can return to at any time for relaxation, guidance and healing.
- And keeping that sense of calm and wellbeing, it is time to head back up the stairs. So moving back up the stairs on my count,
- 1, 2, 3, breathing slowly and deeply,
- 4, 5, 6, your body is starting to feel heavier
- 7, 8, bringing your awareness back to your physical body,
- 9 and 10, on that top step now and when you're ready, step off the top step.
- **Bringing your awareness completely back to your physical body and this room, your contact with the chair, your feet with the floor. Slowly begin to move your fingers and toes, and in your own time, opening your eyes, fully awake and aware and in the physical world.**

(Watch for them starting to wriggle fingers and toes and keep an eye on anyone who doesn't do this. If a member of the group appears not to want to come back to the room simply repeat the last paragraph, in bold, but raising your voice so that it said slightly louder and firmer. Repeat a third time if necessary moving over to the person and at the end just saying their name and asking that they come back now in to the room, placing your hand gently on their shoulder.)

Spend a few minutes sharing experiences of the meditation. Remember that it's okay if someone fell asleep, could see nothing or did their own thing. If you're keeping a personal journal, you may wish to take some time to record you experience. Don't forget to date the entry.

THEORY: MANIFESTATION
The following 'theory' section should be read aloud to the group. You may want to get others to join in and take it in turns to read.

Manifestation in this context is the ability to connect with the universe to create a situation that you desire, or need. Need a job after redundancy? Why not focus some universal energy on the situation? To be fair it may be that you're doing it in some way without thinking. However, you might be focussing the wrong type of energy on the situation by worrying, stressing and wondering 'what if...?' So, why not focus on it in the right way to ensure a positive outcome for all concerned.

The way we see it is that we're all here, on earth, to experience being human beings in physical form, but also to re-connect with, and remember our original state; that of a creative spiritual being and a part of all creation. We're all creative and we're all a part of everything. So it's entirely possible that we're able to harness the energy of the universe to create whatever we wish.

Here's our theory: Thoughts are creative. What you think about comes about. That's why you have to be careful and ensure that you stay positive about life and yourself. Otherwise you may manifest negative events around you. We all know someone, who says to themselves, and to others 'everything always goes wrong for me". Aren't they the one that everything always does go wrong for? Perhaps, if they changed their thought processes things would change? It can be as simple as making sure you go out with a smile on your face. You always have a much more positive day when you do. Your subconscious mind does not understand the difference between fantasy and reality. You'll know this if you've ever watched a sad, or scary film. You know it's not real, don't you? But the feelings that it creates are very real, aren't they? So when you manifest, you turn things around a little, allowing your subconscious to believe you already have the situation that you want. You create the feeling of having it, this feeling is projected into the universe and, in time, you attract the situation to you. Everything that exists started life as a thought.

Because your subconscious mind responds to pictures, you can use visualisation skills to create mental images and feelings of the things and situations that you desire. This programs your subconscious mind to believe that you already have them.

Bear in mind that you must respect the free will of others and that you can't manipulate people into situations by using this method. You can manifest things and events, so if you're looking for your perfect partner you must list details. However, you cannot expect or make a particular person to fall in love with you.

Also, consider that you may need to alter your language slightly when talking to others about the item that you're manifesting. Instead of saying 'I need a job' or 'I want a new car', try saying something like, 'I'm finding the right job,' or 'I'm getting my new car.'

Only share your creative projects with like-minded people. If a friend isn't of the same mindset, they can be negative and knock your confidence and faith. In time, as you understand and believe more fully in your creative influence, you may feel able to be more open with others as their comments won't upset or affect you any longer. You will know just what you're capable of.

Crystals that could assist in manifesting your dreams and desires are citrine, apatite, red chalcedony, tiger's eye and topaz.

Finally, you must believe that the universe will deliver. Don't over-analyse the situation, or sit and worry about it. Whenever you think about your 'order', smile and say 'thank you'. Have a sense of knowing that it will come, then, just let the universe do its thing.

Discuss any personal experiences or thoughts on the subject (but keep any eye on the time).

PRACTICAL WORK
Read out each exercise, one at a time to the group so that you are all clear as to what you are doing, then allocate a time to complete the exercise.

Exercises 1 to 3 should be done as individuals, exercise 4 can be done on your own but with discussion and input from each other and exercise 5 is a team effort.

Exercise 1 - Know what you want
- Each of you should write down what is it that you want to achieve. choose just one thing and write it down in as much detail as possible. For example, if it's a job: what salary, holiday entitlement, what type of people do you wish to work with or for, what do you want the job to do for you, do you need to feel appreciated and recognised? Write every aspect you require down on your list and include a date that you wish to receive it by.
- Give everyone enough time to complete this (within reason).

Exercise 2 - Affirm what you want
- Place this 'request' in an envelope and seal it. On a separate piece of paper come up with an affirmation that will encompass your wish as though it has already been received. Something like, 'I am so grateful for this wonderful new opportunity'. It's important to express your thanks and gratitude for the things you ask for from the universe. By doing this you're acknowledging that what you want already exists, and is out there for you. You're showing your faith in the universe and affirming that it's already yours.
- If anyone is struggling with this it might be a god idea to work in pairs or help each other out to come up with a positive affirmation for each person that they all feel comfortable with.
- Once you've formulated your affirmation write it on the front of your envelope.

Exercise 3 - Connect with the universal catalogue
- Read out the following once everyone is ready:
- Hold your envelope between the palms of your hands.
- Take your awareness to the crown of your head and in your mind's eye see a brilliant white light entering your energy system. It's a magical connection with the higher realms. Its brilliance and its power connects with you and you are naturally connected to it.
- You can sense this energy moving down through the crown, through the throat chakra and in to the heart area. Here it divides and moves in two brilliant streams down each of your arms and in to the palms of your hands.
- Sit quietly and let the universal energy flow through you and into the envelope. As you do this, imagine that you already have the thing you desire. See it as clearly as possible in your minds eye. Feel the feelings that it brings. See it in front of you in as much detail as possible either an object or item that you wish to ohave or a situation that you desire. How does it feel/sound/smell?
- Smile and enjoy the moment as the universal energy enlivens and empowers your request.
- *(Pause for a couple of minutes)*

Exercise 4 - Be practical too
- Read the following out to the group:
- Remember that this isn't something to do instead of going out and looking for a job or taking action to achieve what you require or want. Any positive action you take to achieve your goal will be super charged by the energy being focussed on it, so don't just sit back and do nothing, thinking that the universe will deliver. It still might, but it makes it harder. Think about this. The universe may deliver the perfect job, but if you're not looking at the 'recruitment' section of the paper or sending out your C.V., how are you going to know about it, let alone get an interview? All of your energy will have been wasted and you will think it hasn't worked. So make a list of steps that you can take to help yourself in achieving your request.
- You may want to help each other out with this one, sometimes it is good to have a bit of distance to plan out the steps. Also when you share your requests you never know who in the group may be in a position to help. As if by magic they may be the link that will assist in moving things forward and you may never have known without doing this exercise. It's all part of the process of manifestation, the universe moves in mysterious ways!

Exercise 5 - Team effort
- When you feel that you're finished, sit in a circle and place the envelopes in the middle of the group.
- Read the following out to the group:
- Join hands take your attention to the palms of your hands. Become more aware of the connection you have with the group. As you do so you should feel warmth or tingling as your focus encourages the energy to be pulled fthrough your energy system to your hands.
- Maintain your contact and simply let the energy flow around the circle passing from hand to hand. You may get a sense of it moving round in a particular direction. You may also experience different sensations such as your arms wanting to 'float' or move, or 'power surges' where your body, arms or hands shudder slightly. This is quite normal, just let the energy flow.
- As the energy that you are channelling grows feel it filling the centre of the circle and empowering all of you and your written requests.
- Let the energy flow for a few moments.

Exercise 6 - Be thankful for what you have
- Read the following: 'We thank the universe for responding to our requests. We make them with the hghest intentions and for the highest good. We are grateful for receiving the correct outcome for our individual paths.'

CLOSING & GROUNDING
Once you have completed the exercises everyone should sit comfortably and complete the following meditation to close and ground their energy. Read out the following:
- Sit in a comfortable position and close your eyes.
- Bring your attention to your breathing and focus on this for a few breaths. *(Pause)*
- Take your awareness to the invisible energy field surrounding you and visualise it drawing in close around your physical body. *(Pause)*
- Take your awareness to the area just above your crown and see a sphere of light sitting here.
- Imagine that sphere of light shrinking in size until it's tiny, then sinking down through the crown of your head.
- See it slowly descending down past the brow. *(Pause)*
- Into the throat. *(Pause)*
- Then following the line of the spine, down, through your body, towards your heart area. *(Pause)*
- Down to your solar plexus. *(Pause)*

LESSON NINE - MANIFESTATION

- Through the abdominal area. *(Pause)*
- To the base of your spine. *(Pause)*
- Now visualise the sphere of energy either leaving through the base of your spine, or dividing in two and sinking down through your legs and leaving through the soles of your feet.
- Feel this energy leaving you and connecting with the earth.
- Have a sense of downward movement, deep in to the earth. *(Pause)*
- Become more aware of your feet and your physical body.
- Let us take a moment to thank our Spirit Guides, Angels and loved ones in Spirit for their presence, protection and wisdom whilst we've been working. Knowing that they will always be on hand should we need to call on them. *(Pause)*
- **Now bring your awareness back to your physical body, the chair you are sitting on and your contact with the floor.**
- **Begin to bring some movement back in to your fingers and toes.**
- **In your own time opening your eyes, fully awake and aware and in the physical world.**

(Watch for them starting to wriggle fingers and toes and keep an eye on anyone who doesn't do this. If a member of the group appears not to want to come back to the room simply repeat the last three points, in bold, but raising your voice so that it said slightly louder and firmer. Repeat a third time if necessary moving over to the person and at the end just saying their name and asking that they come back into the room now, placing a hand gently on their shoulder.)

Check to ensure that everyone feels grounded before you finish the session. If not, get them to walk around for a little while. Stamping your feet or jumping up and down helps to bring you back to the physical world. If these don't do the trick, you can ground your energy very readily by eating a small amount of food such as a biscuit.

OTHER THINGS TO TRY:

- You may want to put an actual picture of your 'order' somewhere that you will see it on a regular basis. For example, on the fridge, in your wallet or diary. When you look at it, smile and say 'thank you' to the universe, knowing that it's on the way, much like if you'd ordered an item from a website and were waiting for its delivery. However, if you're the type of person who would obsess about something when faced with it on a regular basis and worry about it not having arrived yet, it may be better to simply write down your order, thank the universe in advance for it, and then place it in a drawer or box and forget about it. Both methods work, it's up to you which one you prefer.
- Download an example of an 'I AM' mirror from www.spreadingthemagic.com. Put it somewhere where you can see it everyday and use it to affirm everything positive in your life. You will manifest a more positive life. Use this one or make your own.
- Start a gratitude or achievement book listing everything you've achieved and are thankful for in your life. Every time you manifest something, add it to your book. If you are having a bad or down day, or need a boost of positivity, look in your book and be thankful. Smile and move on to a more positive day.
- Keep manifesting! The more you do it, the more you know that it works. The more you know that it works, the easier it becomes. But always be grateful, never become complacent.

AND ANOTHER THING...

- Each person should place their envelope somewhere safe. We have friends who have a manifestation box where they place all their 'orders' or 'requests'. This means that whenever you have a moment you can think about the box as a whole, focussing energy onto manifesting all of your dreams within it. You can also bring it along to the group if you decide to spend some time focussing on maifestation again.

- Being receptive to, and aware of signs and opportunities around you will provide evidence for your connection to the universe ensure that you stay in the flow of things, which will greatly increase your success in manifestation.
- Have a look at some books on the subject. We recommend:

The Cosmic Ordering Service - Barbel Mohr
The Secret - Rhonda Byrne
The Power - Rhonda Byrne

FOR DISCUSSION
- What have we got from this lesson? Best bits? Tricky bits?
- Key Concepts - how are we getting on with patience, acceptance, faith?
- Healing - feedback from those in the healing book? Success stories?

Next Time...

The next lesson will be covering PAST LIVES.

You will need to arrange for the following tools to be brought along:
- Pendulums (preferably each person should bring their own)
- An atlas and maps of the country you live in.

Extra tools if you want to do 'other things to try':
- A selection of crystals that may assist in past life discovery such as: amethyst, carnelian, lapis lazuli, double terminated quartz, rutilated quartz, merlinite, herkimer diamonds and purple sheen obsidian.
- Frankincense essential oil & a burner.

LESSON TEN
PAST LIVES

PREPARATION
Well in advance of your meeting ensure that you have all of the tools that you require for this lesson. If not, find out if another group member has access to what you need.

Regular tools:
- Healing book
- Pens and pencils
- Paper
- Candles & matches if desired
- Box of tissues

Tools for this lesson:
- Pendulums (ideally everyone should have their own by now)
- Photocopy the required number of Handout 5 - dowsng charts & Handout 8 - Past life interview scripts
- An atlas and maps of the country you live in.

Extra tools if you want to do 'other things to try':
- Crystals that may help with past life work are amethyst, carnelian, lapis lazuli, double terminated quartz, rutilated quartz, merlinite, herkimer diamonds and purple sheen obsidian.
- Frankincense essential oil in a burner can also assist.

On the day of the meeting ensure that the room is prepared:
Are there enough seats for everyone and enough room for the work you are about to undertake?
Open the windows or burn some incense to freshen the air.
Cleanse the area.
Gather the required tools together. Call and remind anyone who has promised to bring something.
Set out some water and glasses.
Prepare some relaxing background music.
Ensure that the room isn't too cold or too warm.
Ensure that you're not going to be interrupted. Unplugging the phone and turning off mobiles are good ideas.

At the beginning of the meeting:
As people arrive ask them to add the names of anyone they know who needs some healing to the Healing Book. Remember that you don't need to put their full names and private information, first names, initials or nicknames will suffice. Whoever you intend to send the healing to, it will reach.

Once everyone has arrived and is comfortable then you can start.
Work your way through the script and exercises for this lesson as detailed on the following pages.

Read the following scripts out loud to the group. It's a time of meditation so keep your voice calm and relaxed, reading in a fairly slow and controlled manner. Instructions are in brackets and italics.

RELAXATION
- Ensure you're sitting or lying comfortably.
- Take your awareness to your hands, make a tight fist, hold for a count of 3, 2, 1, and release.
- Tense your lower arms, hold for 3, 2, 1, and release.
- Tense your upper arms, hold for 3, 2, 1, and release.
- Tense your shoulders, lifting them up towards your ears, hold for 3, 2, 1, and release.
- Take your awareness to your neck: pull your chin toward chest but keep it from touching chest, hold for 3, 2, 1, and then relax.
- Take your awareness to your lower face and jaw, bite hard and pull back the corners of your mouth, hold for 3, 2, 1, and then relax.
- Screw your eyes up and wrinkle your nose, hold for 3, 2, 1, and then relax.
- Move your awareness to your forehead, lift your eyebrows as high as possible, hold for 3, 2, 1, and then relax.
- Take your awareness to your upper torso, pull your shoulder blades together hold for 3, 2, 1, and then release.
- Tense your stomach muscles, pulling your bellybutton towards your spine, hold for 3, 2, 1, and then release.
- Taking your awareness to your legs tense your thigh muscles, hold for 3, 2, 1, and then release.
- Pull your toes towards your head tensing your calf muscles, hold for 3, 2, 1, and then release.
- Take your awareness to your feet, point and curl your toes downwards, hold for 3, 2, 1, and then release.
- Tense your whole body at once, hands, arms, face, neck, chest, stomach, thighs, calves and feet, screw your eyes up, hold for 3, 2, 1, and completely release.
- Now take your awareness to your breathing, preferably through your nose as this is more relaxing.
- Ensure that you're breathing slowly and deeply.
- As you inhale, your abdomen will gently rise. And as you exhale it will fall.
- If your mind drifts or you lose track during this exercise bring your attention back to refocus on your breathing.
- Take a long, slow, deep inhalation for a count of 1 - 2 - 3 - 4, hold for 1- 2 and exhale for 1 - 2 - 3 - 4.
- In 2 3 4, Hold (pause), Out 2 3 4
- In 2 3 4, Hold (pause), Out 2 3 4
- In 2 3 4, Hold (pause), Out 2 3 4
- In 2 3 4, Hold (pause), Out 2 3 4
- In 2 3 4, Hold (pause), Out 2 3 4
- Continue breathing slowly and deeply.
- *(Move on to the script below.)*

OPENING & PROTECTION
- Let us take a moment to close our eyes and calm our minds.
- Concentrate on your breathing, allowing the breath to become deeper and slower.

(Pause to allow everyone to take a couple of breaths in and out)

- Let us all mentally ask our Spirit Guides and Angels to draw close and create a circle around our own.
- We let it be known that we are happy to work with Spirit and that we only work in love and light. We ask that anyone from the spirit world who wishes to contact us only does so in love and light and with the highest intentions.
- We ask for your protection, guidance and wisdom as we blend our world with yours. *(Pause)*
- Let us blend and harmonise our energies as we sit together in circle.
- Let us send out a note of harmony to the person on our left. Visualise this as a pale pink mist coming from your heart area and moving towards the heart of the person sitting on your left. *(Pause)*

- As you continue to do this, become aware of receiving the same loving energy from the right.
- As we send and receive this energy, be aware of any changes in the atmosphere within the circle. *(Pause)*
- Have a sense of oneness with the group. *(Pause)*
- Now bring your attention back to yourself and the centre of your being, the lower abdominal area.
- Focus on your breathing; become aware of the rise and fall of your abdomen. As you inhale it will gently rise and as you exhale it will fall. *(Pause to allow everyone to take a few breaths in and out)*
- Have a sense of warmth here and in your mind's eye allow a symbol or shape to form. Imagine that this symbol or shape is sitting at and represents your centre. It may be a simple glow of light, a flame or a flower.
- With each in-breath visualise your symbol becoming larger, stronger or more open whichever is appropriate.
- With each out-breath, imagine that you are exhaling any negativity left from your day, or worries that you may have. *(Pause to allow everyone to take a few breaths in and out)*
- Now take your awareness to the soles of your feet, feeling their contact with the floor. Visualise lines of energy extending out from your feet and down into the ground. In your mind's eye, see these lines of energy as roots extending deep into the earth.
- Earth energy also travels back up through these roots revitalising and nourishing you.
- See this energy entering through the soles of your feet and travelling up through your legs to the base of your spine.
- At the base of the spine imagine that the energy becomes a sphere of deep red mist or light, as you visualise it, it becomes more vibrant in colour. *(Pause)*
- From this point a beam of energy leaves the red sphere and travels up towards the sacral area, just below the belly button. Here it forms a sphere of vibrant orange mist or light. As you focus on it, it becomes stronger in colour. *(Pause)*
- Gradually a beam of energy leaves the orange sphere and travels up towards the solar plexus, where it forms a sphere of clear yellow. With each breath, this yellow becomes stronger and brighter. *(Pause)*
- Once more a beam of energy leaves this sphere and continues its journey up to the heart area. Here a sphere of mist or light begins to form, which you may see as either green or pink. Focus on this area for a few breaths allowing the energy to grow stronger and clearer and to expand. *(Pause)*
- Gradually a beam of energy leaves the heart area and moves upwards to the throat. Here it forms a sphere of clear blue. Once more, as you focus on this area, allow the colour to expand and increase in strength. *(Pause)*
- Now, visualise a strand of energy leaving the throat area and linking with the third eye area, just between and slightly above the eyes. Here energy will begin to form as before. You may see this energy as either a rich indigo or violet, whichever you prefer. Concentrate on this energy and visualise it increasing in strength. *(Pause)*
- Again, a beam of light extends upwards from this area moving to the crown. As it does so, become aware of another beam of energy coming down from above to meet the first. As they meet at the crown a sphere of pure energy begins to form. You may see this energy as either violet or pure white light. This connects you with the higher realms of Spirit.
- As you hold this vision for a few breaths the light grows and strengthens. And as it does so, the beautiful pure light begins to overflow down and around you, surrounding you in its wonderful energy. It fills your aura, cleansing, balancing and strengthening it. You feel safe and comfortable. You feel relaxed and light. *(Longer pause before moving on to the script below.)*

CONSCIOUS CONNECTION
- Take your awareness back to the soles of your feet, feeling their contact with the floor. Visualise lines of energy extending out from your feet and down into the ground.
- In your mind's eye, see these lines of energy as roots extending deep into the earth. Maintain this

feeling of energy at the feet and be aware of earth energy moving up through these roots entering your energy system, revitalising and nourishing you. It may help to see them beginning to glow with light as the energy travels up from the earth and enters your energy system.
- Now take your awareness to the crown of your head.
- Imagine that you are being suspended by a piece of string from this point. The piece of string hangs from a point far above you, so far above you that you are unable to see its origin.
- You should have a sense of being lifted upwards.
- In your mind's eye, the string is a brilliant white light, a magical connection with higher realms. Its brilliance and its power connects with and enters into your energy system.
- You can sense this energy entering your energy system through your crown chakra. It feels amazingly empowering.

HEALING
- Slowly open your eyes and join hands with those sitting to either side of you. This increases the flow of healing energy.
- We know that our Guides, Angels and loved ones in Spirit have come forward and that they surround us with their healing energies. We ask them to help us as we send out our healing today. *(Pause)*
- Visualise a pool of brilliant white light forming and growing in the middle of our circle. *(Pause)*
- This is a pool of healing energy from which we can all draw when we need to. Know that this universal healing energy will find its way to all of those for whom we request healing.
- We ask for healing for each of us here, for our minds, bodies and spirit.

(If there are absent members: We ask for healing for the members of our group who cannot be with us today.)
- We ask for healing for all of those on our Absent Healing List. Take a moment to visualise them standing in the healing pool.
- I would also like to ask for special healing for _____

(Mention anyone else that you feel healing is really important for today. Gently squeeze the hand of the person to your left to indicate that it's their turn. Let everyone have a turn at saying this part before continuing with the script.)
- We send our healing thoughts to Mother Earth and to the plant and animal kingdom. Thank you.

THEORY: PAST LIVES
The following 'theory' section should be read aloud to the group. You may want to get others to join in and take it in turns to read.

This is a subject where, when asked a question about it, we take a big breath before answering! It's so subjective and emotive, with any explanation of, beliefs or explanations open to scrutiny, mainly because no-one knows (or can prove) the definitive truth. Most people perceive the idea of past lives in the same way that they perceive the passage of time, as linear. That is, there's a definite sequence of past, present and future. The belief is generally held that you are born into one life, live it, die, and your soul moves on to another incarnation and repeats this process until such time as all lessons are learnt and, in some beliefs, enlightenment is attained. We think that it's probably a bit more complex than that.

We think that a good generic definition of the term 'past life' is: A familiar-feeling vision, or glimpse of an alternate reality, experienced in the first person, from which you gain very personal information and lessons that can help you with your present day situations.

These glimpses or visions can occur in dreams or spontaneously during meditations. They can also appear as little flashbacks, almost like memories, during normal waking hours, usually when the timing is important, or the company that you're in is relevant.

Additionally, some believe that your actions in one lifetime determine your fate in the next (karma), a larger scale version of reaping what you sow. Although, perhaps this belief is constructed by us as humans, so that we can rationalise and justify some of the suffering and inequalities, perceived or otherwise, that we see in life.

Here are some theories on past life glimpses:

a) You lead a series of lives, reincarnating into a new body each time you die. You accumulate knowledge and lessons from each life that are stored away within you on some level. You may repeat similar scenarios in a number of your 'lives' until you have learnt your 'lesson' and changed yourself appropriately. Past life work can help you unlock stored knowledge and learn what you need to.

b) You lead multiple lives all at once, but your conscious mind is more focussed on one. You get glimpses of the others when your conscious focus drifts, through dreams, daydreams or meditations. These glimpses sometimes provide insight and clarity on your current situation.

c) Your subconscious creates an imaginary vision based on a current situation and people in your life. This vision is designed to give you a different perspective or insight into how you might deal with the real situation better or solve a problem. It feels so personal, as though you've actually experienced it because its essence is the same as your current situation, just repackaged.

d) Everything that's ever happened, is happening or will happen is actually happening at the same time. All of the information about everything in the universe forms a massive pool of consciousness that you can access when you dream or meditate. You may then catch glimpses of these 'other lives' from time to time. And on other occasions, because your subconscious is so clever, it may cause you to see certain glimpses that you would benefit from seeing, so that you can gain clarity on your current situation.

Whatever the theory is behind these 'glimpses' or past lives, the information or advice that you extract, the clarity that you receive, or the realisations that occur are what are real and often exceptionally helpful to you. So the mechanics of how, what and why is kind of irrelevant. You can draw your own conclusions given your belief system and experiences. What's more important? How you receive a message or what you choose to do with the information that you're given?

Important points to note
While you may find clarity through past life work, never relinquish responsibility for your own life and circumstances by blaming a past life event. You're always able to choose and mould your life's direction. You can learn things through these exercises and can develop a better understanding of yourself and others, but you shouldn't seek an excuse for your situation in order to give up trying to improve yourself, or taking responsibility for changing it and moving on. Use any information obtained to identify a problem or a pattern that you end up repeating over and over (with friends, family, partners, children, work money etc.) and then work out how to make changes so that you can step out of the cycle of repetition.

Although this subject is very fascinating, it's also important to remember that you're living in this life and not to get caught up in 'other lives,' or allow past experiences to distract you from it.

Past life work can cause you to re-visit traumatic events in your own life, if you haven't rectified or dealt with them. If you're at all concerned about this possibility, don't continue with these exercises.

If you suffer from or are receiving treatment or medication for any mental health issue don't undertake these exercises. Please seek professional assistance if you wish to pursue a past life influence on your current situation. Don't try to deal with it on your own or put friends in a position of assisting you with it as they may become out of their depth. Look for a well recommended and fully qualified past life practitioner or hypnotherapist with a proven background in this type of work.

Whichever of the theories you prefer, or even if you haven't made up your mind about this subject yet, have a go at the practical work. Be open-minded and see what you get from it.

Discuss any personal experiences or thoughts on the subject (but keep any eye on the time).

PRACTICAL WORK
Read out each exercise, one at a time to the group so that you are all clear as to what you are doing, then allocate a time to complete the exercise.

Exercise 1 - A guided visualisation to look at a past life experience
- Ensure that you're sitting comfortably with your hands on your knees, palms facing upwards.
- Close your eyes.
- Take your awareness to your hands, make a tight fist, hold for a count of 3, 2, 1, and release.
- Tense your lower arms, hold for 3, 2, 1, and release.
- Tense your upper arms, hold for 3, 2, 1, and release.
- Tense your shoulders, lifting them up towards your ears, hold for 3, 2, 1, and release.
- Take your awareness to your neck: pull your chin toward chest but keep it from touching chest, hold for 3, 2, 1, and then relax.
- Take your awareness to your lower face and jaw, bite hard and pull back the corners of your mouth hold for 3, 2, 1, and then relax.
- Screw your eyes up and wrinkle your nose, hold for 3, 2, 1, and then relax.
- Move your awareness to your forehead, lift your eyebrows as high as possible, hold for 3, 2, 1, and then relax.
- Take your awareness to your upper torso, pull your shoulder blades together hold for 3, 2, 1, and then release.
- Tense your stomach muscles, pulling your bellybutton towards your spine, hold for 3, 2, 1, and then release.
- Taking your awareness to your legs tense your thigh muscles, hold for 3, 2, 1, and then release.
- Pull your toes towards your head tensing your calf muscles, hold for 3, 2, 1, and then release.
- Taking your awareness to your feet, point and curl your toes downwards, hold for 3, 2, 1, and then release.
- Tense your whole body at once, hands, arms, face, neck, chest, stomach, thighs, calves and feet, screw your eyes up, hold for 3, 2, 1, and completely release.
- Now take your awareness to your breathing, preferably through your nose, as this is more relaxing.
- Ensure that you are breathing slowly and deeply.
- As you inhale, your abdomen will gently rise. And as you exhale it will fall.
- If your mind drifts or you lose track during this exercise bring your attention back to refocus on your breathing.
- Take a long, slow, deep inhalation for a count of 1 - 2 - 3 - 4, hold for 1- 2 and exhale for 1 - 2 - 3 - 4.
- In 2 3 4, Hold (pause), Out 2 3 4
- In 2 3 4, Hold (pause), Out 2 3 4
- In 2 3 4, Hold (pause), Out 2 3 4
- In 2 3 4, Hold (pause), Out 2 3 4
- In 2 3 4, Hold (pause), Out 2 3 4
- Continue breathing slowly and deeply.
- Take a deep inhalation, and breathe out slowly. Continue to breathe slowly and deeply.
- During this meditation you will always be safe and protected, you will feel relaxed and comfortable. If, however, there is anything that does make you feel uneasy, or you wish to come back out of the meditation, you can do so at any time by counting backwards from 3 to 1 and taking a deep breath in and out. You can then bring your awareness back to the physical body, particularly your feet and open your eyes.
- For now though, continue to breathe slowly and deeply, your body feels relaxed and your mind is clear.
- As you breathe, images may begin to form in your mind's eye. Don't try to manipulate or analyse them, simply observe them. If you don't automatically see these images, simply imagine or sense them.
- Ahead of you lies a staircase or series of ten steps. Move towards them. At the bottom you can see a

doorway. We're going to slowly go down these steps towards the door, feeling safe and confident at all times. So moving down the steps on my count,
- 10, 9, 8, with each step feeling lighter and lighter.
- 7, 6, 5, feeling calm and peaceful,
- 4, 3, relaxed and light,
- 2 and 1, you find yourself standing in front of the door. Reaching out you open the door and as you do so, a wonderful, warm light shines through from the other side, bathing your whole being in its rays.
- As you stand in this light for a few moments, your physical body is warmed through and your energy body is nourished and energised. This gives you a sense of comfort and completeness and offers further protection on your journey. *(Pause for a short while.)*
- Today's journey is to help you find out information about the most relevant of your past life experiences that could help you with your current incarnation.
- The rays of light subside and you can now see through the doorway to the other side.
- As your eyes adjust to the change in light, colours begin to form shapes. You can see your sanctuary on the other side of the doorway.
- You step through, closing the door behind you.
- Find a place in your sanctuary that you can sit comfortably, preferably with a nearby wall or vertical surface.
- Make yourself at home in this safe place.
- Ask that your most relevant spirit guide joins you and feel them drawing near.
- Ask your guide to help you in discovering a past life that may help you in your present incarnation.
- As you ask this you begin to see something taking shape on the wall or vertical surface close to you. Gradually you realise that it's something that you can view scenes through that's manifesting in front of you. It may be a door, window or even a large TV or movie screen.
- Your guide has created it for you to show you what you want to see today.
- As you sit here in this comfortable and safe place, with your spirit guide close by, you realise that you are about to see a short glimpse into a lifetime that will help and guide you.
- Ask to be shown the year of this 'glimpse.' On the screen, or other object, a mist will form and as it clears numbers will form to give you a year.
- Ask that this special glimpse into the past begin. Sit back and watch the events unfold, completely safe as though you are watching a film. *(Pause for 3- 4 minutes)*
- Gradually, the images that you have been observing start to fade and a mist falls once more over them. You're in your sanctuary. You're safe and warm.
- Thank your guide for allowing you this insight today. *(Pause)*
- It's time to leave your sanctuary but know that what you have seen will stay with you as you return.
- Make your way towards the doorway to the stairs.
- Open the door. Step through closing the door behind you.
- Know that your sanctuary is your own space that you can return to at any time for relaxation, guidance and healing.
- And keeping your sense of calm and wellbeing, it is time to head back up the stairs. So moving back up the stairs on my count,
- 1, 2, 3, breathing slowly and deeply,
- 4, 5, 6, your body is starting to feel heavier,
- 7, 8, bringing your awareness back to your physical body,
- 9 and 10, on that top step now and when you're ready, step off the top step.
- **Bringing your awareness completely back to your physical body and this room, your contact with the chair, your feet with the floor. Slowly begin to move your fingers and toes, and in your own time, opening your eyes, fully awake and aware and in the physical world.**

(If you are reading this aloud for someone else, watch for them starting to wriggle fingers and toes. If they appear not want to come back to the room simply repeat the last paragraph, in bold, but raising your voice so that it's

said slightly louder and firmer. Repeat a third time if necessary moving over to the person and at the end just saying their name and asking that they come back now into the room, placing your hand gently on their shoulder.)
- Spend a few minutes sharing experiences of the meditation or making notes about it if you are keeping a personal journal. Don't forget to date the entry.

Exercise 2 - Interview
- You may want to take the information you received from exercise 1 and look at it in more detail using this interview technique.
- Working in pairs take it in turns to be the subject whose 'past life' will be looked at. The other is the interviewer.
- Make sure you have some paper and a pen or pencil to make notes about the answers given.
- Make a list of questions that you'd like to ask about your past life. Examples can be found in Handout 8 - version A.
- Sit opposite each other.
- One of the interviewers should read the following script aloud to the past life 'subjects' before each interviewer runs through the questions they have compiled with their partner.

Past life interview script:
- Ensure that you're sitting comfortably.
- Close your eyes.
- Breathe slowly and deeply, allowing your body to relax and your mind to clear.
- Ask your spirit guides to draw close and assist you in finding out about your most relevant past life experience.
- In your mind's eye visualise a mirror and see yourself just as you are now, reflected in it.
- Mist forms slowly across the mirror so that you're unable to see your reflection.
- Ask your spirit guide to use the mirror to reveal information about your most relevant past life experience.
- When you're ready, gently blow the mist away to reveal a reflection of you from your most relevant past life experience.
- Now you will be asked questions to ascertain information about this life experience. Answer with the first impressions that come to mind or you may see the information appear in the mirror, and your partner will make notes for you.
- Interviewers should interview their partners using the pre-prepared questions, making notes of their answers and elaborating where appropriate.
- *(When everyone is finished or your allocated time is up, use the following script to bring everyone back to the room.)*
- Bringing your awareness completely back to your physical body and this room, your contact with the chair, your feet with the floor. Slowly begin to move your fingers and toes, and in your own time, opening your eyes, fully awake and aware and in the physical world.
- Discuss your findings and then swap over and repeat the exercise so that both partners get a go.

Exercise 3 - Dowsing your past lives
Read out: You will have practised dowsing in our 'Beginner's Guide'. It's an extremely useful skill to develop. Use dowsing rods or a pendulum, whichever you prefer. You can either ask questions that require a yes or no answer or dowse over charts, maps or timelines to gain information about your past lives. You may find it beneficial to use the dowsing charts and timelines in Handout 5.
Before you begin, don't forget to orientate your dowsing tool to ensure that you're clear on how to interpret it Typically L-shape rods will cross each other to indicate a positive response but it's as well to make sure that's how they work for you.

a)Decide what you want to know
- Create a list of questions about your past life that you would like answers to. Remember to be as spe-

cific as possible. Then develop questions with a yes or no answer designed to find out the information you require. Examples of questions to ask when discovering your past lives through dowsing can be found in Handout 8 - version B.
- You will learn to fine-tune each subsequent question as you work so that you can get as accurate an answer as possible.

b) Orientate your dowsing tool.
- You can use any of these methods, but you only need to use one.
- Method 1: Simply ask your rods or pendulum to show you the response of 'yes.' Think clearly about the word 'yes' as you do this. Whatever you're using should move in a particular way or direction. Make a note of this 'yes' response. Ask it to stop, or say 'thank you.' Wait for it to stop moving or return to neutral and make a note of the movement for 'yes'. Now do the same for the response 'no'.
- Method 2: Ask a question where you already know the answer is yes. This ascertains the movement for a 'yes' response. Ask it to stop, or say 'thank you.' Wait for it to stop moving or return to neutral and make a note of the movement for 'yes'. Now do the same with a question where you know the answer is 'no'.
- Method 3: Using the yes/no chart in Handout 5, hold your dowsing tool over one, then the other to ascertain the relevant movements.

c) Go dowse!
- Ask question, use maps and timelines and make notes of your discoveries.
- Using maps: You can dowse over maps to establish locations using questions such as: Where did I have a past life that is currently affecting me? Where did I have a past life that is most relevant to my current situation? Where did I have a past life that I can currently learn the most from recalling?
- Using our charts: Try using our charts (Handout 5) to discover the period of your most relevant past life. You can also find out the date of birth, death and other important events for that lifetime. Full instructions are on page 169.
- Bear in mind that when you work with maps and charts, pendulums can behave a little differently. Instead of giving you a 'yes' over the correct information it may change its behaviour so that it suddenly feels heavy, or you get a sense of it being drawn through something sticky, like treacle. (That's the best way we can describe it.) It can feel as though it just wants to stay over this point. Practise and see what you get. You may wish to confirm your answer by moving away from the map or chart and clarifying the point with a yes/no question.

Exercise 4 - Discuss your past lives
- Spend some time discussing your findings and how they might relate to you and help you in your current lifetime. Do any of you think you've been related, had conflict or lived / worked together in past lives? Keep notes in your journal if you're keeping one.

CLOSING & GROUNDING
Once you have completed the exercises everyone should sit comfortably and complete the following meditation to close and ground their energy. Read out the following:
- Sit in a comfortable position and close your eyes.
- Bring your attention to your breathing and focus on this for a few breaths. *(Pause)*
- Take your awareness to the invisible energy field surrounding you and visualise it drawing in close around your physical body. *(Pause)*
- Take your awareness to the area just above your crown and see a sphere of light sitting here.
- Imagine that sphere of light shrinking in size until it's tiny, then sinking down through the crown of your head.

- See it slowly descending down past the brow. *(Pause)*
- Into the throat. *(Pause)*
- Then following the line of the spine, down, through your body, towards your heart area. *(Pause)*
- Down to your solar plexus. *(Pause)*
- Through the abdominal area. *(Pause)*
- To the base of your spine. *(Pause)*
- Now visualise the sphere of energy either leaving through the base of your spine, or dividing in two and sinking down through your legs and leaving through the soles of your feet.
- Feel this energy leaving you and connecting with the earth.
- Have a sense of downward movement, deep in to the earth. *(Pause)*
- Become more aware of your feet and your physical body.
- Let us take a moment to thank our Spirit Guides, Angels and loved ones in Spirit for their presence, protection and wisdom whilst we've been working. Knowing that they will always be on hand should we need to call on them. *(Pause)*
- **Now bring your awareness back to your physical body, the chair you are sitting on and your contact with the floor.**
- **Begin to bring some movement back in to your fingers and toes.**
- **In your own time opening your eyes, fully awake and aware and in the physical world.**

(Watch for them starting to wriggle fingers and toes and keep an eye on anyone who doesn't do this. If a member of the group appears not to want to come back to the room simply repeat the last three points, in bold, but raising your voice so that it said slightly louder and firmer. Repeat a third time if necessary moving over to the person and at the end just saying their name and asking that they come back into the room now, placing a hand gently on their shoulder.)

Check to ensure that everyone feels grounded before you finish the session. If not, get them to walk around for a little while. Stamping your feet or jumping up and down helps to bring you back to the physical world. If these don't do the trick, you can ground your energy very readily by eating a small amount of food such as a biscuit.

OTHER THINGS TO TRY:
- Crystals that may help with past life work are amethyst, carnelian, lapis lazuli, double terminated quartz, rutilated quartz, merlinite, herkimer diamonds and purple sheen obsidian.
- Using frankincense essential oil in a burner is also thought to help induce past life memories and visions.
- Working with another person, make an energetic connection with them, holding hands or placing your hands on their shoulders works well. Ask to receive impressions or information about their most relevant past life experience and then see what comes to you. Give feedback, and if appropriate discuss whether this is relevant to their current situation.
- Alternatively all members of the group can focus on one person at a time. The subject can sit in the centre of the group, one person should state their intention and then each person can make notes on information that they receive intuitively. You may even wish to draw pictures, shapes or images that come to mind. This can be discussed and compared with the subject after the exercise. Bear in mind that with a number of people involved, various different past lives may be picked up on.

AND ANOTHER THING...
- When you have some information about a past life, you may want to research its validity if you can. Some lives are easier to track down than others but it can be fascinating. Don't be disappointed if you can't track down your past life though. As mentioned before, it's the message that you get and how you use it that counts.

- Consider the information that you have and how it is relevant to your current life. How can it help you? What does it help to explain or highlight for you? Keep a note of it in your journal if you have one.
- Connecting with people - Have you ever met someone and just clicked? Felt like you'd known each other forever? Been so comfortable in each other's company that you can't imagine not having known them all of your life? (Or is that for all of your lives?) Some believe that these are people in your 'soul group', who you've re-incarnated with over and over. Because of this you recognise something within each other immediately. Next time you have an experience like this, why not meditate on it and see what information you can find out, perhaps with the help of your spirit guides.
- Keeping a journal can help with past life stories and experiences. Keep a record of any such encounters, meditations and dreams to help identify any patterns or links which may reveal information about your past lives and current situations.
- You may wish to consult a respected and experienced past life therapist or hypnotherapist specialising in this subject.
- This book is one to try: How to Uncover Your Past Lives - Ted Andrews

FOR DISCUSSION

- What have we got from this lesson? Best bits? Tricky bits?
- Key Concepts - how are we getting on with patience, acceptance, faith?
- Healing - feedback from those in the healing book? Success stories?
- Manifestation - Feedback? Success? New projects?

Next Time...

The next lesson will be covering TRANCE MEDIUMSHIP.
You will need to arrange for the following tools to be brought along:
- none required

Extra tools if you want to do 'other things to try':
- Collection of crystals such as blue apatite, fire agate, gold or yellow calcite, opal aura quartz and sodalite to assist in a achieving a deeper meditative state.
- A recording / CD of a single drum beat, or a heartbeat.

LESSON ELEVEN
TRANCE MEDIUMSHIP

PREPARATION
Well in advance of your meeting ensure that you have all of the tools that you require for this lesson. If not, find out if another group member has access to what you need.

Regular tools:
- Healing book
- Pens and pencils
- Paper
- Candles & matches if desired
- Box of tissues

Tools for this lesson:
- Photocopy the required number of Handout 9 - Trance mediumship scripts.

Extra tools if you want to do 'other things to try':
- Collection of crystals such as blue apatite, fire agate, gold or yellow calcite, opal aura quartz and sodalite to assist in a achieving a deeper meditative state.
- A recording / CD of a single drum beat, or a heartbeat.

On the day of the meeting ensure that the room is prepared:
Are there enough seats for everyone and enough room for the work you are about to undertake?
Open the windows or burn some incense to freshen the air.
Cleanse the area.
Gather the required tools together. Call and remind anyone who has promised to bring something.
Set out some water and glasses.
Prepare some relaxing background music.
Ensure that the room isn't too cold or too warm.
Ensure that you're not going to be interrupted. Unplugging the phone and turning off mobiles are good ideas.

At the beginning of the meeting:
As people arrive ask them to add the names of anyone they know who needs some healing to the Healing Book. Remember that you don't need to put their full names and private information, first names, initials or nicknames will suffice. Whoever you intend to send the healing to, it will reach.

Once everyone has arrived and is comfortable then you can start.
Work your way through the script and exercises for this lesson as detailed on the following pages.

Read the following scripts out loud to the group. It's a time of meditation so keep your voice calm and relaxed, reading in a fairly slow and controlled manner. Instructions are in brackets and italics.

RELAXATION
- Ensure you're sitting or lying comfortably.
- Take your awareness to your hands, make a tight fist, hold for a count of 3, 2, 1, and release.
- Tense your lower arms, hold for 3, 2, 1, and release.
- Tense your upper arms, hold for 3, 2, 1, and release.
- Tense your shoulders, lifting them up towards your ears, hold for 3, 2, 1, and release.
- Take your awareness to your neck: pull your chin toward chest but keep it from touching chest, hold for 3, 2, 1, and then relax.
- Take your awareness to your lower face and jaw, bite hard and pull back the corners of your mouth, hold for 3, 2, 1, and then relax.
- Screw your eyes up and wrinkle your nose, hold for 3, 2, 1, and then relax.
- Move your awareness to your forehead, lift your eyebrows as high as possible, hold for 3, 2, 1, and then relax.
- Take your awareness to your upper torso, pull your shoulder blades together hold for 3, 2, 1, and then release.
- Tense your stomach muscles, pulling your bellybutton towards your spine, hold for 3, 2, 1, and then release.
- Taking your awareness to your legs tense your thigh muscles, hold for 3, 2, 1, and then release.
- Pull your toes towards your head tensing your calf muscles, hold for 3, 2, 1, and then release.
- Take your awareness to your feet, point and curl your toes downwards, hold for 3, 2, 1, and then release.
- Tense your whole body at once, hands, arms, face, neck, chest, stomach, thighs, calves and feet, screw your eyes up, hold for 3, 2, 1, and completely release.
- Now take your awareness to your breathing, preferably through your nose as this is more relaxing.
- Ensure that you're breathing slowly and deeply.
- As you inhale, your abdomen will gently rise. And as you exhale it will fall.
- If your mind drifts or you lose track during this exercise bring your attention back to refocus on your breathing.
- Take a long, slow, deep inhalation for a count of 1 - 2 - 3 - 4, hold for 1- 2 and exhale for 1 - 2 - 3 - 4.
- In 2 3 4, Hold (pause), Out 2 3 4
- In 2 3 4, Hold (pause), Out 2 3 4
- In 2 3 4, Hold (pause), Out 2 3 4
- In 2 3 4, Hold (pause), Out 2 3 4
- In 2 3 4, Hold (pause), Out 2 3 4
- Continue breathing slowly and deeply.
- *(Move on to the script below.)*

OPENING & PROTECTION
- Let us take a moment to close our eyes and calm our minds.
- Concentrate on your breathing, allowing the breath to become deeper and slower.

(Pause to allow everyone to take a couple of breaths in and out)

- Let us all mentally ask our Spirit Guides and Angels to draw close and create a circle around our own.
- We let it be known that we are happy to work with Spirit and that we only work in love and light. We ask that anyone from the spirit world who wishes to contact us only does so in love and light and with the highest intentions.
- We ask for your protection, guidance and wisdom as we blend our world with yours. *(Pause)*
- Let us blend and harmonise our energies as we sit together in circle.
- Let us send out a note of harmony to the person on our left. Visualise this as a pale pink mist coming from your heart area and moving towards the heart of the person sitting on your left. *(Pause)*
- As you continue to do this, become aware of receiving the same loving energy from the right.
- As we send and receive this energy, be aware of any changes in the atmosphere within the circle. *(Pause)*
- Have a sense of oneness with the group. *(Pause)*

- Now bring your attention back to yourself and the centre of your being, the lower abdominal area.
- Focus on your breathing; become aware of the rise and fall of your abdomen. As you inhale it will gently rise and as you exhale it will fall. *(Pause to allow everyone to take a few breaths in and out)*
- Have a sense of warmth here and in your mind's eye allow a symbol or shape to form. Imagine that this symbol or shape is sitting at and represents your centre. It may be a simple glow of light, a flame or a flower.
- With each in-breath visualise your symbol becoming larger, stronger or more open whichever is appropriate.
- With each out-breath, imagine that you are exhaling any negativity left from your day, or worries that you may have. *(Pause to allow everyone to take a few breaths in and out)*
- Now take your awareness to the soles of your feet, feeling their contact with the floor. Visualise lines of energy extending out from your feet and down into the ground. In your mind's eye, see these lines of energy as roots extending deep into the earth.
- Earth energy also travels back up through these roots revitalising and nourishing you.
- See this energy entering through the soles of your feet and travelling up through your legs to the base of your spine.
- At the base of the spine imagine that the energy becomes a sphere of deep red mist or light, as you visualise it, it becomes more vibrant in colour. *(Pause)*
- From this point a beam of energy leaves the red sphere and travels up towards the sacral area, just below the belly button. Here it forms a sphere of vibrant orange mist or light. As you focus on it, it becomes stronger in colour. *(Pause)*
- Gradually a beam of energy leaves the orange sphere and travels up towards the solar plexus, where it forms a sphere of clear yellow. With each breath, this yellow becomes stronger and brighter. *(Pause)*
- Once more a beam of energy leaves this sphere and continues its journey up to the heart area. Here a sphere of mist or light begins to form, which you may see as either green or pink. Focus on this area for a few breaths allowing the energy to grow stronger and clearer and to expand. *(Pause)*
- Gradually a beam of energy leaves the heart area and moves upwards to the throat. Here it forms a sphere of clear blue. Once more, as you focus on this area, allow the colour to expand and increase in strength. *(Pause)*
- Now, visualise a strand of energy leaving the throat area and linking with the third eye area, just between and slightly above the eyes. Here energy will begin to form as before. You may see this energy as either a rich indigo or violet, whichever you prefer. Concentrate on this energy and visualise it increasing in strength. *(Pause)*
- Again, a beam of light extends upwards from this area moving to the crown. As it does so, become aware of another beam of energy coming down from above to meet the first. As they meet at the crown a sphere of pure energy begins to form. You may see this energy as either violet or pure white light. This connects you with the higher realms of Spirit.
- As you hold this vision for a few breaths the light grows and strengthens. And as it does so, the beautiful pure light begins to overflow down and around you, surrounding you in its wonderful energy. It fills your aura, cleansing, balancing and strengthening it. You feel safe and comfortable. You feel relaxed and light. *(Longer pause before moving on to the script below.)*

CONSCIOUS CONNECTION

- Take your awareness back to the soles of your feet, feeling their contact with the floor. Visualise lines of energy extending out from your feet and down into the ground.
- In your mind's eye, see these lines of energy as roots extending deep into the earth. Maintain this feeling of energy at the feet and be aware of earth energy moving up through these roots entering your energy system, revitalising and nourishing you. It may help to see them beginning to glow with light as the energy travels up from the earth and enters your energy system.

- Now take your awareness to the crown of your head.
- Imagine that you are being suspended by a piece of string from this point. The piece of string hangs from a point far above you, so far above you that you are unable to see its origin.
- You should have a sense of being lifted upwards.
- In your mind's eye, the string is a brilliant white light, a magical connection with higher realms. Its brilliance and its power connects with and enters into your energy system.
- You can sense this energy entering your energy system through your crown chakra. It feels amazingly empowering.

HEALING

- Slowly open your eyes and join hands with those sitting to either side of you. This increases the flow of healing energy.
- We know that our Guides, Angels and loved ones in Spirit have come forward and that they surround us with their healing energies. We ask them to help us as we send out our healing today. *(Pause)*
- Visualise a pool of brilliant white light forming and growing in the middle of our circle. *(Pause)*
- This is a pool of healing energy from which we can all draw when we need to. Know that this universal healing energy will find its way to all of those for whom we request healing.
- We ask for healing for each of us here, for our minds, bodies and spirit.

(If there are absent members: We ask for healing for the members of our group who cannot be with us today.)

- We ask for healing for all of those on our Absent Healing List. Take a moment to visualise them standing in the healing pool.
- I would also like to ask for special healing for _____

(Mention anyone else that you feel healing is really important for today. Gently squeeze the hand of the person to your left to indicate that it's their turn. Let everyone have a turn at saying this part before continuing with the script.)

- We send our healing thoughts to Mother Earth and to the plant and animal kingdom. Thank you.
- Release your hands but keep your eyes closed so that you remain relaxed and peaceful as we go in to our meditation.

THEORY: TRANCE MEDIUMSHIP

The following 'theory' section should be read aloud to the group. You may want to get others to join in and take it in turns to read.

Trance mediumship is when a medium goes in to a trance and allows a spirit to 'overshadow' or 'overlay' their energy. The spirit effectively takes up the same physical space as the medium but at a higher vibratory rate. The medium can, if they wish, hand over partial control of their body to the spirit allowing them to speak through them. It causes their speech to change, by tone, accent, speed, vocabulary etc. Working in this way isn't a necessary requirement of being a medium, it's just another method for spirit communication. Working in a light to medium trance will allow the gap to remain whereby the medium is aware of the spirit and able to pass on their message without being completely overshadowed. Guides will help to facilitate this. Trance mediumship (often called channelling) is not a possession. Trance mediumship is done with the consent of the medium and on the understanding that they're sharing the experience with the person in spirit.

Observers of a medium in trance, even light trance, may notice changes in their physical appearance. For example, some of things we've observed in others who are in trance are thickening of the features, the shape of the face altering, different hair style and colour, a change in height or build. This is the spirit making their presence known by overshadowing the medium (also known as transfiguration). These changes are often validated by information provided by the trancing medium about the spirit they're channelling.

Light / Medium trance is quite hard to describe; what you hear, or see, in your mind's eye or from the world around you may be hard to recall afterwards. If you do hear anything around you, for example a phone or doorbell, it will seem distant (although if there was an emergency your body would soon react). You may start to lose a sense of feeling in parts of your body, become more sensitive to atmospheric pressure and temperature changes around you and if someone was to move your arm you really wouldn't be bothered about moving it back again.

In a deeper trance you can open your eyes without affecting the state that you're in. If you wanted to you would be able to recall lost memories and will probably experience feelings of lightness, floating or flying. You can stimulate dreams and visions, while in this state, or request that they come to you in your sleep later on. There can be varying degrees of consciousness, a lowering of the body's temperature, slow deep steady breathing and a slower heart rate. When in this state for mediumship or channelling the person may well appear to have left their body entirely, speak in another accent and in a voice that isn't their own.

At this stage in your development we would advise that it is only appropriate to work in a light / medium trance and only then if you have the agreement of all other members of your group. You may in fact find that some of your group will naturally progress into a light / medium trance as a result of deeper meditation exercises. Remember, as always that you're fully in control of any such occurrences. It's important that at least two of you remain in a fully conscious state at all times if your group is attempting any trance work.

Being able to attain and control these deeper altered states of consciousness takes regular mental and physical training over time. It's no different to any other form of training, such as running marathons, or weightlifting. Regular practise over time allows you to improve, less practise or ceasing completely will cause your abilities to wane.

This type of work is really an extension of deep meditation combined with continued practice at connecting with spirit. It can take years. Lack of self-confidence and any level of fear about trance work will put a huge obstacle in your path. If you're not ready for this work keep going with other things until you are. Be honest with yourself. Act as a facilitator for others for a while until you feel okay with it. Then work with those same people but swap roles, this will ensure that you have absolute trust in them.

Crystals that may help to facilitate trance work are apatite and yellow labradorite.

Important points before you start
- Work in a quiet place where you won't be disturbed.
- Ensure phones are turned off or unplugged. It can be quite a jolt and very disconcerting for anyone in trance to be disturbed from it.
- Don't attempt trance work if you are tired or unwell. Some people find this type of work emotionally and / or physically draining.
- Work with a group of people: one to scribe for you as you will often not be able to recall the messages that you give; At least one other to watch over you, ask questions of anyone who makes contact through you and talk you back into the room should they feel it necessary using the closing & grounding stage (this is the facilitator); and others who will lend their energy to the process. At the very least work with a facilitator; do not attempt this on your own.
- Be aware of any feelings or sensations that you have and where in your body they are focussed, for example around a particular chakra.
- You may find that you have to cough or clear your throat or you may get a tickly throat. Have a glass of water to hand.
- Trust your guides to help you with this work as they understand the process of trance work even if you don't.

Discuss any personal experiences or thoughts on the subject (but keep any eye on the time).

PRACTICAL WORK
Read out each exercise, one at a time to the group so that you are all clear as to what you are doing, then allocate a time to complete the exercise.

Read out: There are two ways you can go through the practical exercises: The first is to work in pairs. One partner will go into trance while the other interviews them. One of the interviewers will also act as the overall facilitator, reading out the scripts from this workbook - or operating the audio version. The second way (which you may prefer once you have more experience) is that there is just one (possibly two) of the group who 'stays back'. Quite often we find there are only one or two members who actually go into trance anyway; the others are in deep meditation but must still be observed for signs of stress or discomfort. The facilitators in this case focus primarily on the one(s) that 'go', asking them questions and making notes. Decide as a group how you would like to proceed.

The following practical exercises will take you through a staged process preparing for trance. You can either use our audio CD/MP3 downloads for stages 1 to 6 or a facilitator can read them out taking the participants through the process. The interviewers must be proactive and observant at stage 7. Read through the stages before you start to familiarise yourself with the process. Ensure that each interviewer has a copy of Handout 9 - 'Trance mediumship script' so that they know what sort of questions to ask. Make sure everyone is sitting or laying comfortable before you start.

Stage 1 - Protection Request
- Take a moment to close your eyes and calm your mind.
- Concentrate on your breathing, allowing the breath to become deeper and slower.
- Mentally ask your spirit guides and angels to draw close and offer their assistance using the following script:

"I call upon my spirit guides, angels and loved ones in spirit to draw close to me and to create a circle of protection around me ensuring that I am safe and protected at all times and on all levels, while I work and afterwards. I ask for your protection, guidance and wisdom. I am happy to work with guidance from the spirit world and to communicate with them, but I do so only in love and light and with the highest intentions. I ask that anyone from the spirit world who wishes to assist or communicate does so with the same intentions, and that my guides and angels enforce this on my behalf."
- *(Move straight on to the next stage.)*

Stage 2 - Simple Physical Relaxation
- Take your awareness to your hands, make a tight fist, hold for a count of three and release.
- Tense your lower arms, hold for three, and release.
- Tense your upper arms, hold for three, and release.
- Tense your shoulders, lifting them up towards your ears, hold for three, and release.
- Take your awareness to your neck: pull your chin toward chest but keep it from touching chest, hold for three and then relax.
- Take your awareness to your lower face and jaw, bite hard and pull back the corners of your mouth hold for three and then relax.
- Screw your eyes up and wrinkle your nose, hold for three and then relax.
- Move your awareness to your forehead, lift your eyebrows as high as possible, hold for three and then relax.
- Take your awareness to your upper torso, pull your shoulder blades together hold for three and then release.
- Tense your stomach muscles, pulling your bellybutton towards your spine, hold for three and then release.
- Taking your awareness to your legs tense your thigh muscles, hold for three and then release.
- Pull your toes toward head tensing your calf muscles hold for three and then release.

- Taking your awareness to your feet, point and curl your toes downwards, hold for three and then release.
- Tense your whole body at once, hands, arms, face, neck, chest, stomach, thighs, calves and feet, screw your eyes up, hold for three, two, one, and completely release.
- *(Move straight on to the next stage.)*

Stage 3 - The Breath
- Take your awareness to your breathing, preferably through your nose, as this is more relaxing.
- Ensure that you are breathing slowly and deeply.
- As you inhale, your abdomen will gently rise. And as you exhale it will fall.
- If your mind drifts or you lose track during this exercise bring your attention back to refocus on your breathing.
- Take a long, slow, deep inhalation for a count of 4 - 3 - 2 - 1, hold for 1- 2 and exhale for 4 - 3 - 2 - 1.
- In 2 3 4, Hold (pause), Out 2 3 4
- In 2 3 4, Hold (pause), Out 2 3 4
- In 2 3 4, Hold (pause), Out 2 3 4
- In 2 3 4, Hold (pause), Out 2 3 4
- In 2 3 4, Hold (pause), Out 2 3 4
- Continue breathing slowly and deeply. *(Pause for a few breaths.)*
- *(Move straight on to the next stage.)*

Stage 4 - Elevating Your Energy
- Take your awareness to your feet and to the energy entering through your soles; imagine it travelling up through your legs to the base of your spine.
- At the base of the spine imagine that the energy becomes a sphere of deep red mist or light. As you visualise it, it becomes more vibrant in colour.
- From this point a beam of energy leaves the red sphere and travels up towards the sacral area, just below the belly button. Here it forms a sphere of vibrant orange mist or light. As you focus on it, it becomes stronger in colour.
- Gradually, a beam of energy leaves the orange sphere and travels up towards the solar plexus, where it forms a sphere of clear yellow. With each breath, this yellow becomes stronger and brighter.
- Once more a beam of energy leaves this sphere and continues its journey up to the heart area. Here a sphere of mist or light begins to form, which you may see as either green or pink. Focus on this area for a few breaths allowing the energy to grow stronger and clearer. It may begin to expand.
- Gradually, a beam of energy leaves the heart area and moves upwards to the throat. Here it forms a sphere of clear blue. Once more, as you focus on this area, allow the colour to expand and increase in strength.
- Now, visualise a strand of energy leaving the throat area and linking with the third eye area, just between and slightly above the eyes. Here energy will begin to form as before. You may see this energy as either a rich indigo or violet, whichever you prefer. Concentrate on this energy and visualise it increasing in strength and energy.
- Again, a beam of light extends upwards from this area moving up to the crown. As it does so, become aware of a beam of energy coming down from high above to meet the first at the crown, A sphere of pure energy begins to form in this area. You may see this energy as either violet or pure white light. This connects you with the higher realms of spirit.
- *(Move straight on to the next stage.)*

Stage 5 - Expanding Your Awareness
- As you hold this vision for a few breaths the light grows and strengthens. The sphere becomes larger and brighter and as it does so, the beautiful pure light begins to overflow down and around you, sur-

- rounding you in this wonderful energy.
  - It fills your aura, cleansing, balancing and strengthening it. The light around your physical body grows stronger and brighter. It extends out in all directions around you.
  - See in your mind's eye how far it extends.
  - Now take a deep slow breath in and as you slowly exhale, imagine your aura expanding further as though you're blowing it up like a balloon but maintaining its strength and brightness.
  - Continue to breathe in this way to expand your energy further. As you do so, you feel safe and comfortable. You feel relaxed and light.
  - *(Move straight on to the next stage.)*

Stage 6 - Visualisation
- In your mind's eye allow an image of one or more candles to form. Each candle is lit and gives off a gentle glow. *(Pause)*
- The candlelight is soothing and as its energy envelops you, you have a sense of comfort and wellbeing.
- You're safe and content. *(Pause)*
- Your aura and body are one, and they feel as though the same gentle glowing energy of the candle is filling them. You are becoming lighter and lighter. *(Pause)*

Stage 7 - For The Facilitator
- Be aware of any subtle changes, overshadowing, temperature or pressure changes in the room. Usually the person in trance will be sitting very still, you'll be able to see that they're in a deep meditative state. It's important that you speak to them very gently and quietly. Begin by asking if they have someone with them or working through them and allow them time to answer (responses are often slower than normal). Ask questions to establish who the person is, what their message is, and who it's for, also who in the group they are connected to and how. The person in trance will most likely answer as themselves (especially in the beginning) and tell you about the person who is with them. (See Handout 9 - example trance script a). This is light trance. With practice they may eventually go into deep trance and become a channel for the person in spirit, in which case they will answer in the first person. If this is the case change your language slightly so that you are asking direct questions (see Handout 9 - example trance script b). Ensure that you or someone else present makes notes on the information that's given.
- If at any point you feel uncomfortable with the messages, or the situation, or your trancing medium appears to be uncomfortable or distressed, bring your medium back to the room by calmly but firmly saying the following:

"Name of medium, it's time to ask spirit to leave you now. Your spirit guide is close and is assisting you. Name, step forward now please and bring your awareness back to the room. Step forward now. Bring your awareness back to your physical body, the chair you are sitting on and your contact with the floor. Begin to bring some movement back in to your fingers and toes. In your own time opening your eyes, fully awake and aware and in the physical world."

- Then use the closing & grounding technique to bring them back fully to the room before moving on to step 8.
- Once they have finished delivering their message you will probably be aware of a subtle change indicating that the person in spirit is leaving the person in trance. Once finished you may need to talk them back to the room using the closing & grounding script (although we would recommend closing & grounding again after the next stage.

Stage 8 - Discuss
Refer to the notes and discuss your experiences, see if anyone in the group can take the messages.

CLOSING & GROUNDING
Once you have completed the exercises everyone should sit comfortably and complete the following meditation to close and ground their energy. Read out the following:
- Sit in a comfortable position and close your eyes.
- Bring your attention to your breathing and focus on this for a few breaths. *(Pause)*
- Take your awareness to the invisible energy field surrounding you and visualise it drawing in close around your physical body. *(Pause)*
- Take your awareness to the area just above your crown and see a sphere of light sitting here.
- Imagine that sphere of light shrinking in size until it's tiny, then sinking down through the crown of your head.
- See it slowly descending down past the brow. *(Pause)*
- Into the throat. *(Pause)*
- Then following the line of the spine, down, through your body, towards your heart area. *(Pause)*
- Down to your solar plexus. *(Pause)*
- Through the abdominal area. *(Pause)*
- To the base of your spine. *(Pause)*
- Now visualise the sphere of energy either leaving through the base of your spine, or dividing in two and sinking down through your legs and leaving through the soles of your feet.
- Feel this energy leaving you and connecting with the earth.
- Have a sense of downward movement, deep in to the earth. *(Pause)*
- Become more aware of your feet and your physical body.
- Let us take a moment to thank our Spirit Guides, Angels and loved ones in Spirit for their presence, protection and wisdom whilst we've been working. Knowing that they will always be on hand should we need to call on them. *(Pause)*
- **Now bring your awareness back to your physical body, the chair you are sitting on and your contact with the floor.**
- **Begin to bring some movement back in to your fingers and toes.**
- **In your own time opening your eyes, fully awake and aware and in the physical world.**

(Watch for them starting to wriggle fingers and toes and keep an eye on anyone who doesn't do this. If a member of the group appears not to want to come back to the room simply repeat the last three points, in bold, but raising your voice so that it said slightly louder and firmer. Repeat a third time if necessary moving over to the person and at the end just saying their name and asking that they come back into the room now, placing a hand gently on their shoulder.)

Check to ensure that everyone feels grounded before you finish the session. If not, get them to walk around for a little while. Stamping your feet or jumping up and down helps to bring you back to the physical world. If these don't do the trick, you can ground your energy very readily by eating a small amount of food such as a biscuit.

OTHER THINGS TO TRY:
To help achieve an altered state of consciousness:
Any of the techniques mentioned in our chapter on deeper meditation will assist in this activity. Such as:
- Using healing energy: Receive healing energy from an individual or group while meditating to encourage a deeper meditative state.
- Black Out: Try meditating in complete darkness.
- In a beat: Meditate to a recording of a simple drum beat or heartbeat. Have it playing while you work through a physical relaxation and breathing exercise then simply focus your attention on the beat for as long as you wish.
- Bang it out: Try drumming out a simple rhythm on a small drum over and over again with your

hands - if you have enough drums for each person in the group to do this it's very powerful. Go past the boredom point and just keep going. Allow your consious mind to be taken out of the equation. You will go in to a state of deep meditation.

To help connect and communicate with spirit:
- When in a trance-like state, if you feel as though you want to speak, or you get a strong sense of energy building up in your throat area (sometimes this can feel like a lump in your throat or make you want to cough) start to speak in your own voice, say whatever comes in to your head. This may be a message from spirit, or it may encourage one to come through. With experience it can also encourage complete overshadowing whereby the spirit uses you to speak in something like their own voice. Don't worry though, this will only happen when you're ready and allow it to.
- You could try holding an object belonging to someone in spirit while working in this way, in an attempt to tune in to their energies and help them to bring a message to a loved one in the physical world.

AND ANOTHER THING...
- It's simply a case of keeping practising with the right people and in a safe environment. Don't practise every day to begin with, but having a go on a regular basis is advised.
- Rhythmic dancing to the point of exhaustion, or chanting can also be worth a try to induce trance.

FOR DISCUSSION
- What have we got from this lesson? Best bits? Tricky bits?
- Key Concepts - how are we getting on with patience, acceptance, faith?
- Healing - feedback from those in the healing book? Success stories?
- Manifestation - Feedback? Success? New projects?

Next Time...
The next lesson will be covering the OUT OF BODY EXPERIENCES.

You will need to arrange for the following tools to be brought along:
- One or more candle in a sturdy holder (and matches).

LESSON TWELVE
OUT OF BODY EXPERIENCES

PREPARATION
Well in advance of your meeting ensure that you have all of the tools that you require for this lesson. If not, find out if another group member has access to what you need.

Regular tools:
- Healing book
- Pens and pencils
- Paper
- Candles & matches if desired
- Box of tissues

Tools for this lesson:
- One or more candle in a sturdy holder (and matches).

On the day of the meeting ensure that the room is prepared:
Are there enough seats for everyone and enough room for the work you are about to undertake?
Open the windows or burn some incense to freshen the air.
Cleanse the area.
Gather the required tools together. Call and remind anyone who has promised to bring something.
Set out some water and glasses.
Prepare some relaxing background music.
Ensure that the room isn't too cold or too warm.
Ensure that you're not going to be interrupted. Unplugging the phone and turning off mobiles are good ideas.

At the beginning of the meeting:
As people arrive ask them to add the names of anyone they know who needs some healing to the Healing Book. Remember that you don't need to put their full names and private information, first names, initials or nicknames will suffice. Whoever you intend to send the healing to, it will reach.

Once everyone has arrived and is comfortable then you can start.
Work your way through the script and exercises for this lesson as detailed on the following pages.

Read the following scripts out loud to the group. It's a time of meditation so keep your voice calm and relaxed, reading in a fairly slow and controlled manner. Instructions are in brackets and italics.

RELAXATION
- Ensure you're sitting or lying comfortably.
- Take your awareness to your hands, make a tight fist, hold for a count of 3, 2, 1, and release.
- Tense your lower arms, hold for 3, 2, 1, and release.
- Tense your upper arms, hold for 3, 2, 1, and release.
- Tense your shoulders, lifting them up towards your ears, hold for 3, 2, 1, and release.
- Take your awareness to your neck: pull your chin toward chest but keep it from touching chest, hold

- for 3, 2, 1, and then relax.
- Take your awareness to your lower face and jaw, bite hard and pull back the corners of your mouth, hold for 3, 2, 1, and then relax.
- Screw your eyes up and wrinkle your nose, hold for 3, 2, 1, and then relax.
- Move your awareness to your forehead, lift your eyebrows as high as possible, hold for 3, 2, 1, and then relax.
- Take your awareness to your upper torso, pull your shoulder blades together hold for 3, 2, 1, and then release.
- Tense your stomach muscles, pulling your bellybutton towards your spine, hold for 3, 2, 1, and then release.
- Taking your awareness to your legs tense your thigh muscles, hold for 3, 2, 1, and then release.
- Pull your toes towards your head tensing your calf muscles, hold for 3, 2, 1, and then release.
- Take your awareness to your feet, point and curl your toes downwards, hold for 3, 2, 1, and then release.
- Tense your whole body at once, hands, arms, face, neck, chest, stomach, thighs, calves and feet, screw your eyes up, hold for 3, 2, 1, and completely release.
- Now take your awareness to your breathing, preferably through your nose as this is more relaxing.
- Ensure that you're breathing slowly and deeply.
- As you inhale, your abdomen will gently rise. And as you exhale it will fall.
- If your mind drifts or you lose track during this exercise bring your attention back to refocus on your breathing.
- Take a long, slow, deep inhalation for a count of 1 - 2 - 3 - 4, hold for 1- 2 and exhale for 1 - 2 - 3 - 4.
- In 2 3 4, Hold (pause), Out 2 3 4
- In 2 3 4, Hold (pause), Out 2 3 4
- In 2 3 4, Hold (pause), Out 2 3 4
- In 2 3 4, Hold (pause), Out 2 3 4
- In 2 3 4, Hold (pause), Out 2 3 4
- Continue breathing slowly and deeply.
- *(Move on to the script below.)*

OPENING & PROTECTION
- Let us take a moment to close our eyes and calm our minds.
- Concentrate on your breathing, allowing the breath to become deeper and slower.

(Pause to allow everyone to take a couple of breaths in and out)

- Let us all mentally ask our Spirit Guides and Angels to draw close and create a circle around our own.
- We let it be known that we are happy to work with Spirit and that we only work in love and light. We ask that anyone from the spirit world who wishes to contact us only does so in love and light and with the highest intentions.
- We ask for your protection, guidance and wisdom as we blend our world with yours. *(Pause)*
- Let us blend and harmonise our energies as we sit together in circle.
- Let us send out a note of harmony to the person on our left. Visualise this as a pale pink mist coming from your heart area and moving towards the heart of the person sitting on your left. *(Pause)*
- As you continue to do this, become aware of receiving the same loving energy from the right.
- As we send and receive this energy, be aware of any changes in the atmosphere within the circle. *(Pause)*
- Have a sense of oneness with the group. *(Pause)*
- Now bring your attention back to yourself and the centre of your being, the lower abdominal area.
- Focus on your breathing; become aware of the rise and fall of your abdomen. As you inhale it will gently rise and as you exhale it will fall. *(Pause to allow everyone to take a few breaths in and out)*
- Have a sense of warmth here and in your mind's eye allow a symbol or shape to form. Imagine that this symbol or shape is sitting at and represents your centre. It may be a simple glow of light, a flame or a flower.
- With each in-breath visualise your symbol becoming larger, stronger or more open whichever is appropriate.

- With each out-breath, imagine that you are exhaling any negativity left from your day, or worries that you may have. *(Pause to allow everyone to take a few breaths in and out)*
- Now take your awareness to the soles of your feet, feeling their contact with the floor. Visualise lines of energy extending out from your feet and down into the ground. In your mind's eye, see these lines of energy as roots extending deep into the earth.
- Earth energy also travels back up through these roots revitalising and nourishing you.
- See this energy entering through the soles of your feet and travelling up through your legs to the base of your spine.
- At the base of the spine imagine that the energy becomes a sphere of deep red mist or light, as you visualise it, it becomes more vibrant in colour. *(Pause)*
- From this point a beam of energy leaves the red sphere and travels up towards the sacral area, just below the belly button. Here it forms a sphere of vibrant orange mist or light. As you focus on it, it becomes stronger in colour. *(Pause)*
- Gradually a beam of energy leaves the orange sphere and travels up towards the solar plexus, where it forms a sphere of clear yellow. With each breath, this yellow becomes stronger and brighter. *(Pause)*
- Once more a beam of energy leaves this sphere and continues its journey up to the heart area. Here a sphere of mist or light begins to form, which you may see as either green or pink. Focus on this area for a few breaths allowing the energy to grow stronger and clearer and to expand. *(Pause)*
- Gradually a beam of energy leaves the heart area and moves upwards to the throat. Here it forms a sphere of clear blue. Once more, as you focus on this area, allow the colour to expand and increase in strength. *(Pause)*
- Now, visualise a strand of energy leaving the throat area and linking with the third eye area, just between and slightly above the eyes. Here energy will begin to form as before. You may see this energy as either a rich indigo or violet, whichever you prefer. Concentrate on this energy and visualise it increasing in strength. *(Pause)*
- Again, a beam of light extends upwards from this area moving to the crown. As it does so, become aware of another beam of energy coming down from above to meet the first. As they meet at the crown a sphere of pure energy begins to form. You may see this energy as either violet or pure white light. This connects you with the higher realms of Spirit.
- As you hold this vision for a few breaths the light grows and strengthens. And as it does so, the beautiful pure light begins to overflow down and around you, surrounding you in its wonderful energy. It fills your aura, cleansing, balancing and strengthening it. You feel safe and comfortable. You feel relaxed and light. *(Longer pause before moving on to the script below.)*

CONSCIOUS CONNECTION
- Take your awareness back to the soles of your feet, feeling their contact with the floor. Visualise lines of energy extending out from your feet and down into the ground.
- In your mind's eye, see these lines of energy as roots extending deep into the earth. Maintain this feeling of energy at the feet and be aware of earth energy moving up through these roots entering your energy system, revitalising and nourishing you. It may help to see them beginning to glow with light as the energy travels up from the earth and enters your energy system.
- Now take your awareness to the crown of your head.
- Imagine that you are being suspended by a piece of string from this point. The piece of string hangs from a point far above you, so far above you that you are unable to see its origin.
- You should have a sense of being lifted upwards.
- In your mind's eye, the string is a brilliant white light, a magical connection with higher realms. Its brilliance and its power connects with and enters into your energy system.
- You can sense this energy entering your energy system through your crown chakra. It feels amazingly empowering.

HEALING
- Slowly open your eyes and join hands with those sitting to either side of you. This increases the flow of healing energy.
- We know that our Guides, Angels and loved ones in Spirit have come forward and that they surround us with their healing energies. We ask them to help us as we send out our healing today. *(Pause)*
- Visualise a pool of brilliant white light forming and growing in the middle of our circle. *(Pause)*
- This is a pool of healing energy from which we can all draw when we need to. Know that this universal healing energy will find its way to all of those for whom we request healing.
- We ask for healing for each of us here, for our minds, bodies and spirit.

(If there are absent members: We ask for healing for the members of our group who cannot be with us today.)
- We ask for healing for all of those on our Absent Healing List. Take a moment to visualise them standing in the healing pool.
- I would also like to ask for special healing for _____

(Mention anyone else that you feel healing is really important for today. Gently squeeze the hand of the person to your left to indicate that it's their turn. Let everyone have a turn at saying this part before continuing with the script.)
- We send our healing thoughts to Mother Earth and to the plant and animal kingdom. Thank you.
- Release your hands but keep your eyes closed so that you remain relaxed and peaceful as we go in to our meditation. *(Brief pause before moving on to the Meditation script.)*

MEDITATION
- Ensure that you're sitting comfortably with your hands on your knees, palms facing upwards.
- Close your eyes.
- Take a deep inhalation, and breathe out slowly. Continue to breathe slowly and deeply.
- During this meditation you will always be safe and protected, you will feel relaxed and comfortable. If, however, there is anything that does make you feel uneasy, or you wish to come back out of the meditation, you can do so at any time by counting backwards from 3 to 1 and taking a deep breath in and out. You can then bring your awareness back to the physical body, particularly your feet and open your eyes.
- For now though, continue to breathe slowly and deeply, your body feels relaxed and your mind is clear.
- As you breathe images may begin to form in your mind's eye. Don't try to manipulate or analyse them, simply observe them. If you do not automatically see these images, simply imagine or sense them.
- Ahead of you lies a staircase or series of ten steps. Move towards them. At the bottom you can see a doorway. We're going to slowly go down these steps towards the door feeling safe and confident at all times. So moving down the steps on my count:
- 10, 9, 8, with each step feeling lighter and lighter.
- 7, 6, 5, feeling calm and peaceful,
- 4, 3, relaxed and light
- 2 and 1, you find yourself standing in front of the door. Reaching out you open the door and as you do so, a wonderful, warm light shines through from the other side, bathing your whole being in its rays.
- As you stand in this light for a few moments, your physical body is warmed through and your energy body is nourished and energised. This gives you a sense of comfort and completeness and offers further protection on your journey. *(Pause for a short while)*
- Today's journey is to help you reveal and begin to explore the astral realm.
- The rays of light subside and you can now see through the doorway to the other side.
- As your eyes adjust to the change in light, colours begin to form shapes. You can see your sanctuary on the other side of the doorway.
- You step through, closing the door behind you

LESSON TWELVE - OUT OF BODY EXPERIENCES

- Moving through your sanctuary you soon discover something new. A spiral staircase leading upwards has appeared here just for you.
- It has a slightly sparkling energy about it and although you cannot see where it leads, you know that it is safe.
- Stepping on to the spiral staircase you begin your ascent, moving slowly up the stairs.
- The stairs lead higher and higher, spiralling ever upwards.
- You feel lighter with each step. You're happy and don't tire.
- You can see above you that there is now a mist or area of cloud surrounding the staircase.
- You reach the cloud and continue to climb the stairs through it, feeling safe and secure at all times.
- You move through the cloud and eventually emerge from it into a dark night sky.
- You appear to be on a rooftop or cliff top but cannot see below you as you're surrounded by gently rolling clouds. It's as though you're walking on clouds.
- The night sky feels as though it is coming down to meet you, it is a vast expanse of deep indigo all around you, scattered with millions of bright sparkling stars.
- You feel as though you could reach out and pluck one of the stars from its dark blanket.
- Take a few moments to explore this celestial world. It's a higher level of existence which you can return to at any time to gain inspiration and wisdom. You may meet others who are journeying here or spirit guides who will show you around. It is a safe place for you to explore. *(Pause for 2-3 minutes)*
- It will shortly be time to return to your sanctuary. Thank any guides that you have communed with.
- Make your way back towards the spiral staircase, or simply ask for it to appear before you.
- Move down the staircase, descending slowly through the clouds.
- Continue moving down from this higher level towards your sanctuary.
- You see your sanctuary begin to come into view and eventually step from the spiral staircase into your special place.
- Make your way towards the doorway to your usual stairs.
- Open the door. Step through closing the door behind you.
- Know that your sanctuary is your own space that you can return to at any time for relaxation, guidance and healing.
- And keeping that sense of calm and wellbeing, it is time to head back up the stairs. So moving back up the stairs on my count,
- 1, 2, 3, breathing slowly and deeply,
- 4, 5, 6, your body is starting to feel heavier
- 7, 8, bringing your awareness back to your physical body,
- 9 and 10, on that top step now and when you're ready, step off the top step.
- **Bringing your awareness completely back to your physical body and this room, your contact with the chair, your feet with the floor. Slowly begin to move your fingers and toes, and in your own time, opening your eyes, fully awake and aware and in the physical world.**

(Watch for them starting to wriggle fingers and toes and keep an eye on anyone who doesn't do this. If a member of the group appears not to want to come back to the room simply repeat the last paragraph, in bold, but raising your voice so that it said slightly louder and firmer. Repeat a third time if necessary moving over to the person and at the end just saying their name and asking that they come back now in to the room, placing your hand gently on their shoulder.)

Spend a few minutes sharing experiences of the meditation. Remember that it's okay if someone fell asleep, could see nothing or did their own thing. If you're keeping a personal journal, you may wish to take some time to record you experience. Don't forget to date the entry.

THEORY: OUT OF BODY EXPERIENCES
The following 'theory' section should be read aloud to the group. You may want to get others to join in and take it in turns to read.

The term 'out of body experience' is generally used interchangeably with 'astral projection' to describe the energetic body leaving the physical body and to travel independently.

However, there are two levels of out of body experiences. The first would be better described as 'etheric projection', where the etheric body is projected away from the physical allowing it to travel in the physical world of its own accord while continuing to be energetically linked. A bit like a living ghost your etheric body can travel in the physical world, or venture backwards and forwards in time, and even into space. It can be experienced involuntarily such as at times of great physical or emotional stress or trauma, the most commonly reported being when the subject is close to death. During such events the subjects etheric body projects away from their physical body typically floating above the activity and observing it or sometimes leaving the area entirely and escaping the scene. This may occur in those who undergo surgery or who are subjected to torture or abuse. Equally etheric projection can occur spontaneously without any known trigger, often at night when the person is falling asleep. Have you ever had that 'jolt' awake as though you've just landed on the bed? Who's to say that isn't you snapping back into your body? Etheric projection can also be deliberate and it's quite possible, with perseverance and regular practice, to teach yourself this skill.

The second, 'astral projection is the projection of your consciousness, possibly via the mental (or causal) energetic body, on to the astral plane of existence.

The astral plane is said to be a level of existence just beyond human perception where the spiritual side of you may exist outside of the body and your rational mind. Here it's believed that you can access universal philosophy, knowledge and wisdom through what are described as the 'akashic records'.

The 'akashic records' are a compilation of all mystical and universal knowledge, including the truth about your own existence and destiny. Sometimes referred to as a library of universal wisdom and knowledge or the 'book of life'.

The presence of different, more subtle planes of existence could be seen as similar to the theory that each individual exists at different vibrational levels as covered in our 'Beginner's Guide', physical, etheric, mental or causal and spiritual. Astral projection therefore could not only propel you beyond the physical plane, but to any of the higher dimensions to gain any amount of wisdom and knowledge. Who's to say that 'alien' visitors aren't higher evolved beings from the higher levels, visiting this physical dimension, or that there aren't dimensions that are more dense than ours existing at a lower vibrational frequency?

Like etheric projection, astral projection can be learnt and developed, or it can be spontaneous. How many times has your mind wandered to... who knows where? And you suddenly snap back to reality knowing the answer to a question or a solution to a problem? Many scientists talk about this need to go 'out of their mind' when seeking solutions to very complex theories.

We're going to focus on etheric projection in more detail in this workbook, although you may find that in doing so, astral projection also occurs. You may also wish to investigate the more advanced subject of astral projection yourself to develop your skills even further.

Why learn astral or etheric projection?
- Maybe it happens to you spontaneously and you would like to control or understand it better, or learn more about the mechanics of it.
- Maybe it's helpful in learning to connect with your true self on all levels as well as possibly gaining an insight into the bigger picture and universal law and wisdom.
- Perhaps you're just intrigued and fancy giving it a try.
- It could be a discipline that you feel would help to strengthen your abilities and have a positive effect on other practices as well as your mental focus.

- It could help you to intimately know and appreciate that you're more than just your physical body. (Although, if you've come this far, we're sure that you have some knowledge of this already.)
- To have a greater understanding that life is more than what you see on a daily basis.
- To raise your level of consciousness and awareness.
- To diminish a fear of death.

Is it dangerous?

Many people from all walks of life, including scientists, and from all civilisations and cultures have experienced out of body experiences (some spontaneously and some deliberately) for many years with no ill effects.

While it's mooted that it's theoretically possible for someone or something to step into your physical body while you're travelling there's no evidence of this having happened and seems very unlikely. We think that any interference with the physical body on any level would cause your etheric body to snap back into it so fast that any 'intruder' simply wouldn't be able to stay. It's your body after all! However, to give yourself more confidence you should always ensure that you set up protection around you before you start attempting to project.

There are commonly held beliefs that you shouldn't touch a person's physical body while they're travelling. It's said that it's highly dangerous to do so and can cause serious damage to their health. While researching this further we haven't found any evidence for this. However, it's reported that as it causes the traveller to return to their body alarmingly quickly, it's an uncomfortable and unpleasant experience that's best avoided.

There are some reports of unpleasant sensations that can occur with etheric projection and it would be unfair of us not to mention them, and how best to address them:

- The initial feeling of the etheric projecting can be unpleasant and take a bit of getting used to.
- 'Etheric slippage' is the etheric energetic body pulling away partially from the physical but not fully projecting. If 'etheric slippage' occurs while you're awake it can cause nausea, disorientation or balance problems. Firm pressure on the top of the head is said to alleviate these symptoms although they will pass. Grounding techniques and crystals will also help.
- Following 'etheric slippage', if the etheric pops back suddenly it can causing a jolting sensation. A lot of people experience this as they're drifting off to sleep.
- It has been reported that following frequent etheric projecting the subjects can experience involuntary unexplained sensations of vibrations through a part or the whole of their body. It isn't a visible shaking but an energetic sensation. Whilst a little disconcerting it will pass. Always ensure that you close and ground your energies after working to help prevent this and if it does occur use grounding techniques and crystals (such as haematite) to bring your vibrations back to a physical level. Receiving healing or other energy work to rebalance your energy may also help.

What is the 'silver cord'?

Many reports and stories involving etheric projection mention a silver cord that connects the physical body with the etheric. It never tangles and is as long as it's needed to be for your journey. Some say that it's attached at the naval of both bodies, some at the 3rd eye of the physical body and base of the brain area of the etheric. The cord is said to be severed only on death. However, many seasoned travellers have never seen a cord. In his in-depth book on the subject 'Discover Astral Projection', J H Brennan muses that perhaps "what is perceived as a cord seems to be no more than the subjective impression of a definite link – and an impression moreover that is not always present" He surmises that it's the link that's important. We suppose that for some, a visual confirmation of this link is required while for others it isn't necessary, therefore they don't see one.

The energetic link or cord from the physical body maintains a degree of tension or a magnet-like pull on the etheric at all times, ensuring your easy and safe return to your physical body. You can re-trace your steps, think yourself back or for a more casual return, follow the cord if you do see one. Physical recalls can also occur, for example if your physical body is hungry or if you think about moving your big toe (as an example) you will swiftly return to your body. You'll still need to close and ground properly though.

How do I move around when projecting?
When E.P.'ing you'll find that you can move in a number of ways, either at regular walking pace, or at a kind of 'fast forward' speed. Alternatively you can focus your attention on a particular place (and time) and you will simply be there. It's quite common to notice that you levitate while travelling, whereby your etheric body floats a few inches above where your physical body would be, but that's not always the case.

TIPS:
- Regular consistent practice if you're serious about the subject – a min of 30 minutes each time.
- Ensure there are no distractions or noises.
- Work in a darkened room.
- If working in a group you will want at least one person to remain behind as a non-traveller to talk you back at a set time.
- Relaxation is paramount as this type of work relies on your ability to 'let go'.
- A desire to travel and a lack of doubt or fear is important otherwise you will hold yourself back.
- Cover yourself with a blanket to ensure your physical body stays warm.
- Crystals to aid out of body experiences are: angelite, amethyst, celestite, blue obsidian, merlinite, and chiastolite. (Helen personally experienced the power of chiastolite which caused an etheric slippage as soon as she picked it up for the first time. It was so intense that she physically stumbled backwards so be careful with it.)

Discuss any personal experiences or thoughts on the subject (but keep any eye on the time).

PRACTICAL WORK
Read out each exercise, one at a time to the group so that you are all clear as to what you are doing, then allocate a time to complete the exercise.

Read out: These exercises will start you off. They are progressive so work through them in order, and then it's a case of regular practice. However, before you begin, ensure that you familiarise yourself with the 'Come back and ground' process just in case you wander off and want to get back or in case you wish to return to the room between exercises. Don't forget to always put protection in place, as always, before you start.

Be aware that you could project during any of these exercises, especially if you have a natural tendency for it. You should be generally experienced enough that you can enjoy the experience, but if you don't, simply use the 'Come back and ground' technique. These exercises should be read out by a non-traveller who can also observe those who're travelling to ensure that they're not experiencing any discomfort. If a couple of people don't feel ready to travel yet they can also assist in observing the travellers. In a large group it's advisable for 2 or 3 people to stay back and observe. Again, if you're overseeing this exercise and suspect that someone isn't enjoying it, use the 'Comeback & ground' technique to bring them back to the room.

You could use our audio CD / MP3 tracks for these exercises but you should still have someone observing, at least while you're learning and until you get used to travelling.

'Come back and ground' technique
- Think about your body, your energy body will return to it immediately.
- Bringing your awareness completely back to your physical body and this room, your contact with the

chair, your contact with the floor.
- Take a deep inhalation, hold and exhale the breath.
- Feel your physical body.
- Take your awareness to your feet, your contact with the floor. Imagine roots extending out from the soles of your feet extending deep down into the earth. These roots are a rich, dark, earthy brown colour. See this colour filling your energy body now. It becomes heavier and heavier.
- **You can feel every part of your physical body now, your legs, stomach, chest, arms, hands, head and neck. Slowly begin to move your fingers and toes, and in your own time, opening your eyes, fully awake and aware and in the physical world.**

(If you are reading this aloud for someone else, watch for them starting to wriggle fingers and toes. If they appear not want to come back to the room simply repeat the last paragraph, in bold, but raising your voice so that it's said slightly louder and firmer. Repeat a third time if necessary moving over to the person and at the end just saying their name and asking that they come back now into the room, placing your hand gently on their shoulder.)

Ensure that everyone is comfortable and warm. they should be sitting or laying down. The read through each stage in turn ansuring that you keep an eye on all the travellers.

Stage 1 - Intention and protection
- Once again we ask our spirit guides to draw close to use and offer their protection. Our intention is to etherically project from out physical bodies. We know that you will protect and watch over us on all levels as we work and thank you for your assistance.

Stage 2
Exercise 1- Simple Physical Relaxation
- Take your awareness to your hands, make a tight fist, hold for a count of three and release.
- Tense your lower arms, hold for three, and release.
- Tense your upper arms, hold for three, and release.
- Tense your shoulders, lifting them up towards your ears, hold for three, and release.
- Take your awareness to your neck: pull your chin toward chest but keep it from touching chest, hold for three and then relax.
- Take your awareness to your lower face and jaw, bite hard and pull back the corners of your mouth, hold for three and then relax.
- Screw your eyes up and wrinkle your nose, hold for three and then relax.
- Move your awareness to your forehead, lift your eyebrows as high as possible, hold for three and then relax.
- Take your awareness to your upper torso, pull your shoulder blades together hold for three and then release.
- Tense your stomach muscles, pulling your bellybutton towards your spine, hold for three and then release.
- Taking your awareness to your legs tense your thigh muscles, hold for three and then release.
- Pull your toes toward head tensing your calf muscles hold for three and then release.
- Taking your awareness to your feet, point and curl your toes downwards, hold for three and then release.
- Tense your whole body at once, hands, arms, face, neck, chest, stomach, thighs, calves and feet, screw your eyes up, hold for three, two, one, and completely release.
- *(Move on to the next exercise.)*

Exercise 2 - Breathing
- Take your awareness to your breathing, preferably through your nose, as this is more relaxing.
- Ensure that you are breathing slowly and deeply.
- As you inhale, your abdomen will gently rise. And as you exhale it will fall.
- If your mind drifts or you lose track during this exercise bring your attention back to refocus on your

breathing.
- Take a long, slow, deep inhalation for a count of 4 - 3 - 2 - 1, hold for 1- 2 and exhale for 4 - 3 - 2 - 1.
- In 2 3 4, Hold (pause), Out 2 3 4
- In 2 3 4, Hold (pause), Out 2 3 4
- In 2 3 4, Hold (pause), Out 2 3 4
- In 2 3 4, Hold (pause), Out 2 3 4
- In 2 3 4, Hold (pause), Out 2 3 4
- Continue breathing slowly and deeply. *(Pause)*
- *(Move on to the next exercise.)*

Stage 3

Exercise 1 - 'Being of Light' visualisation
- Continue to breathe slowly and deeply.
- As you breathe in visualise the air as pure bright light, silvery and sparkling.
- Visualise it filling your body.
- As you exhale, your body relaxes further, feeling lighter and lighter.
- Breathe in - brighter and brighter.
- Breathe out - lighter and lighter.
- In - brighter and brighter.
- Out - lighter and lighter.
- In your mind's eye begin to see your body filling with tiny sparkling silvery white particles, as though every cell and molecule are becoming pure light.
- Breathe in - brighter and brighter.
- Breathe out - lighter and lighter.
- In - brighter and brighter.
- Out - lighter and lighter.
- You feel as though you could float away, but you don't.
- You are a beautiful being of light.
- Continue to breathe and enjoy this sensation for a few moments.
- *(When you're ready move on to the next exercise.)*

Exercise 2 - Sensing the energy
- You may begin to lose awareness of your physical body and instead begin to experience a sensation of a gentle vibration throughout your entire energetic being. It's as though each tiny sparkle is vibrating or moving around. *(Pause)*
- The feeling may begin as a slight humming sound or sensation.
- Connect with these vibrations or waves of energy, allowing them to move through you.
- Feel them move through your entire being. *(Pause)*
- Now see if you can alter their frequency? Can you slow them right down until they are almost imperceptible? *(Pause)*
- And then speed them back up again so that they are pulsing more quickly through your energy system once more. *(Pause)*
- *(Move on to the next exercise.)*

Stage 4 - Letting go
- Allow your body to relax and sink into the sensations that you're feeling. *(Pause)*
- Surrender to them, and allow yourself to let go entirely. *(Pause)*
- At this point your etheric body may project and go for a wander. You can come back whenever you wish. *(Pause for 2 minutes to start with. Watch over the group, should you see or sense that anyone is agi-*

tated or distressed in any way, use the come back and ground technique to bring everyone back to their bodies and the room.)

You can try this again, close and ground, or take a look at our alternative suggestions if this hasn't worked for you so far. Or you might just like to try a different technique to see which one works best for you.

Alternative 1 - Go through Stage 1 & 2 then try this alternative sequence:
Candle Gazing
(Use a candle or try gazing at a crystal associated with travelling.)
- Place a candle in a stable holder on a flat surface so that each person can sit about two to three feet away from it. It should be just at or below your eye level when you're seated. (If you have room you can use more than one at different points around the group.)
- Light the candle and ensure that you're all sitting comfortably and with good posture. Your back should be straight and your hands resting gently, palms up, on your knees. Read out stage 1 & 2 first, then the following:
- Close your eyes and take a deep inhalation, hold it, and then exhale.
- Slowly open your eyes and with a soft gaze look at the flame of the candle in front of you.
- Let any thoughts that you may have drift from your mind as though they were a wisp of cloud floating in a clear blue sky. Do not try to analyse these thoughts, but take your focus back to the candle's flame.
- Keep your eyes relaxed.
- Your eyes become heavy and tired, allow them to gently drift shut.
- You may see fluctuations in light and colours with your eyes closed. Simply allow these images to come and go.
- Eventually you may see nothing.
- You may begin to lose your awareness of your physical body and instead begin to experience a sensation of a gentle vibration throughout your entire energetic being. It is as though each cell within you is vibrating or moving around. *(Pause)*
- The feeling may begin as a slight humming sound or sensation.
- Connect with these vibrations or waves of energy, allowing them to move through you.
- Feel them move through your entire being. *(Pause)*
- Now see if you can alter their frequency? Can you slow them right down until they are almost imperceptible? *(Pause)*
- And then speed them back up again so that they are pulsing more quickly through your energy system once more. *(Pause)*
- Allow your body to relax and sink into the sensations that you're feeling. *(Pause)*
- Surrender to them, and allow yourself to let go entirely.
- At this point your etheric body may project and go for a wander. You can come back whenever you wish. *(Pause for 2 minutes to start with.)*
- *(Watch over the group, should you see or sense that anyone is agitated or distressed in any way, use the come back and ground technique to bring everyone back to their bodies and the room.)*

Alternative 2 - Conscious projection
- Read through stage 1 to 3 from the original exercise then read the following:
- Close your eyes and in your mind's eye see your etheric energy body. It takes up the same space as your physical body and its aura extends just beyond that, making it appear to glow.
- Focus mentally on the thought of exiting your physical body.
- Focus your attention on the energy in your hand. Visualise yourself stretching it towards something close to you, a wall, the floor or an object. You may even find that it passes straight through

- the object. *(Pause for 20 - 30 seconds.)*
- Now bring it back inside your physical body
- Play with this exercise for a couple of minutes, practise extending your etheric body out of your physical in different directions. *(Pause for 1 - 2 minutes.)*
- Now fix your attention on a point in the room around you, it may be the far corner or a particular object. Slowly count to 20, keeping your focus on this point and projecting yourself towards it. *(Pause for 20 - 30 seconds.)*
- Now visualise your etheric body floating out of, or standing up from and moving slightly away from your physical body. *(Pause for 20 - 30 seconds.)*
- Allow yourself to turn and look at your physical body and then to explore the physical world in your new guise. *(Pause)*
- *(At this point the subjects etheric body may project and go for a wander, they will come back in time, of their own accord, but if you are someone left behind and responsible for bringing them back at a set time, 2 minutes should be fine to start with, or indeed should you sense that they are agitated or distressed in any way, use the come back and ground technique.)*

Discuss

Once you start to be able to consciously project you can refine your technique to what works best for you. Discuss your experiences and compare notes. Someone may have found something that they did slightly differently that worked for them. Share your thoughts but don't worry if you didn't go anywhere this time. Guess what? It takes practice!

CLOSING & GROUNDING

Once you have completed the exercises everyone should sit comfortably and complete the following meditation to close and ground their energy. Read out the following:

- Sit in a comfortable position and close your eyes.
- Bring your attention to your breathing and focus on this for a few breaths. *(Pause)*
- Take your awareness to the invisible energy field surrounding you and visualise it drawing in close around your physical body. *(Pause)*
- Take your awareness to the area just above your crown and see a sphere of light sitting here.
- Imagine that sphere of light shrinking in size until it's tiny, then sinking down through the crown of your head.
- See it slowly descending down past the brow. *(Pause)*
- Into the throat. *(Pause)*
- Then following the line of the spine, down, through your body, towards your heart area. *(Pause)*
- Down to your solar plexus. *(Pause)*
- Through the abdominal area. *(Pause)*
- To the base of your spine. *(Pause)*
- Now visualise the sphere of energy either leaving through the base of your spine, or dividing in two and sinking down through your legs and leaving through the soles of your feet.
- Feel this energy leaving you and connecting with the earth.
- Have a sense of downward movement, deep in to the earth. *(Pause)*
- Become more aware of your feet and your physical body.
- Let us take a moment to thank our Spirit Guides, Angels and loved ones in Spirit for their presence, protection and wisdom whilst we've been working. Knowing that they will always be on hand should we need to call on them. *(Pause)*
- **Now bring your awareness back to your physical body, the chair you are sitting on and your contact with the floor.**
- **Begin to bring some movement back in to your fingers and toes.**

◦ **In your own time opening your eyes, fully awake and aware and in the physical world.**
(Watch for them starting to wriggle fingers and toes and keep an eye on anyone who doesn't do this. If a member of the group appears not to want to come back to the room simply repeat the last three points, in bold, but raising your voice so that it said slightly louder and firmer. Repeat a third time if necessary moving over to the person and at the end just saying their name and asking that they come back into the room now, placing a hand gently on their shoulder.)

Check to ensure that everyone feels grounded before you finish the session. If not, get them to walk around for a little while. Stamping your feet or jumping up and down helps to bring you back to the physical world. If these don't do the trick, you can ground your energy very readily by eating a small amount of food such as a biscuit.

OTHER THINGS TO TRY:
- Ask one person to place a particular object outside of the room you're working in. Attempt to project out of your body and wander off to find where the particular object is placed.
- Alternatively someone can draw a simple picture and place it outside of the room. Now you must find where it is, observe the drawing and report back what you saw.

AND ANOTHER THING...
- Grou members could pair up and arrange an etheric visit to each other's homes. Agree a day (a different one each) but not a time that you will visit each other using etheric projection. Ensure that you do this during the daytime. Project and travel to each other's home using the route you would normally use. You may find yourself flying, or even being instantly transported there. See if you notice anything different about their home. If they're in gently kiss or touch them on the cheek.
- Find out from them later if anything that you saw was correct, or if they mention that they were thinking of you at a particular time in the day. Did they sense your presence?
- Try it another time and ask them to leave an object in an unusual position and report back to see if your findings were correct.
- Being enveloped with classical or other appropriate music is said to induce projection so why not try a deep relaxation with music with the intention of projecting and returning able to recall your journey.
- Rhythmic dancing to the point of exhaustion, or chanting can also be worth a try as it can induce projection.

FOR DISCUSSION
- What have we got from this lesson? Best bits? Tricky bits?
- Key Concepts - how are we getting on with patience, acceptance, faith?
- Healing - feedback from those in the healing book? Success stories?
- Manifestation - Feedback? Success? New projects?
- To finish read out 'Where next?' on the following page and perhaps have a discussion about your next steps as a group.

WHERE NEXT?

We hope that this and our Beginners Workbook have given you a good grounding in the basics and a variety of spiritual and psychic development subjects. You should also be confident enough to put together your own sessions with your group choosing things you would like to repeat or develop futher or something new that you would like to explore. You can either go back to the beginning and repeat the lessons from the start (of either workbook) with more experience and knowledge this time, or you can decide on new activities on an ad hoc basis, dipping in and out of these books as a point of reference.

More often than not our group nights are fairly unplanned, now that we are more established. We use a structure as a base but will often decide what we are going to do once we are together. Someone will usually 'create' the meditation as they go along and see what springs to mind or we will use a CD of a guided visualisation or other audio meditation such as gongs, drumming or a binaural beat. We might do card readings, some psychometry, automatic writing or trance work, whatever we feel drawn to do on the night. It can also depend on what is going on for our group members. Sometimes someone might need help with a manifestation project, or some healing or energy work for themself or someone outside of the group (which we can do remotely). Even past members can link up and join in the energy if they are further away. Helen quite often drops in (so to speak) to 'Petals' to assist with a project despite living on the other side of the country now. Once you are attuned with the group and have some experience you can join energies wherever you are in the world.

With experience and confidence you will become flexible and adaptable. You will also become more adventurous. Providing you practise good basics: protection, closing & grounding etc. feel free to experiment and find news ways to work. And let us know how you and your group get on, we love to hear wonderful stories about the groups all around the world who are working towards improving themselves and their abilities for positive change.

FINAL THOUGHTS

There are so many directions that your journey of spiritual discovery could take you in. We hope that this book has given you some ideas of things you might like to develop or are good at. Keep practising all of the subjects from this and 'A Beginner's Guide' on your own or with others.

As you open your mind to the possibilities of what you can do and achieve, and how this will help you in all aspects of your life, even more opportunities will come to you. As you begin to trust your own feelings and judgements or intuition, you will find more and more that you're in the flow of the universe. No choice is a bad choice if you learn from the situations that you find yourself in. The people you meet along the way will teach you many things, about human nature, about spirituality and about yourself.

We hope that you can take this information and develop your own thoughts, your own belief system, your own understanding of the universe and its amazing beauty, complexity and simplicity. We hope that you can find true meaning for your life and make it the best that you can.

If you look at the world and wish to make it a better place, you must start with you, as Ghandi famously said, "You must be the change you wish to see in the world". We believe that by developing your wisdom, your skills and your connection with the universe, you will be shining brighter from within, and that in turn illuminates the world around you.

With Bright Blessings on your path, wishing you love and light always,
Helen & Diane

APPENDICES

HANDOUT 1
INTRODUCTION

WHAT WE WILL COVER
Deep meditation, energy work, increasing your sensitivity. 3rd eye chakra development, past lives, psychokinesis, manifestation, angelic energy, psychic art, automatic writing, out of body experiences, trance mediumship.

RULES
1) Do not mix your spirits!
In other words, no alcohol, or other mind-altering substances for that matter! Being under the influence whilst working in circle affects your ability and judgement. It also lowers your energy vibration and your defences (in much the same way as it lowers inhibitions). This can leave you and the rest of the group open to less positive energies or influences. This rule is non-negotiable.

2) Confidentiality.
Anything of a personal nature must not be spoken of outside of the group. This will allow everyone to work with trust and develop a safe and supportive environment. This does not mean that spirit are going to divulge your innermost secrets to everyone, they don't work like that, but discussions can arise which can bring up sensitive issues and everyone needs to know that they can be open and honest with each other.

3) Stay Positive!
This is extremely important. Positive energy is essential when working in circle. If you feel negative, depressed or simply under the weather, tell the group or take a break and get an early night instead. You will be told how to bring yourself out of a meditation should you feel the need, and if ever feel worried or uncomfortable in the group you must mention it. It would be wise to change the subject for a few minutes or to lighten the mood a little.

GUIDELINES
- Please be Prompt - If you know that you're going to be late let a group member know in advance so that they can wait for you.
- Keep it Regular - whilst it's understandable that things do crop up which can't be helped, it's preferable for group members to attend regularly to maintain group harmony.
- Food - it isn't advisable to eat a large meal *just* before circle, equally a rumbling tummy during a meditation can be off-putting. Many people prefer to avoid eating meat before circle as they believe that it lowers their vibratory rate making it more difficult to work with the higher, faster spiritual energies.
- Health - if you're unwell it isn't advisable to work in circle as your energy levels will be low, but let the group know and they'll send you healing energy to help you feel better! If a person suffers from depression, anxiety or a similar mental health issue, especially if they are on medication for any of these conditions, we would strongly suggest that they avoid working with Spirit. They're more vulnerable to energy dips and should concentrate on getting well before developing in this way. However, learning about and taking part in healing groups would be beneficial.
- Personal Hygiene - a lot of books and teachings say that one should ritually prepare for spiritual work by bathing and dressing in particular clothing before starting work. This is not always possible, or necessary, however, cleanliness is always appreciated! Heavy perfumes can interfere with psychic work so should be avoided.

HANDOUT 1 CONTINUED
INTRODUCTION

- Sharing - please do! Don't be worried about saying something silly, all contributions are welcome.
- Comparing - please don't! Everyone develops at different rates and finds certain things easier than others. Don't feel that you have to be the same as someone else or that you're not good enough, learn from and encourage each other.
- Working Space - it's ideal to use the same room each week. Before the meeting the room should be prepared. If possible, open the windows and air the room earlier in the day. Ensure that the room is warm and comfortable and that there is enough seating for everyone in the circle. You may want to burn some incense or place some fresh flowers in the room or to cleanse the area.

You may like to keep your own journal. One of the best ways to do this is to use an A4 ring binder. Then you can section it off as you wish with dividers, and use it to keep the handouts that are included on this course. You can add interesting magazine and newspaper articles that you find and record your own meditations and discoveries. Also, if you forget to take your folder to a lesson or on a course, you can make notes and slot them in at a later date. You will soon build up an amazing reference guide for yourself as well as documenting your journey and development.

APPENDICES

HANDOUT 2
BODY / CHAKRAS OUTLINE

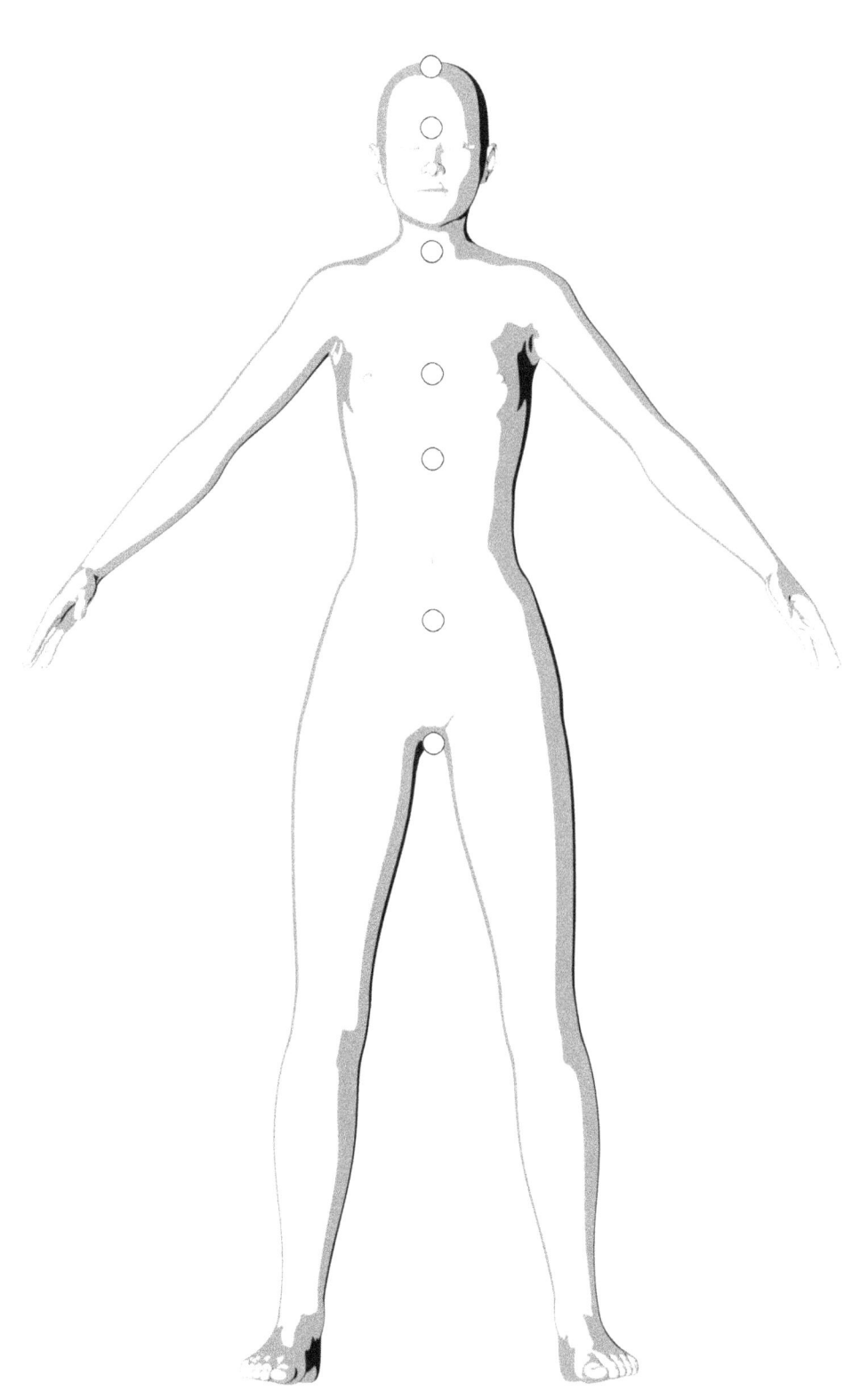

© 2011 www.spreadingthemagic.com

HANDOUT 3
SENSING PROMPTS

Where relevant, make notes of what you physically see as well as the impressions that you get. Sometimes you may find that one contradicts the other and it is interesting to see if you can ascertain why this might be.

What are your instant feelings or observations about this area?

Is the room light or dark?

Where is the light source?

What colours are in the room?

What is the temperature like?

What sounds can you hear?

What smells can you sense?

Place one hand on your solar plexus. What you do you feel in this part of your body as you walk around the area?

Are you relaxed or tense?

Are you comfortable or uneasy?

What emotions are you feeling?

HANDOUT 3
SENSING PROMPTS

Do you have any new feelings about this area?

Is your physical or emotional state different from when you arrived here?

How would you describe the personality of the room?

What function does the area have?

What kind of things do you think occur here?

Are the people who use this area generally happy? Or are you picking up other emotions?

Does this area encourage people to feel comfortable, happy, or otherwise?

What do you feel or see has happened here in the past?

Is it still having an influence on the area today?

Do you feel that people may be affected emotionally, physically or in any other way when they come here?

Is there anything else that you sense, see, hear, feel, taste or smell?

APPENDICES

HANDOUT 1
ANGEL CARDS

GRATITUDE	JOY
LOVE	FAITH

© 2011 www.spreadingthemagic.com

THE SPIRITUAL & PSYCHIC WORKBOOK – A COURSE COMPANION

HANDOUT 4
ANGEL CARDS

PEACE	HOPE
SELF-ACCEPTANCE	CHARITY

© 2011 www.spreadingthemagic.com

APPENDICES

HANDOUT 1
ANGEL CARDS

CREATIVITY	MANIFESTATION
ABUNDANCE	PATIENCE

© 2011 www.spreadingthemagic.com

THE SPIRITUAL & PSYCHIC WORKBOOK – A COURSE COMPANION

HANDOUT 4
ANGEL CARDS

AWARENESS	PROGRESSION
REFLECTION	GENEROSITY

© 2011 www.spreadingthemagic.com

APPENDICES

HANDOUT 1
ANGEL CARDS

LISTEN	COMMUNICATE
FULFILMENT	LAUGHTER

© 2011 www.spreadingthemagic.com

APPENDICES

HANDOUT 5
DOWSING CHARTS FOR PAST LIFE RESEARCH

INSTRUCTIONS

You can use these charts for all sorts of dowsing exercises once you have more experience. If you're quite new to this, here is a simple way to use them in your past life research.

- To discover when your most relevant past life occurred, keep this question in mind while you are dowsing for information; 'When was my past life that is most relevant to my current situation?'
- Use chart 1 to orientate your pendulum: Holding the pendulum over 'yes' ask that the pendulum indicate a positive response. Then holding it over 'no', ask that it indicate a negative response. Make a note of its movements.
- Use chart 2 to establish whether this most relevant past life was in AD or BC.
- Then move on to charts 3 & 4: Firstly hold your pendulum over each page in turn and ask if it is the chart you need to establish the correct century for this most relevant past life. Work with whichever one you get a positive response from. While keeping the original question in mind hold the pendulum over the centre point of the chart, ask that the pendulum moves in the direction of the segment indicating the century in which you lived. If your penduum does not appear to work in this way, hold it over the outer section of each segment in turn until you get a positive response.
- If you're unsure as to which century it is referring to (perhaps it could be 1100 or 1200) use a yes / no question to clarify the information: Move the pendulum away from the chart and ask a specific question: 'Was my past life that is most relevant to my current situation in 1100?' If it was you will get a postive, 'yes' response. If not, change the question to 1200 and you should clarify the answer.
- Chart 5 & 6 will indicate the decade and year of the period in your past life that you can learn the most from given your situation in this lifetime. If you wish to you can also use these charts (and chart 7 & 8) to establish your date of birth and death and other relevant events during that incarnation.
- You can use the idea behind these charts to create your own if you wish to work further with dowsing.

© 2011 www.spreadingthemagic.com

THE ADVANCED COURSE COMPANION

HANDOUT 5
DOWSING CHARTS FOR PAST LIFE RESEARCH - 1

YES

NO

© 2011 www.spreadingthemagic.com

DOWSING CHARTS FOR PAST LIFE RESEARCH - 2

HANDOUT 5

A.D.

B.C.

THE ADVANCED WORKBOOK - A COURSE COMPANION

HANDOUT 5
DOWSING CHARTS FOR PAST LIFE RESEARCH - 3

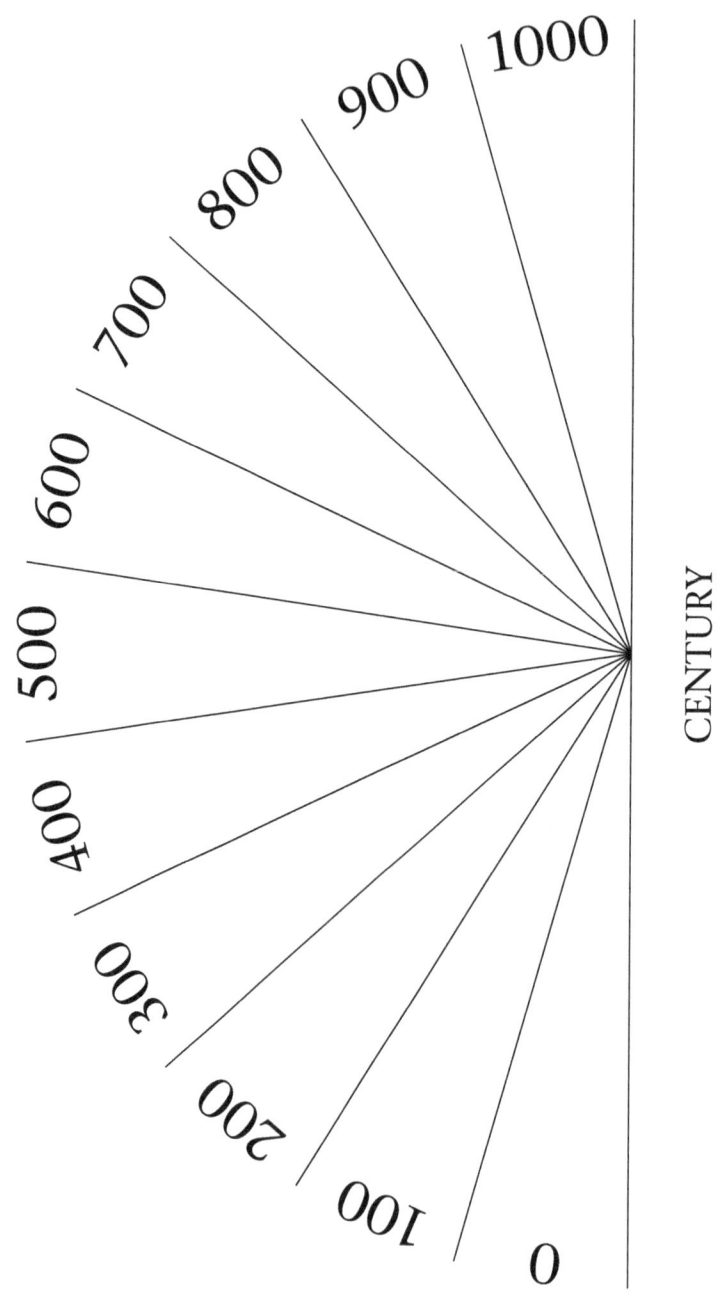

© 2011 www.spreadingthemagic.com

APPENDICES

HANDOUT 5

DOWSING CHARTS FOR
PAST LIFE RESEARCH - 4

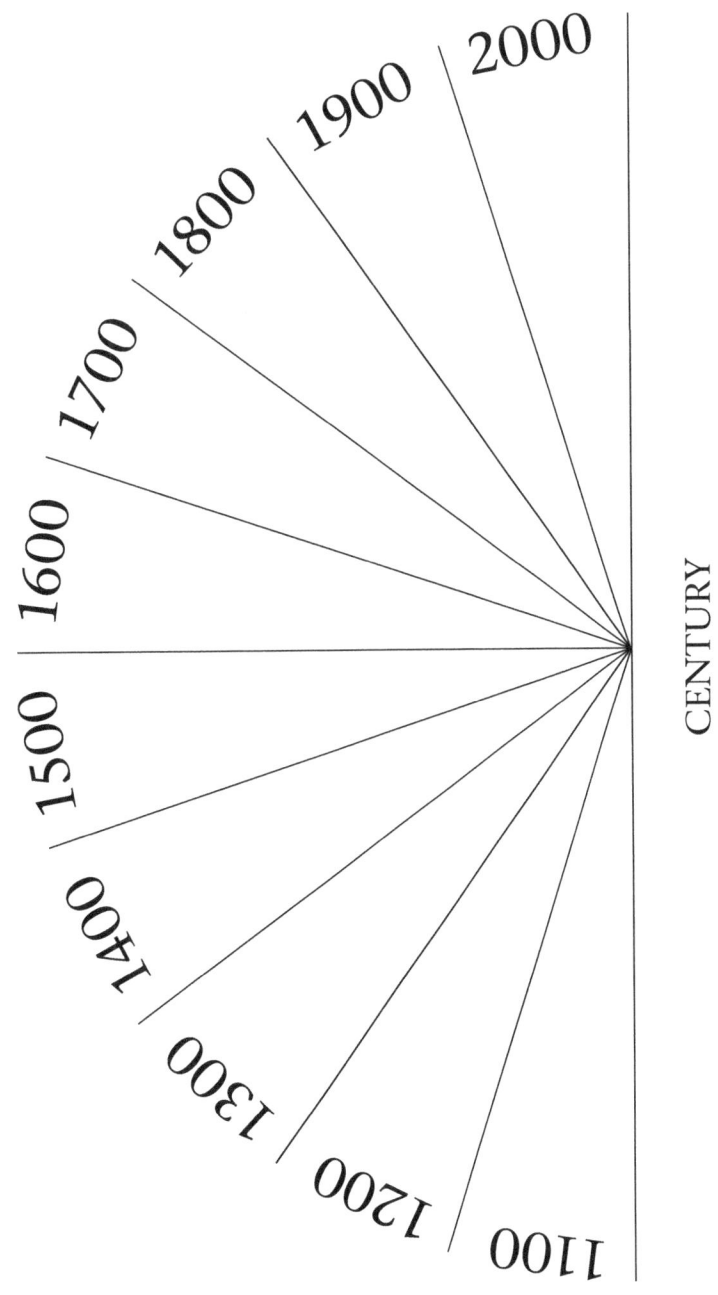

© 2011 www.spreadingthemagic.com

THE ADVANCED WORKBOOK - A COURSE COMPANION

HANDOUT 5

DOWSING CHARTS FOR PAST LIFE RESEARCH - 5

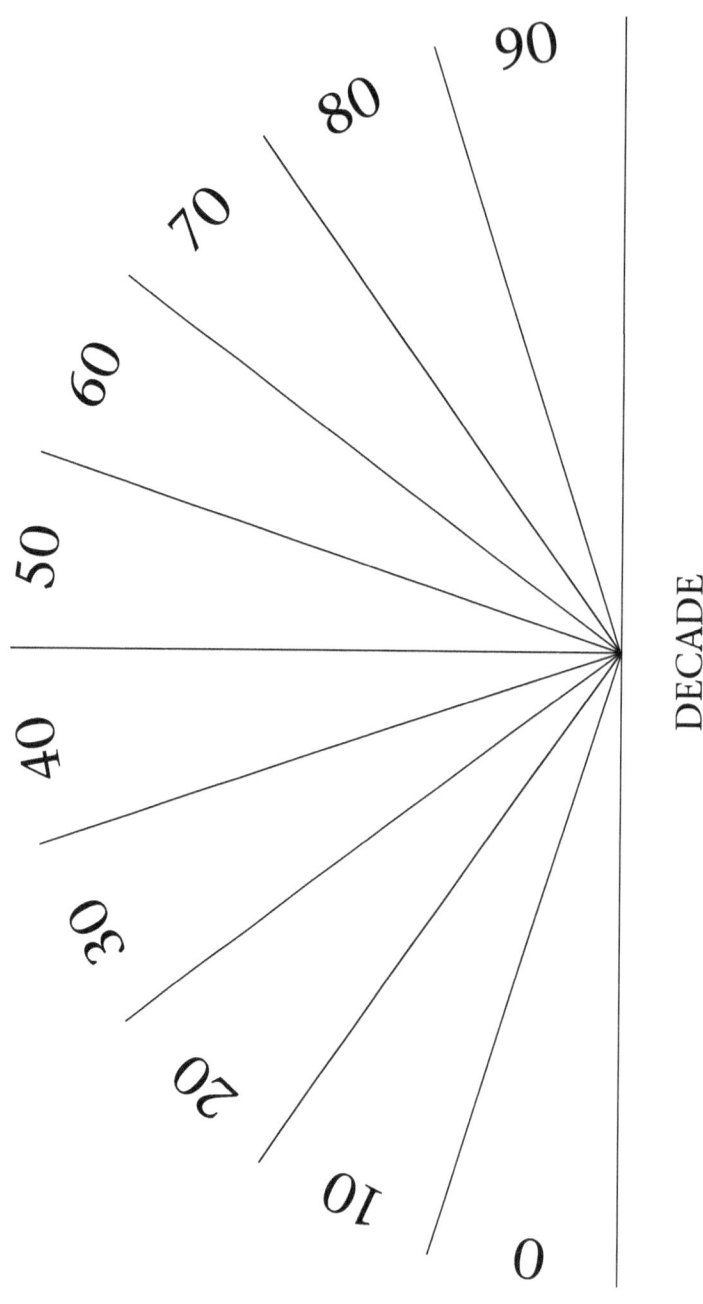

APPENDICES

HANDOUT 5

DOWSING CHARTS FOR
PAST LIFE RESEARCH - 6

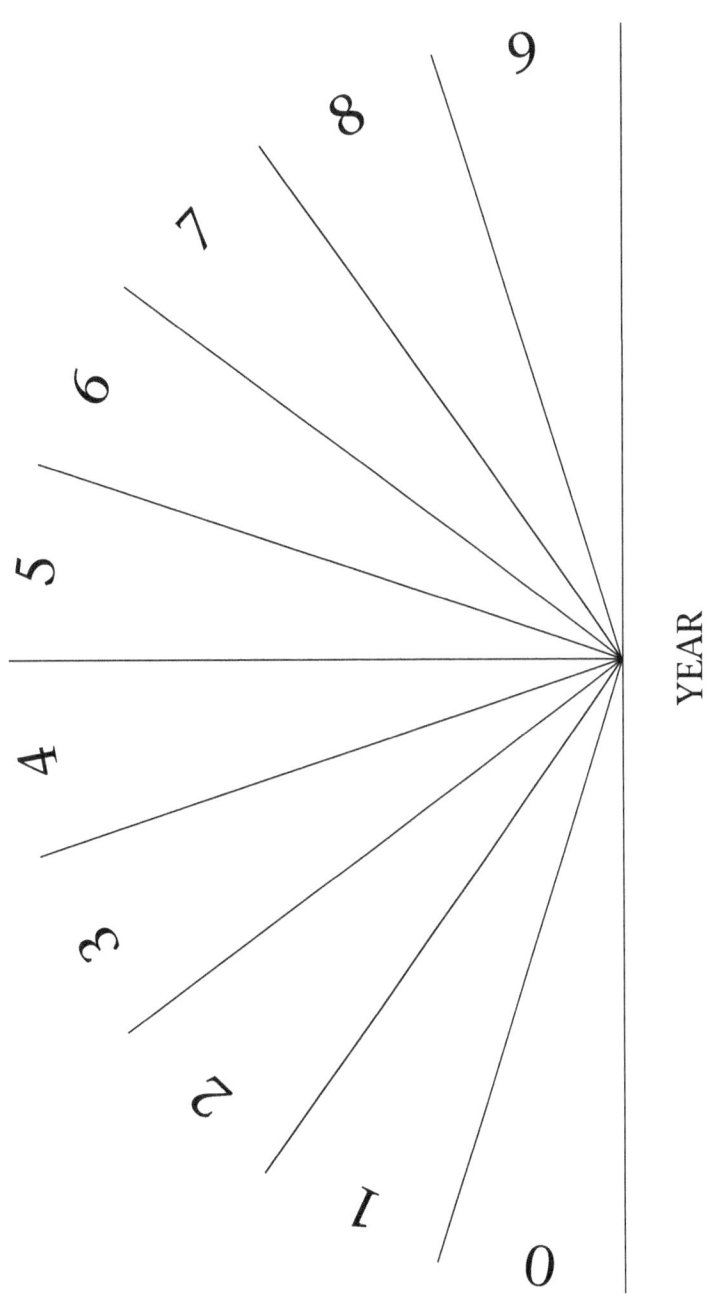

HANDOUT 5
DOWSING CHARTS FOR PAST LIFE RESEARCH - 7

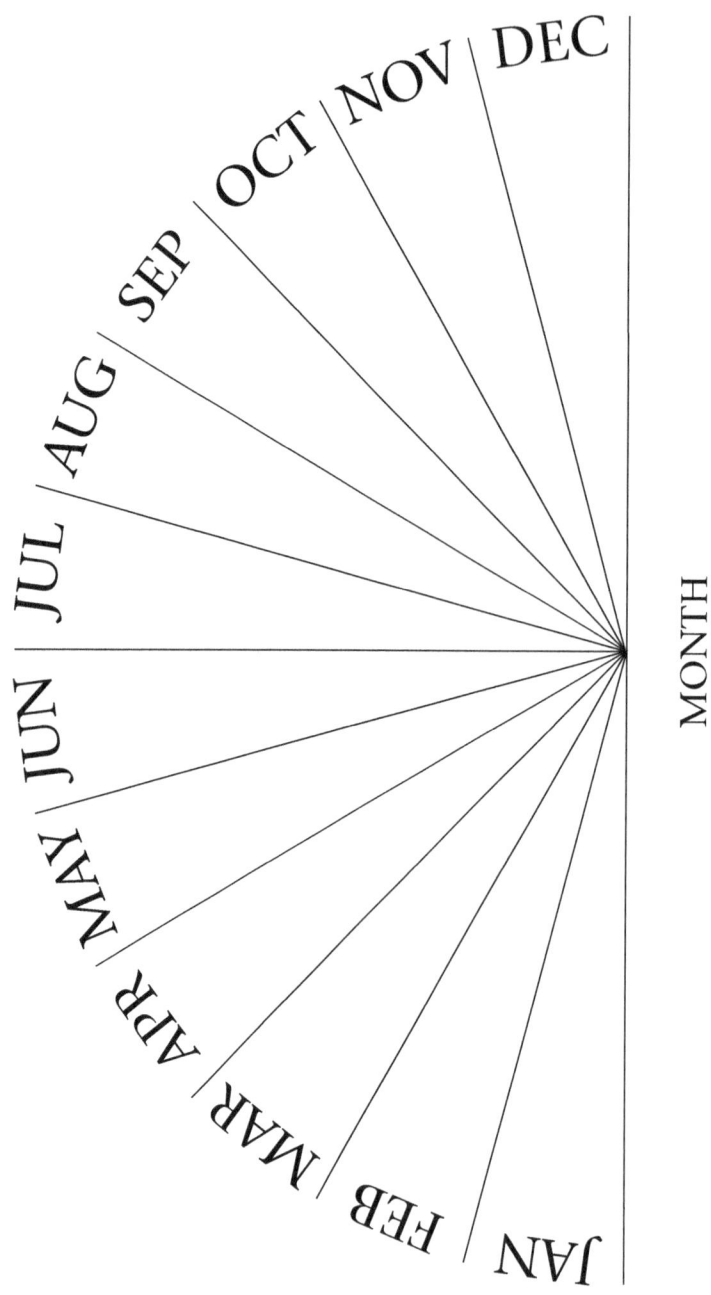

APPENDICES

HANDOUT 5

DOWSING CHARTS FOR
PAST LIFE RESEARCH - 8

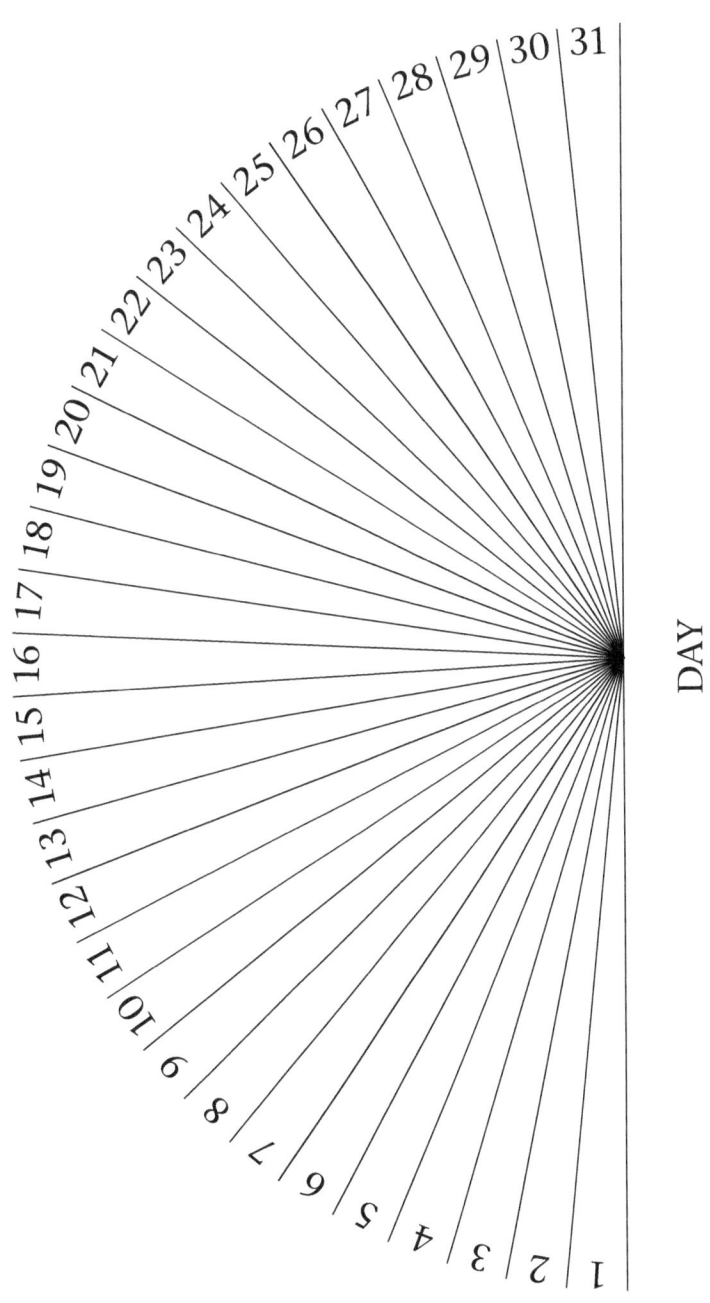

DAY

© 2011 www.spreadingthemagic.com

APPENDICES

HANDOUT 5
FACE OUTLINE

© 2011 www.spreadingthemagic.com

HANDOUT 7
BASIC COLOUR INFORMATION

RED
If you surround yourself with, love the colour or have lots of **RED** in your aura you are: Passionate, active, courageous and strong with lots of vitality.
Caution: Too much exposure can cause anger, impulsiveness and hunger.
Use RED to: Add some get up and go to your life.

ORANGE
If you surround yourself with, love the colour or have lots of **ORANGE** in your aura you are: Joyful and happy, an optimistic, independent and social person.
Caution: Too much can cause restlessness.
Use ORANGE to: Cheer yourself and give you confidence.

YELLOW
If you surround yourself with, love the colour or have lots of **YELLOW** in your aura you are: Intellectual, creative and artistic. An open and articulate person.
Caution: Over exposure can cause over-thinking, over-analysis or being too open to the affect that others can have on you.
Use YELLOW to: awaken clairsentient abilities and to bring happiness into your life.

GREEN
If you surround yourself with, love the colour or have lots of **GREEN** in your aura you are: Affectionate, loyal and trustworthy. You are full of sympathy and compassion and strive for health and harmony.
Caution: Too much green can mean that you let others walk all over you or have a tendency to seek peace at any price.
Use GREEN to: Promote calm, relaxation, healing and balance.

PINK
If you surround yourself with, love the colour or have lots of **PINK** in your aura you are: Charming and delicate, a peacemaker, full of love and compassion,
Caution: Over exposure can lead to indecisiveness, immaturity and lack of focus.
Use PINK to: Attract love, protection and security and to learn to appreciate the finer things in life.

HANDOUT 7
BASIC COLOUR INFORMATION

BLUE

If you surround yourself with, love the colour or have lots of **BLUE** in your aura you are: Good at communication, listening skills and self-expression. You are serious and cautious. Blue is linked with clairaudience.
Caution: Too much can mean someone who is over cautious, a worrier or is oversensitive.
Use BLUE to: attract tranquillity, and to learn to communicate your concerns.

PURPLE

If you surround yourself with, love the colour or have lots of **PURPLE** in your aura you are: Strong, sensitive, spiritual and intuitive. It is linked with clairvoyance and E.S.P. You're a visionary and are passionate about your beliefs.
Caution: Over exposure can cause you to be overbearing, feel misunderstood and become aloof.
Use PURPLE to: Develop your spiritual and psychic side.

WHITE

If you surround yourself with, love the colour or have lots of **WHITE** in your aura you are: A very spiritual person, an idealist and an innovator. You may seem shy but you do voice your opinions. You are seeking and are aware of the process of enlightenment.
Caution: Over exposure may cause you to begin to think of yourself as more important than others.
Use WHITE to: Help simplify your life, seek the truth and awaken greater creativity.

BLACK

If you surround yourself with, love the colour or have lots of **BLACK** in your aura you are: Seeking knowledge, intense, introspective and have hidden depths.
Caution: You may be trying to hide in the shadows or be suppressing your desires.
Use BLACK to: Look within.

APPENDICES

HANDOUT 8
PAST LIFE INTERVIEW SCRIPTS

Past life meditation:
- Ensure that you're sitting comfortably.
- Close your eyes.
- Breathe slowly and deeply, allowing your body to relax and your mind to clear.
- Ask your spirit guides to draw close and assist you in finding out about your most relevant past life experience.
- In your mind's eye visualise a mirror and see yourself just as you are now, reflected in it.
- Mist forms slowly across the mirror so that you're unable to see your reflection.
- Ask your spirit guide to use the mirror to reveal information about your most relevant past life experience.
- When you're ready, gently blow the mist away to reveal a reflection of you from your most relevant past life experience.

Past life questions (version A):
Are you male or female?
What are your initials?
What is your name?
What year is it?
Are you married?
Do you have a family?
How many children do you have?
Do you work?
What job do you do?
What are you wearing?
What nationality are you?
Where do you live?
Are any of your friends or family part of your present life?
How do you know them in this life?
What situation is similar in this past life that may help you in this one?

Past life questions (version B):
Am I male? Am I female?
Am I older than 10 / 20 / 30 / 40 / 50 / 60 (etc. until you can narrow it down.)
Do I have children? 1? 2? 3? (etc. until you can pinpoint it.)
Am I married?
Am I english/ (or your nationality in your current life)
Where do you live?
Are any of my friends from this life part of my past life?
Are any of my family from this life part of my past life?

© 2011 www.spreadingthemagic.com

TRANCE MEDIUMSHIP SCRIPT

Example Trance Script (a)
Is there someone with you?

Are they male or female?

Do you know their name? (Sometimes this will elicit a yes or a no so you may need to be more direct) What is their name?

Do they have a connection with someone here? (Who is that?)

If they are not clear in their answer, mention the people present until you get a positive response e.g. Are they connected to Jane? Are they connected to Jim? How are they connected?

Do you have a message for _____? (the person they have said they are connected to)

If they say they aren't connected to a person in the room then ask, do they have a message for one of us? If yes, which one of us is the message for? If no, do they have a message for all of us?

If none of the above have had a yes, ask, do they have a message for someone we know? (Ask more questions to find out who that is.)

What is it that they would they like to pass on?

Example Trance Script (b)
If you have asked 'Is there someone with you?' and you feel that the person is in deep trance you may need to change your language so that you are addressing the spirit presence direct, as below:

Are you male or female?

What is your name?

Are you connected to someone here? Are you connected to Jane? Are you connected to Jim?

How are you connected? Do you have a message for that person?

Do you have a message for one of us? If so, which person is the message for?

Do you have a message for someone we know? (Ask more questions to find out who that is.)

What is it that you would like to share with us?

© 2011 www.spreadingthemagic.com

ABOUT THE AUTHORS

About Helen

From as far back as I can remember I have seen and communicated with spirit. Our family home had a number of ghosts, one of which was a wonderful gentle nurse from the early 1900s. Seeing, hearing and sensing ghosts, prophetic dreams and trusting my intuition and inner guidance to avoid potentially negative situations were all a part of my life from very early on. I had devoured all of Doris Stokes' books on mediumship well before I was 12. I started reading Tarot when I was 14 and also discovered a natural ability for dowsing with a pendulum. I attended courses and workshops whenever I could from the age of 18 and found a deep affinity with crystals and the native pagan culture of the British Isles. I trained as an alternative therapist and became a Reiki Master. I loved Reiki straight away and knew without a doubt that I had to teach others about it. The self-empowerment, the wonderful healing stories, and the changes that it facilitates in people are all amazing. I started running courses as soon as I could and continue to do so, seeking to make it as accessible to everyone as possible.

Over the years my psychic side became more prevalent and I also realised how empathic I was. I feel the emotions of others, the joy, the fear, and the pain. This can be difficult sometimes but I'm also able to see their potential, which is inspiring. Throughout my twenties I worked closely with friends of like mind, some much more experienced and some at a similar point to me. We discovered more and more about ourselves, our abilities and how to tap into our inner power and knowledge. We debated spiritual philosophy and universal mysteries long into the night. I continued to do card readings and dowsing but also developed other skills including psychometry and mediumship. I was invited to join a psychic development circle where I met and started working with Diane and others. I found that I was drawn to and had the ability to do rescue work. In layman's terms this is performing something like an exorcism, a horrible phrase conjuring many negative and scary images, but one that most people will understand. Basically I'm good at getting rid of unwanted and problem ghosts. A haunted antique cauldron being the first and most unusual situation that I came across.

At 30 I relocated to Shropshire I found myself with a very definite purpose. I had to share my acquired knowledge and understandings with a larger audience. Apart from running businesses, I was running workshops and a website for personal, spiritual and psychic development and had also started writing. Books began to take shape and I knew this was the next step for me.

My journey so far, punctuated by many paranormal experiences, has been a massive learning and development process, and I continue in this every day. I know that I'm connected to the Universe as many seeming coincidences continue to put me in front of the right person at the right time, in a better place, or out of harm's way. I don't consider myself to be special, I have simply chosen to actively pursue this avenue, to open to and connect with the Universe and to develop my own natural abilities, to ask more questions and look for more answers. I enjoy helping others to do the same.

About Diane

I guess I've always had psychic and spiritual experiences, though for many years I didn't understand them, or even acknowledge them. I had an idyllic childhood, was blessed with a wonderful family, and did well at school, but I always felt different somehow. I didn't feel better than anyone else, nor indeed worse, just different. Perhaps the sensitivity to spirit around me, strange dreams and even stranger trance experiences that I had, all contributed to my 'feeling different'. That feeling stayed with me until I embraced my spiritual side during my mid 20s, and as clichéd as it may sound, finally found my true self.

ABOUT THE AUTHORS

My spiritual journey began in earnest when facing upheaval in my personal life. I felt drawn to have a Tarot reading, the first one I'd ever had. The cards told an amazing story, describing exactly what I was going through at that time. I was also told that I was a healer, but at that point I had no understanding of what this meant. Upon returning home, my sister jokingly said "Well if you're a healer, heal my headache before it turns into a migraine." I didn't even know how to go about it, so, between us we kind of guessed that I should put my hands on her head. To our immense surprise her headache did disappear!

My curiosity and a series of amazing synchronicities led me to 'Petals in the Wind', a group that was run by Carol, a medium and healer. Carol was kind enough to teach me all she knew about healing, and I quickly became a permanent fixture at Petals' meetings. I was fortunate to have plenty of time to pursue my new found interests, and over the next few months I went to every workshop I could, joined circles, read books, visited spiritualist churches, debated with like-minded new friends – anything that could further my knowledge. It was a time of rapid learning, facilitated by amazing teachers. To this day I remain passionate about teaching people beginning their spiritual journey as a way of returning some of what I was given when I was starting out.

I became part of Petals more than ten years ago now, and although it has evolved and changed in many ways since those early days, I'm proud to still be a part of it. I owe a huge amount to my wonderful special fellow members who I always count as my second family. I was also blessed to meet Helen through 'Petals'. Years later we found out that the first time we had worked together we had secretly been in awe of each other. We had both felt nervous as we'd perceived the other to be far more spiritually advanced than ourselves! Interestingly, our great friend Janice predicted that we would work together in a business venture, before she had even introduced us to one another. Our books prove her prediction right.

I was also lucky to have Helen become my Reiki Master, passing her knowledge and love of Reiki on to me. My passion for Reiki remains with me and I run regular Reiki courses. I feel privileged to be able to pass on my knowledge of this wonderful healing method to as many people as possible. Additionally I run psychic development workshops with 'Petals', as part of my 'mission' to help people who are exploring their spiritual pathway. Through these workshops I have learnt as much as I have taught.

Over time I have developed many aspects of my spiritual and psychic side, including rescue work, Angel Card readings, trance mediumship, automatic writing, crystal healing and reading auras to name but a few. I have worked with some amazing spirit guides who have patiently helped me along the way! It is a lifelong journey and I am always eager to discover more, and to help others do the same.

RESOURCES

WHERE TO GO FOR HELP:
It's difficult for us to recommend a particular place or person without knowing them personally and having had some experience of their work. However, these are some points of contact for you that will start you off if you're in need of help. Do a bit of research in your local area, ask for recommendations and trust your intuition. (UK only)

To help you find a local Spiritualist Church visit the Spiritualist National Union's website: www.snu.org

For courses, seminars and demonstrations take a look at The Arthur Findlay College in Stansted, Essex. www.arthurfindlaycollege.org

The Pagan Federation for honest and reliable information about the many types of pagan faith. www.paganfederation.org

Other Websites associated with and personally recommended by the authors:

www.spreadingthemagic.com
An on-line resource for personal, spiritual and psychic development. Books & products, courses, workshops and other events. Plus, sign up for a free e-newsletter.

www.stmpublishing.co.uk
For all books & products by Spreading The Magic.

www.protectedbyangels.co.uk
Find out more about healing, and put someone in the online healing book if you feel they could benefit from help by our angels.

www.petalsinthewind.co.uk
Information on courses and workshops on psychic development held in Hertfordshire.

www.lighting-the-way.co.uk
A website offering enlightenment and upliftment to those wishing to explore their spiritual side.

ACKNOWLEDGEMENTS

FROM HELEN

As with all my books, my thanks and acknowledgements must start at the beginning. To my Mum and Dad for allowing me to be and become 'me', and especially to Mum for giving me my first set of Tarot and my crystal ball, one day I may even be able to see something in it! To my brother and sisters for accepting my 'being weird'.

To John for travelling most of the journey so far with me, and for joining me for the one ahead, for all your love & support and for putting up with my book writing obsession.

To all those who I've met on my journey so far who I have learnt so much from, Stan, Christina, Marion, Bea, Jane, Lynn, Beth, Lynne Wakerly, my Reiki Master, Vivienne, Sue Lean and your wonderful meditation group that triggered this writing bug. To Sara for being a sounding board on the occasional moments when I got stuck in my own thoughts. Also to Jan, Pete, Rosemarie, Andrea, Jacqui, Eileen. And of course to Diane, who has taught me so much including self-belief, a wonderful friend, our paths are so similar yet so diverse and I'm sure we will continue to work together, learn from and lean on each other for much time to come.

FROM DIANE

Firstly, thanks to my dearest husband Barry, always there to listen and support, always hugely encouraging of my many projects. To my beautiful daughters, Alicia and Louise who entertain me, teach me and inspire me. You all mean the world to me.

To my Mum and Dad, amazing parents. To the rest of my special family, thank you for your words of encouragement and support.

For Helen, a most cherished friend, always there to advise, encourage and inspire me. Thank you for your patience and enthusiasm whilst we have worked on this project, may there be many more to follow.

To all the wonderful teachers that I have encountered along the way. I have been blessed with so many, and each has helped me to reach the path I am on today. In the words of Henry Brooke Adams, "A good teacher affects eternity, he never knows where his influence stops". So many people have affected my eternity and for that I will always be grateful.

To the many special people who continue to help me to grow and develop spiritually, Rosemarie, Jan, Pete, Jacqui, Andrea, Jo, Rachel, Nicky and Ruth amongst many others. I am so pleased that we have chosen to tread this path together, long may it continue.

FROM US BOTH

Heartfelt thanks go to the following wonderful people:

For taking time to review and comment on the manuscript for this book and to assist us with some corrections and editing, your generosity, expertise and wisdom are very much appreciated; Dori Scott-Morgan, Andrea Allen, Vivien Leyland-Green, Janice Allgood, Debbie White, Allison Harris & Ros Healy.

For an inspired yet simple idea, Janette Oakman (psychic artist) whose face template has proved a wonderful tool in developing our psychic art skills.

John Leathers, once more for your design genius in putting another of our projects together in a beautiful way, with love, understanding and endless patience.

All of 'Petals', who continue to help us grow and develop in a safe, loving and trusting environment.

ABOUT 'SPREADING THE MAGIC'

Started in 2005 by Helen Leathers, 'Spreading The Magic' began life as an online resource for personal, spiritual and psychic development. Courses and workshops and a small range of products were available. Helen was also writing and had a number of projects on the go at once. But she knew it was extremely difficult to get an agent or publisher in the literary world. So she decided to create what she wanted and pull the two concepts together turning 'Spreading The Magic' into a publisher for her and Diane's specialist books on the spiritual side of life.

'Spreading The Magic' is a vehicle with which we seek to help others find and develop their own spirituality and integrate it into their daily life.

Our core values are open-mindedness and acceptance.

We want everyone to find their own path and know their own truth. To find the magic in themselves and to see it in others.

The 'magic' is our connection with life, our oneness with the universe and everything within it.
Through our courses, workshops, articles, books, products, websites and events we aim
To encourage, inform and inspire
To simplify and demystify the unknown
To open hearts and minds
To promote non-judgement, acceptance and understanding
To transform and enlighten
To leave a positive impact
To teach others to create their reality
To raise consciousness, personally, socially and globally
To remember
To Be
To spread the magic

Become part of the change at www.spreadingthemagic.com

OTHER PRODUCTS FROM HELEN & DIANE

BOOKS

These can be ordered online at www.stmpublishing.co.uk

Help! I Think I Might Be Psychic
101 Frequently Asked Questions About Spiritual, Psychic & Spooky Stuff
Answered by Helen Leathers & Diane Campkin

This book is for everyone who has ever asked. "What's it all about?", "Is there life after death?", "What's it like to see a ghost?" and other virtually unanswerable questions.

Do you have fascination with or passing interest in the paranormal?

Do you have a more pressing concern and don't know where to turn for the answers?

Do you suspect you have a talent, a path, a dream or desire that you are not fulfilling and you really wish there was more to life?

Whether you have had supernatural experiences or not, this book will give you the basics, and a whole lot more. This is our take on the often confusing and occasionally egotistical world of the paranormal. A reference point that's open and honest and that looks to blow away some of the cobwebs surrounding the more esoteric side of life and death, as we see it. This book is for everyone. Do you want to know more...?

RRP £7.95

Bright Blessings
Spiritual Thoughts, Inspirational Quotes and Philosophical Observations on Life.
from Helen Leathers

Ever wonder about the bigger picture and the spiritual side of life?

Do you need inspiration? Are you happy?

Do you truly know who you are and where you're heading?

This is a collection of articles, observations and quotes which aim to make you stop and think. Whether you need inspiration, a quiet moment, a focus for meditation, spiritual or philosophical advice or support, or maybe something different to do this weekend, this is the book to have within easy reach.

RRP £5.95

The Spiritual & Psychic Development Workbook
A Beginners Guide
Helen Leathers & Diane Campkin

An introduction to the theory and practical basics of spiritual and psychic development. From meditation to dowsing, card readings to working with the chakras, understanding crystals to connecting with your spirit guides.

Do you want to increase your intuition, work with healing energy, learn how to meditate or develop your own clairvoyant ability?

This book will facilitate an opening up to and development of your own natural spirituality and psychic skills. Essential basics, simple to understand theory and practical exercises make this a beginners guide for everyone. And there's not too many long words either.

This is the book we've been looking for for years.

RRP £9.95

OTHER PRODUCTS FROM HELEN & DIANE

THE SPIRITUAL & PSYCHIC DEVELOPMENT WORKBOOK
A COURSE COMPANION
Helen Leathers & Diane Campkin

An in-depth course book for workshop leaders, development groups or a bunch of like-minded friends. Based on our 'Beginners Guide', the course companion is a step-by-step guide to running your own group, circle, or series of workshops on spiritual & psychic development - or just use it for yourself!

You don't have to think about it, we've done all the planning for you, a 12 part course of lessons including:

- Preparation • How to open and close meetings • Essential basics
- Easy to understand theory • Practical exercises • Handouts / worksheets
- Extra ideas and activities to complement each lesson and develop your skills further.

An essential workbook based on our experience of running groups, courses and workshops.
A4 and spiral bound for easy use.
RRP £19.95

THE ADVANCED SPIRITUAL & PSYCHIC DEVELOPMENT WORKBOOK
Helen Leathers & Diane Campkin

Building on our 'Beginners Guide' this workbook looks at the more advanced subjects within spiritual & psychic development. In an easy step-by-step process you can venture into subjects such as:
- Deep Meditation • Energy work • 3rd eye chakra development • Past lives
- Psychokinesis • Manifestation • Angelic energy • Psychic art
- Automatic writing • Out of body experiences • Trance mediumship.

In this workbook we want to continue to help you develop your own spiritual ethos and understanding as well as your natural psychic skills in a safe and supported way. Endeavouring to keep things as simple as possible, we provide various theories and practical exercises, include our top tips and share some personal experiences of our own.
RRP £9.95

MEDITATIONS AVAILABLE ON CD & AS MP3 DOWNLOADS
Available to order from www.stmpublishing.co.uk

THE SPIRITUAL & PSYCHIC DEVELOPMENT MEDITATION COLLECTION
Read by Helen & Diane
CD1 Essential Beginners

Suitable for use on its own or to accompany either our 'Beginners Guide' or 'Course Companion'. Includes 'opening & protection', and 'closing & grounding' visualisations, 'Creating Your Sanctuary' PLUS a bonus track.

CD2 Individual meditations from our Course Companion Lessons 2 - 7.
Includes 'Meeting Your Spirit Guide', 'Extending Your Senses' & 'Connect with the Energy of the Earth'

CD3 Individual meditations from our Course Companion Lessons 8 - 12.
Includes 'Awaken Your Psychic Senses' & 'Connect With Your Totem Animal'.

WATCH OUT FOR...

THE ADVANCED SPIRITUAL & PSYCHIC DEVELOPMENT AUDIO COLLECTION
Read by Helen & Diane.

This audio collection is taken from and complements 'The Advanced Workbook' & its 'Course Companion'. Some tracks are guided visualisations that will help revitalise & inspire as well as assist in your spiritual & psychic development: 'Enlightenment', 'A walk down memory lane', 'Journeys through the 3rd eye', 'Meet your guardian angel', Transforming potential', 'The inner scribe', 'The garden of abundance' & 'Discover a past life'.

Other tracks are sets of meditative development exercises or processes designed with a specific goal in mind: Deeper meditation exercises - Assistance with trance mediumship - Out of body experience exercises.

THE POWER IN YOUR HANDS
An Experiential Guide to Energy Work
Helen Leathers

This book is an introduction to the basics of energy work for aspiring healers, lightworkers and anyone seeking personal, spiritual or psychic development.

It's a hands-on, practical approach to understanding the theory behind the subtle energy systems of the universe. Learn how to connect to, channel and consciously focus universal energy and integrate energy work into all aspects of your life.

Whether you feel that you personally need more energy or you would like to work with energy for healing, spiritual or psychic work, this is a great place to start.

This book provides the building blocks of theoretical and practical understanding which will allow you to make your journey at your own pace, develop your own ideas and skills and enjoy your path to enlightenment and empowerment.

Want a more fulfilling life? The power is in your hands.

THE POWER IN YOUR HANDS AUDIO COLLECTION
Read by Helen

A collection of guided visualisations and development exercises taken directly from 'The Power In Your Hands' and read by the author. These tracks include energy and development work for aspiring healers, lightworkers and anyone seeking personal and spiritual growth.

- Simple physical relaxation • The breath • conscious connection
- harmonising group energy • creating an energy souce as a group
- creating an energy source on your own • elevate your energy • expand your energy • close & ground

Use this audio collection to help you connect with universal energy and rediscover your limitless power.

Register for updates and offers on these or find out more at: www.stmpublishing.co.uk

www.ingramcontent.com/pod-product-compliance
Lightning Source LLC
Chambersburg PA
CBHW080910230426
43666CB00013B/2661